THE SWEET AND TWENTIES

ALSO BY BEVERLEY NICHOLS

THE SWEET
AND TWENTIES

BEVERLEY NICHOLS

WEIDENFELD AND NICOLSON
7 CORK STREET LONDON WI

PRINTED IN GREAT BRITAIN
IN 11 POINT BEMBO
BY WYMAN AND SONS, LIMITED
LONDON, FAKENHAM AND READING
N. 6384

CONTENTS

ACKNOWLEDGMENTS

THE PHOTOGRAPHS listed opposite are reproduced by courtesy of the following: those facing pages 49, 113, 144 (upper), 145, 193, 208 (lower) and 209, Cecil Beaton; 64, 65, 96, 97, 112, 144 (lower), 160 (upper), 161 and 192, the Picture Post Library; 160 (lower) and 208 (upper), the Keystone Press; and 48, Eliot & Fry Ltd. The drawings on pages 29, 31, 32, Dame Laura Knight; and 26, 127 and 178, *Punch*.

I RECORD my thanks to the following for permission to quote from their publications:

Associated Newspapers Ltd, for extracts from *The Weekly Dispatch* and *The Sunday Dispatch*; *The Daily Mail*; *The New Statesman*; The Public Trustee and The Society of Authors for extracts from an article by George Bernard Shaw; Messrs Jonathan Cape, *Twenty-five* by Beverley Nichols; Mr C. D. Medley for extracts from George Moore's works and Mr Siegfried Sassoon for permission to reproduce his poem *Blighters*.

ILLUSTRATIONS

To

JAMES WEDGWOOD DRAWBELL

who knew it all

FOREWORD

On November 10th, 1920, four British ratings stood with bowed heads on the deck of the French destroyer *Verdun*. A cold wind from the Channel flicked the flag of the Union Jack that was draped over the coffin they were guarding. Inside the coffin lay a British soldier from the battlefields of France. Nobody knew who he was, but already tens of thousands of mothers whose sons were missing claimed him, in their secret hearts, as their own. Across the Channel the scene was set for the greatest act of homage that has ever been accorded to a man of arms. No Caesar, no Napoleon, ever went to his last resting-place with such solemn glory as the Unknown Warrior.

This was perhaps the last occasion in history when the heart of a great nation was enobled and uplifted by the contemplation of war and its tragedy. A great deal more was buried in the tomb of the Unknown Warrior, in Westminster Abbey, than the body of a solitary hero. Into that grave, though few people realized it at the time, were piled all the pride, all the pomp and all the circumstance of war, from which the glory had finally departed. True, in a few years time the clouds would be gathering again; the nations would be locked in an even more desperate struggle, and the young men would be falling, falling. But at the end of the second World War there was no unknown warrior, because the illusions that had created him, and fashioned him into a figure of hope and beauty, were shattered for all time. To have laid a second hero by the side of the first would have been an act of irony too bitter to contemplate.

Who first conceived the idea of the Unknown Warrior? The credit has sometimes been given to the Dean of Canterbury;

in fact it should go to the Reverend David Railton, who was then Vicar of Margate. Railton was himself a brave soldier who had won the Military Cross. When he first mentioned his plan, in all modesty, to the Dean, he could hardly have guessed the extent to which it would capture the world's imagination. The Cenotaph became a place of pilgrimage for the whole nation. For four days Whitehall was closed to traffic, and all through the days and nights of November 11th and 12th a vast crowd filed past in silence. When dawn came on November 13th, over 100,000 wreaths were piled high round the monument, a carpet of colour shining through the mist. For months afterwards, when traffic was nearing the monument, the drivers of cars and buses instinctively slowed down, while the men raised their hats and the women bowed their heads. As late as 1925 there were reports of 'incidents' in buses caused by some man who had omitted to raise his hat. How many men raise their hats today?

The whole country was setting up statues to its dead. Some of these statues were ambitious, like Sir George Frampton's memorial to Nurse Cavell. He described his work as a 'labour of love'; but when it was unveiled by Queen Alexandra it was betrayed as a singularly loveless erection. The general feeling of the British public was that it would act as 'a salutory memorial to the brutishness of the Hun'. This attitude of mind incurred a mild reproof from a writer in *The Illustrated London News* who remarked: 'Those who look upon the Nurse Cavell statue as something put up merely to shame the Germans surely take too low a view of it.' He added, somewhat obscurely: 'On the other hand, perhaps they take too high a view of the German mentality, *as it is at present.*'

Those statues of the early twenties still stand in the cities and market towns of Britain, and each one is a lasting memorial not only to the death of a soldier but to the death of a faith. Men do not set up statues in a mood of despair; they set them up in a spirit of hope. The mood of the twenties, as far as war was concerned, was buoyant with hope; it was reflected in words by the phrase 'Never again', and it was given visual expression, however crude and ugly, in thousands of these monuments. But very few statues were set up in the forties. Another list of names was chiselled round the base, and that was all. And instead of the Cenotaph we were given Mr Roosevelt, the conquering American, dominating the shambles of Grosvenor Square, for whose ruins, in the opinion of some of us, his country was not entirely unresponsible.

II

This is not intended as a serious history of a decade, but rather as an album of snapshots and memories which may offer, at least to the middle-aged, some moments of nostalgic entertainment. However, even in so slight a compilation, seriousness 'creeps in'. As one turns the pages of the album some of the pictures seem to darken; a shadow falls across them—the shadow of the present obscuring the brightness of the past. It is as though we are looking at the portrait of a laughing boy who is destined to die of a terrible disease; in his smile we can see his tragedy foretold. Thus, as I have been making this little collection I have been constantly struck by the fact that some of the pictures and scraps of dialogue seem to be invested with a poignancy that cannot be explained by their context. Even a light-hearted group of undergraduates, taken at Oxford when I was President of the Union, has this strange suggestion of brooding melancholy. Why? Not because any of the group were destined for tragic ends; most of them are still alive and some of them have risen to the highest office. (The lad sitting cross-legged in the front row, whom I once called to order, rather sharply, for wandering from the point, is now Her Majesty's Lord Chancellor[1].) Nor is this strange *patine* of sadness due—I trust—to any tiresome hankerings after my own youth. I have been sentimental about many things but never about growing old. The advent of senility has always seemed

[1] Lord Kilmuir.

to me better treated as a comedy than a tragedy . . . in so far, at least, as one's own faculties are concerned.

Why then this shadow over the group? I think the answer was hinted at above. It is the shadow of the present over the past. All the young men in that group had the light of faith in their eyes, and in all of them that light has been extinguished. We were destined to be duped, every man Jack of us.

That is the fundamental difference between the average intelligent young man of the twenties and his modern counterpart. It is a difference of faith—not of religious faith, but of faith in the civilized world at large and the possibility of its ever making sense.

Let us come from the general to the particular. The faith which animated the intelligent young man of the twenties was faith in the League of Nations. It was axiomatic. When he lifted up his eyes and looked to the hills, he saw, gleaming on the horizon, the white Palace of Peace, where all the troubles of the world would find solution. This Palace was not a dream to him, it was a reality; he was actually living in the era which Tennyson had so comfortably foretold, and the phrase 'the parliament of man, the federation of the world' was constantly on his lips. Indeed, it was almost impossible for the intelligent young man to make a speech without using it.

This faith in the future was greatly comforting to us; when we were angry with our elders and betters we had only to look to the horizon and see the white towers of our palace, and we felt much better, like persecuted Christians who console themselves with visions of the pearly gates. Whatever trials and tribulations we might be called upon to endure, nobody could take *that* from us. The palace stood firm, guarding us for ever from war. We knew that we could live out our lives in peace, to the end.

The modern young man can comfort himself with no such illusions. He would be a fool if he did. When he lifts up his eyes to the modern version of the League of Nations, which bears the grossly misleading title of UNO, what does he see?

No gleaming palace, but a gaunt, jerry-built edifice, already tottering on its foundations, with the rain pouring in through the roof. Half of this sorry structure is empty and deserted; from the other half comes a perpetual uproar of vituperation. High above, in the darkening sky, looms the lurid shadow of a cloud shaped like a mushroom.

How can any young man, however idealistic his bent, gain any comfort from the contemplation of such a monstrosity? One of those 'angry young men' who, at the time these words are written, has been attracting the attention of the newspapers, summed up his attitude to me in these words:

'How can we regard UNO as anything but a joke in atrocious taste? Look at the cast! Every fourth child that is born into the world is a Chinese, but China is not even represented! Nor is Western Germany, which is the guts of Europe! Every fifth child that is born into the world is an Indian. India *is* a member, but when India commits flagrant aggression, all they say is 'Naughty, naughty!' They said the same to Russia over the rape of Hungary . . . and then proceeded to welcome the Hungarian delegation! America's role has been almost more repellent than Russia's, with President Eisenhower sweeping a low curtsey to King Ibn Saud on the steps of the White House. King Ibn Saud of all people! Hasn't Eisenhower ever heard of the slave-trade? Don't speak to me of UNO. It's a collection of gangsters and their molls. It ought to be called the Harlot's House. I spit on it.'

The language is extreme but the facts, alas, cannot be faulted.

Nor is it only the young who feel this contempt for UNO. Perhaps the most striking illustration of the revolution in what may be called 'international ideology' is provided in the person of one man—the late Dr Gilbert Murray.

When I was at Oxford, Gilbert Murray was a man to whom the young idealist went with a sense of pilgrimage. He was the figure-head of all our dreams—a great classical scholar who might lead us forward to the golden age. Though the world scene darkened Murray remained always incorruptible in his championship of the international idea; for ten years he was chairman of the League of Nations Union and for eighteen years its co-president; and after the last war he was among the leaders of sentiment for organizing the United Nations.

And then—what did he say, in the fullness of his years? In one of the last interviews that he ever gave[1] he proclaimed that the UN Assembly 'no longer speaks with the voice of morality', that its vote is determined by 'illiterate prejudice and narrow national self-interest' and that by obeying its decisions the civilized nations of the world are bowing to the will of countries that are 'semi-barbarous, anti-Christian, anti-white.' One would have thought that such words, coming from one of the greatest figures of twentieth-century Europe, would have created an international sensation. As far as I am aware, they were not even quoted.

What interests us, however, for the purposes of this survey, is that if any young man in the twenties had talked like that about the League of Nations, he would have been regarded as mentally deranged. But then, of course, he couldn't have talked like that. The twenties were an Age of Innocence. And though the League of Nations, in the fullness of time, was to reveal its corruption and its total incompetence, it was, by comparison, a harmless institution. It was not, like UNO, an active menace to peace. And in some minor respects it actually did good; it raised the expenses of the white slave traffickers, and it made it rather more difficult for the drug-sodden peoples of Egypt to obtain their necessary ration of hashish.

The twenties, then, were politically an Age of Innocence, and the great illusion persisted—the illusion that the parliament of man was already in existence, on the shores of the Lake of Geneva. This illusion I shared, and was to keep until the end of the decade, when I went to Geneva to see for myself. (Among

[1] *Life*, April 15, 1957.

the things I saw were a number of delegates furtively reading dirty French magazines under their desks, while they debated the best ways to ensure the certainty of another war. I wonder what they read at UNO?)

But though we were in the grip of an illusion, we were not milk-and-water idealists; we were just as angry as the young men of the fifties, but we were angry about different things. Because we believed so passionately in the League of Nations we struck out fiercely at all those who seemed to be undermining its authority . . . in particular the international ring of the armament makers. If the modern young man had the same faith in UNO, he might show a similar indignation. Having no such faith his anger finds very different objects of attack.

Moreover, strange as it may seem, I believe that in the twenties we had a far more vivid realization of the bare physical agonies of war for the common soldier. Were those agonies, in fact, greater in the first war? Or were we more sensitive? Or were our feelings in the last war blurred and deadened by the fact that the soldier was no longer isolated in his agony—that he was merely a unit in a common crucifixion of the human race?

These questions seem worth answering.

One cannot compile statistics of human agony, and therefore one cannot compare the first World War with the second, in terms of sheer pain. When one thinks of the destruction of Berlin, the miseries of Dachau, and the macabre aftermath of Hiroshima, it is possible that the second war produced refinements of bestiality unknown to the first, practiced on an even wider scale.

In spite of this, as we have observed, the revulsion from agony, when it was all over, was far less keen after the second World War than after the first. Perhaps this was due, in part, to the difference between the physical conditions of the combats. The main horror of the first World War was the long drawn-out torture of the trenches in France, which was enacted on our very doorstep; it was as though the screams of the wounded could be heard across the Channel; the stench of the corpses in No-Man's-Land might have been blowing over the Sussex Downs. To an island population, living in comparative comfort—and they included the intelligent young men, who were still at school—this gave to the tragedy a specially hideous twist; it was as though we were sitting impotent in the stalls watching a body being slowly done to death on a brightly lighted stage.

This particular horror was not present in World War Two, and I think it is due to the reason suggested above . . . the whole civil population was involved. Our sensitive youth of 1940, bending over his Latin verbs at Eton, was aware that at any moment the sirens might be sounding and hell break loose over his head. As for his mother, reading her morning newspaper in London, the accounts of yesterday's battles abroad seemed less harrowing because she was reading them in a house from which the roof had just been blown off. The world, it is true, was supping on horrors, but we were all sitting at the same table. Because of this, even Hiroshima did not make so lasting an emotional impact as Passchaendaele.

(As a nauseating example of this I may quote the fact that on my last visit to New York, I heard a cabaret artist use the word Hiroshima as a comic gag in a point number. The audience laughed heartily.)

There was another reason why our intelligent young man, who was a schoolboy during the first World War, carried with him this poignant awareness of the physical agonies of war; he was being eloquently reminded of them by a series of brilliant writers who themselves had experienced those agonies. No novel of the fifties had a fraction of the emotional impact of Remarque's *All Quiet on the Western Front*, which revealed the naked reality of war as vividly as if a bandage had been ripped from an open wound. No poet of the fifties distilled such concentrated bitterness as Siegfried Sassoon. I can still remember Siegfried sitting on the floor of an undergraduate's room at Oxford, with the firelight flickering on his face, reciting one of his war poems to a group of students who had been too young to go to war. 'Reciting' is perhaps the wrong expression; Siegfried was a shy, diffident young man whose spirit had been brutally maimed; he spoke his verses as flatly as though he were an adjutant giving out the orders of the day. Perhaps, for that reason, their effect was all the more shocking.

'BLIGHTERS'

The House is crammed: tier beyond tier they grin
And cackle at the Show, while prancing ranks
Of harlots shrill the chorus, drunk with din;
'We're sure the Kaiser loves our dear old Tanks!'

I'd like to see a Tank come down the stalls,
Lurching to rag-time tunes, or 'Home, sweet Home',
And there'd be no more jokes in Music-halls
To mock the riddled corpses round Bapaume.

After that evening, as we walked back to our colleges through the cold moonlit streets, we renewed our vows of 'Never Again!' Nor were those vows lightly made; as the decade progressed they were strengthened and extended, leading us to expound causes and pass resolutions which greatly shocked our elders and betters, culminating in the notorious Oxford Union debate in which a large majority of undergraduates voted that in no circumstances would its members fight for King and country.

It is hard to imagine such a motion being passed today; indeed, it is hard to imagine its even being debated. Not because the modern young man is more virile or more 'patriotic'; on the contrary. Rather is it because the whole subject has become academic. The circumstances no longer exist in which any group of young men can fool themselves that it is possible to change the world by a resolution in a students' debating hall. Pacifism has gone the way of all the other

B

'isms', and the white flag has gone the way of all the other flags, national and international; throw them into the cauldron and they all come out a dirty grey.

Whatever else may be said against the twenties, they were not grey; the whole decade is drenched in colour. True, we had our 'poets of disillusionment', of whom T. S. Eliot was perhaps the most eminent. Eliot's philosophy was summed up in three lines which have been quoted more often than they deserve:

> For I have known them all already, known them all
> Have known the evenings, morning, afternoons,
> I have measured out my life with coffee-spoons.

Some contemporary historians have attached too much importance to these liverish lines. The vast majority of us were not measuring out our lives with coffee-spoons; we were dreaming, dancing, composing, campaigning. Needless to say, we were constantly informed by the press that we were a collection of worthless dilettantes, whose morbid eccentricities would soon be forgotten. 'A flimsy crew, these moderns.' That was the verdict of H. G. Wells on one occasion, and it was heartily endorsed by the majority of the critics. Among those destined for the curtain of oblivion were such figures as Edith Sitwell, Noel Coward, Epstein, Cecil Beaton, Graham Sutherland, William Walton, Oliver Messel . . . and indeed the great majority of those whose names are still household words today. One wonders how many of the young men and women of the fifties will still be in the bright lights in 1988?

However, there is a hint of middle-aged disgruntlement in such a question. And our foreword has begun to bore me as much as it has doubtless begun to bore you. This book, as I hinted before, is really only a light-hearted collection of snapshots. Let us open it. If an occasional shadow falls across the pages, maybe you will not notice it . . . maybe it is in my eyes alone.

CHAPTER ONE

LET'S ALL GO DOWN THE STRAND

SUPPOSING that a modern young man could be transported to 1920 by a magic carpet, and set down near Trafalgar Square on some blustery day of spring, what would strike him most? That would depend, of course, on his temperament. If he were interested in the theatre he might be surprised by the number of familiar names which in those days were already in bright lights. Names like the enchanting Yvonne Arnaud. In those days she was as slim as a straw, kicking up her heels with Leslie Henson in a show called 'Kissing Time'. Names like Marie Löhr, whom he has probably seen on television, and Gerald du Maurier, of whom he has certainly heard through the cigarettes. And over the Haymarket he would see the name of Gladys Cooper, who was at the beginning of her life-long struggle to prove to the world that she could act, in spite of her beauty.

It must be difficult for the modern young man to realize the impact on contemporary society, in the twenties, of beauty such as Gladys Cooper's. When Gladys played Magda, and put on a black wig to do so, the event was front page news. She looked fabulously beautiful in the wig, especially as Edward Molyneux had designed some very brilliant dresses to go with it. But should she have done it? Had she, indeed, the *right* to do it? Gladys, after all, belonged to the whole country, and the British public felt that it ought to have been consulted on the matter.

The mechanical means by which this beauty was disseminated was the picture postcard, which was the modern equivalent of the pin-up. There were two essential differences between the picture postcard and the pin-up. Firstly, the picture postcards were all as clean as a whistle. Breasts were indicated, of course, but only mistily, behind discreet layers of tulle; they were not protruded like battering-rams.

The other difference was psychological. The smiles and gestures of the picture-postcard ladies almost always indicated a mood of coyness, of whimsicality. If they were portrayed smoking a cigarette, the lips were pursed, the eyes were slightly askew, and the caption might well have been 'Oh, what a naughtee, naughtee little girl I am!' The comparative rarity of women smokers is indicated by the dialogue of a typical cigarette advertisement.

He: Cigarette, darling?

She: Well . . . perhaps just one, somewhere where nobody can see us! (Aside) I *do* hope he smokes Kensingtons!

Coyness, coyness everywhere! The ladies of the fashion plates were so coy that they seemed to be dislocating their bones, screwing round on their hips, slanting their necks at impossible angles. One of the most popular advertisements of the day showed the evergreen Miss Dorothy Ward biting . . . yes, *biting* . . . a long string of Ciro pearls. She was not biting them, like a sensible modern girl, to see if they were real; no, she was biting them in a frenzy of insouciance, with an ever so roguish smile, and her eyelids obviously fluttering. In the background one seemed to hear the twirling of ghostly Edwardian moustaches.

Roguishness reached its peak in a song of the period called 'I've never been kept waiting'. This was 'created' by a rather tragic girl called Teddie Gerrard. Teddie was a sort of Tallulah of the Twenties. (Now one comes to think of it, Tallulah herself was also a Tallulah of the Twenties; I saw her debut with Gerald du Maurier, and *that* was a first night to remember.) But whereas Tallulah's wickedness is really a pose—a mask to *épater les bourgeois*, for no woman can remain beautiful and gay and vital in her fifties on a diet of cocktails and cocaine . . . Teddie was, in actual fact, a stupidly naughty girl. She really did take drugs, and she really did drink to excess. I once saw her so drunk at a matinee that she could not remember the chorus of *Limehouse Blues*, which she must have sung at least a thousand times. As for her lovers, to say that she had catholic tastes would be a screaming understatement.

The general public, of course, did not know the facts. All they knew was that Teddie was a 'naughtee, naughtee' little girl. Hence the sensation caused by 'I've never been kept waiting'. Do you know how Teddie sang it? She sang it in a very revealing dress and . . . hold your breath . . . she paused for a whole bar between the words 'kept' and 'waiting'! Did you ever hear of such naughty naughtiness? There she was, the delicious creature, singing . . .

'I've never been *kept* . . .waiting!'

The members of White's Club, thronging the stalls, tied themselves into knots of lubricity at this announcement. 'D'you hear that? Never been kept, what? Ha! Ha! Never been *kept*! You're telling me! Ho! Ho!'

Then came the next line, to the hushed house . . .

'I've never been *kept* . . . hesitating.'

By now the whole house was in a state of panting expectation, and even the members of the Reform Club, in the dress circle, were moistening their lips and reflecting how far we had come since the days of Mr Gladstone.

We had, indeed, come a long way since the days of Mr Gladstone. And when one thinks of that frightful little song, we can be thankful that we have come a long way since the days of Teddie Gerrard. For Teddie, in spite of her aforesaid catholic tastes in sexual relations, was adopted as the symbol of all that arch, roguish, pouting, chase-me attitude to sex which, today, seems so curiously dirty.

This dreadful ultra-femininity has vanished from the world, one trusts for ever. It was a hangover from that horror . . .

Scott's 'woman in our hours of ease, uncertain coy and hard to please.' Such a woman today would find herself the odd girl out.

Still walking down the Strand, in the spring of 1920, our young man from the fifties, if he happened to have an interest in female beauty, would find himself constantly blinking in astonishment at one feature of the then 'modern girl', her hair. Did women really have so much hair? And did they really think it an asset? We are still, you see, in the shadow of Scott, when her hair was a woman's 'crowning glory'. On a hoarding across the road there is a gigantic poster for Harlene Hair Drill, portraying a female monster violently scratching her head, rubbing in the precious liquid in order, presumably, to encourage her hair to even greater excesses, for it already stretches to her waist. Such a creature might well fill our modern young man with bewilderment. How did women support such loads in those days? How did they keep up their strength? How did they discipline such a mass of material? He would have found the answer in the shops around him, which would have been filled with mysterious devices like Hinde's Curlers and—of course—an array of hair-nets big enough to cover the whole of Britain.

And though he might not agree with the late Mrs Somerset Maugham, who observed sharply that 'all hair is obscene', he would probably agree that when women, later in the twenties, decided to cut their hair, they took as important a step to freedom as when they got the vote.

This may seem a trivial journey, this little stroll down the Strand in the spring of 1920, and obviously it must have many diversions. And yet, in some of these apparently trivial details, in the sights and sounds of the streets, we may be able to recognize symptoms that are not so unimportant.

Thus, as we near Aldwych, it is more than possible that we

may be greeted, from the gutter, by the strains of Ivor Novello's *Keep the Home Fires Burning*, played by a derelict ex-soldier on a cracked mouth-organ. All over London there were these tragic bands of forgotten men, playing Ivor's tune to passers-by who were heartily sick of it. Ivor once told me that it nearly drove him mad. 'I made £18,000 out of that tune,' he said, 'and if I hadn't spent the lot, I'd give it to those poor devils.'

And here, because of this agreeable little melody, echoing from the gutter, we are reminded of a highly disagreeable fact —the fact of unemployment. Here too, perhaps for the first time, we are made to realize one of the fundamental differences between ourselves and our young friend. Unemployment, to the vast majority of young men born at any time after 1936, can only be a word in a dictionary. Naturally, if he were the son, say, of a Welsh miner, the word might be more familiar to him, but it could have no personal application; it must always remain academic. Unemployment was by no means academic to us. I hope that I am not claiming any exceptional sensibility when I say that it entered into our souls. Even if we came from families which were comparatively well-to-do, it was always at the back of our minds, like a feeling of guilt.

Moreover, unemployment in those days was ... as it were ... dramatized by an accident of history, for the echoes of the bugles of the first World War had scarcely died away; the gilt had not had time to tarnish on the medals; and over the head of the ex-serviceman there was still to be seen the faint glimmer of the halo with which a grateful population had invested him during the actual conflict. Now, almost over-night, he was unwanted. By the end of the year, there were unemployed riots in Downing Street, and in the *Daily Mail* was published for the first time the word 'malnutrition' ... a genteel euphemism for a grim fact. Particularly sickening was the attitude of some of the glossy magazines. During the coal strike of October 1920, these were filled with sneering pictures of miners getting into motor-cars after 'spending an evening at the cinema', and of their wives, in fur coats, enjoying themselves on shopping sprees. The readers of these pitiful productions might have been surprised to learn that the average wage of a putter—and in those days the work was often dangerous—was no more than £4 a week.

We seem to be hearing some ugly echoes from Ivor's little tune, drifting towards us from the gutter. Our young companion might well feel justified in remarking: 'You must have been a pretty hard-fisted lot in those days.' He would be right, in so far as he was referring to middle-aged people of the 'upper classes'. In the twenties the ghost of Lady Clara Vere de Vere had not been wholly laid, and I need not recall to you . . . or need I? . . . the awful words which Lord Tennyson addressed to *her.* 'Go, teach the orphan boy to read! Go, teach the orphan girl to sew!' There was still a very definite conviction, among the Lady Claras of the time, that the lower classes were the lower classes and should never expect to be anything else. One of the most nauseating features of the decade was the fury with which the upper classes regarded the lower for their refusal to become domestic servants, although they were unemployed. The papers were full of letters from outraged householders protesting that the lower classes did not want to work, that they would rather 'live in luxury on the dole' than take a job as a cook or a housemaid or even a second footman.[1]

Fifty pounds a year was still considered a fair wage for a 'cook-general'. For this remuneration she was expected to rise at seven, to make the fires, tidy up the house, prepare all the meals and work a six-and-a-half-day week. She had an 'afternoon off', and she must be back, at the latest, by eleven o'clock. The idea of giving her a latchkey would have been regarded as immoral. My own mother, who was the kindest and gentlest of women, was horrified when one of the housemaids asked

[1] The extent to which they were 'living in luxury on the dole' may be gauged by the fact that in some cases a family of five had to support themselves on fifteen shillings a week.

for a latchkey. 'I should not be able to sleep,' she said, 'if I felt that she was still out.'

In short, Britain was still, to some extent, a slave state. True, there were Christian households with devoted retainers who were, in fact as well as in name, 'members of the family'. But they were few and far between. Domestic service, as a general rule, was another name for slavery. How else can one describe a state in which tens of thousands of under-privileged females were chained in cellars in order to minister to their mistresses? The chains may have been economic but they were none the less real, and though the cellars were dignified by the name of basements they were still cellars. I remember walking round a London square on one occasion with Arnold Bennett. It was a blustery evening in April, and he trailed his umbrella along the railings. From time to time the white face of a servant would peer up through a grimy window, startled by the rat-tat-tat. He turned to me and said: 'One day those slaves will revolt. It may not be in my time, but it will certainly be in yours.'

He was right; the slaves have revolted; 'domestic service'— except in a few households that are exceptionally rich or exceptionally understanding—is a dead profession, and it will never be revived. Some Balzac yet unborn might do worse than choose it as a theme for a novel; here, surely, is the setting for a major tragi-comedy. The 'period' notes which occur to me at random for such a work would include:

1. The 'character'. This was a pathetic piece of paper, much creased, from the former employer, stating that Mary Jones, or whatever her name might be, was a good plain cook, honest and sober, with a cheerful disposition. She probably burned the toast, drank like a fish, and was permanently sunk in Stygian gloom. In spite of this her employer, having dismissed her, usually gave her a good 'character'. This deception was not considered at all improper; it was merely a way of saving 'unpleasantness'.

2. The 'follower'. This is a word that will soon have 'obs.'

after it in the *Oxford Dictionary*. But in the twenties *Punch* was still using it. 'Follower' meant boy friend. There was a great deal of hissing, shocked conversation about 'followers' coming into the kitchen. It seems to me a rather beautiful word . . . suggesting a faithful shadow, pursuing a trail of love, even down the basement steps. But to the upper middle classes it was a term of ridicule and reproach. 'No followers' was still a common phrase in the advertisements for domestic help. This meant that never, in any circumstances, could a respectable, healthy young woman invite a young man to share a cup of tea in her basement. 'No followers!' When one considers the inhuman arrogance of those two forgotten words, one is almost reconciled to living in the atomic age.

3. The 'uniform'. Parlourmaids of the middle classes still wore aprons which tied in long bows at the back, collars and cuffs, and caps. If a parlourmaid had answered the door or

MAY 2, 1923.]   PUNCH, OR THE LONDON CHARIVARI.   419

"HOW DO YOU LIKE YOUR NEW MAID?"
"SHE'S A PERFECT TREASURE, BUT I DO WISH SHE WOULDN'T CALL ME 'OLD THING.'"

served tea in any less formal attire her mistress would have considered herself *déclassée*. These uniforms were usually black, but sometimes a 'daring' hostess would dress her maids in grey or plum colour. The maid, of course, was never consulted about her own preference.

Those of us who are as old, or nearly as old, as the century, will probably never quite accustom ourselves to the strange apparitions who nowadays present themselves when we ring our friends' front door bells. Low comediennes with rolled-up sleeves and dirty aprons, bewildered stable-boys, butlers so old that one feels one should assist them across the hall, haughty young ladies, heavily made up, who stare at one as though one had come to tune the piano.

For myself, I welcome the death of domestic service. There is no reason why it should have been a degrading profession, but society—with those few Christian exceptions—made it so. And society was ably assisted by the press, in particular by that darling of the middle classes, *Punch*. Throughout the twenties, *Punch*—not for the first time in its history—was faithfully championing all the most deplorable aspects of British social life. The war was over, so it could no longer continue its shameful jibes at the 'temporary gentleman'—the 'comic' buffoon whose crime was that his gallantry had earned him promotion from the ranks. So it turned its coarse savagery on to the domestic servant . . . ridiculing every suggestion that a servant might perhaps be also a human being. Those who are inclined to lament the passing of the 'good old days' might do worse than turn up the old volumes of *Punch*. They will be reminded not only that a social revolution has taken place but that it was long overdue.

Still walking down the Strand, our modern young man would have been reminded that the revolution in society has been matched by the revolution in art. Artistic London was still under the shadow of Lord Leighton. There were no cheap reprints of Picasso, and though Van Gogh's 'Sunflowers' were beginning to shed their golden rays in a few little shops of the *avant-garde*, they only made people gape and giggle. Today this flaming masterpiece is a commonplace of suburban decoration; it is delivered along with the 'modernist de luxe dining sweet' and hung on ten thousand walls above the inevitable rubber plant. I preferred it when it was less popular.

The artist who attracted the fiercest thunderbolts of contemporary criticism was . . . believe it or not . . . Jacob Epstein. The first showing of his 'Christ', in the first few weeks of the decade, was greeted with a hullaballoo of abuse, and if our modern young man had passed by the galleries where it was exhibited, he would have seen the public emerging into the street in a frenzy of indignation. From the letters in the popular press you would have thought that this work, a psalm in stone, conceived with the utmost reverence, was some form of obscene phallic symbol. Even the most sober journals appeared to be totally unable to understand it.

'Had he lived in the time of Torquemada and the Inquisition,' boomed the *Morning Post*, 'Mr Epstein would have ended his career in the flames of an *auto de fe*. The head is elongated and of a *negroid* type. Nothing could be less Christ-like . . .'

The critic of *The Times* threw up his hands in despair. 'We feel a bewilderment, an incongruity, between the vivid reality of the face and the *Byzantine* feeling and attitude.'

Whereas the *Sunday Times* dismissed it as 'gaunt, ascetic, with a suggestion of the *Mongolian* in type.'

Here were three critics of three great newspapers tying themselves into knots over one of the most direct and eloquent sculptures of the century, and finding it respectively negroid, Byzantine, and Mongolian! I doubt if there could be quite so grotesque an exhibition today.

I took time off from Oxford to see the Epstein, and I had luck in the choice of day, for there, standing by the Christ, was one of my idols . . . Pavlova. She was escorted by an endearing

Pavlova, by Dame Laura Knight

man called Rudolf Kommer, who was afterwards associated with Max Reinhardt. I had only the slightest acquaintance with Kommer, but this was too exciting an opportunity to let pass, and after a few moments I had got myself introduced.

How did Madame like the Epstein? It seemed the obvious thing to say and I said it.

Pavlova sighed and made no reply.

'She is sad,' observed Kommer cryptically.

And indeed, she looked very sad indeed—very sad, and very small and very white.

'She is sad about her swans,' observed Kommer.

Then Pavlova spoke. 'They have forgotten me,' she said in husky tones.

Kommer nodded. 'All of them,' he said. There was an impish gleam in his eye.

'But I will make them remember me again,' proclaimed Pavlova. With which, she turned and walked out. She did not walk very prettily; few great dancers do.

I had little doubt that Pavlova would make the swans remember her again. (These creatures, I afterwards learned, resided on a lake in the gardens of her house at Hampstead.) I certainly remembered her myself, for I had seen her when I was nine years old. She was then at the snowy peak of her career, and she remained in that rarified atmosphere for another twenty years. I was taken to a matinee at the Palace Theatre where she was supposed to be dancing with Mordkin; but she didn't dance with Mordkin. She floated on to the stage, slapped his face and floated off again. She was having one of her celebrated temperaments. Down came the curtain, out came Mordkin shrugging his shoulders, and one little boy in the audience burst into tears. But I cheered up again later on, when she danced solo, and I came out of the theatre in a trance which lasted, on and off, for the rest of my adolescence.

How great was Pavlova? How did she compare with Ulanova or Margot Fonteyn? Presumably the modern generation must sometimes ask this question. (I have constantly asked it about Nijinski. Did he really do that legendary leap in *L'Apres-midi*? Did he really remain suspended in the air? Time and again I have pestered Edwardian dowagers with those questions. 'Yes, he did,' they have always told me, and each time that I receive their assurance, I sigh with relief.)

I may be able to answer the question about Pavlova . . . though whether the answer will be interesting is another matter. Perhaps it can be made more so by saying that I believe there to be certain artists who are, as it were, of the blood royal. These artists are very rare; they are instantly recognizable; and they differ from other artists not in degree but in kind . . . which means *in toto*. This is most easily illustrated in the case of singers. Patti died when I was a child, but I trusted the legend about her, and years later I was to prove it, from a cracked old record in the gramophone library of the BBC. Patti was seventy when she made it, and all she could manage was *Home Sweet Home*. The voice was almost inaudible through the scrapes and scratches. But the instant it came through, I smiled and nodded to myself. Here was the real thing, here was the blood royal, and only two other women since then had been born with it—Melba and Tettrazini. Your Flagstadts, your Maggie Teytes, your Schumanns and Schwarzkopfs and even—dare I say it?—your Maria Callas . . . are all a lot of commoners. Fine artists, lovely voices, exciting personalities—agreed. But compared with the old lady panting *Home Sweet Home* into an Edison Bell phonograph . . . commoners.

So now we can answer the question. Pavlova was of the blood royal, and it was not till almost the present day that any artist has appeared who can make the same boast. Age for age . . . and I saw her when she was over forty . . . she would have danced Ulanova off the boards. She could do things that no other dancer could even approach. When she danced 'The Dying Swan' the effect was of a figure floating across a sheet of ice, the flicker of the toes was so fantastically swift that it completely evaded the eye. Markova, at her best, was ethereal, Pavlova was more . . . she seemed, at times, to be transparent.

Rarest of all, she was at every moment a complete melodic unit. One appreciated this most in her adagios; her body was a single melodic line that flowed from her toes to her fingertips.

The younger generation must take my word for it, just as I take the word of the Edwardians about Nijinski. And lest they think that I am besotted, I am very well aware of her limitations. She was a royal dancer but a very silly woman. Her taste in decor was atrocious and she liked a lot of ghastly music. Though she danced to Brahms

and Strauss and Dvorak, she was much happier with Glazunov.

The last time I saw her was almost the last time that she danced in London. I was given the opportunity to watch her dance 'The Dying Swan' from the wings. It was a rare privilege, but I wish that I had not taken it. When she came off, she was totally exhausted; sweat was pouring down her face and her eyes were glazed. Dame Laura Knight once caught this glimpse of her in a masterly drawing called 'Expense of Spirit'. This brilliant artist knew Pavlova in every mood; with a twist of her pencil she could capture her in flight and pin her down for all posterity. I am deeply indebted to her for permission to reproduce two revealing sketches, hitherto unpublished. True, Pavlova always 'danced herself out', but on this occasion she was dancing very near to death.

The slender link of the Strand, my technical device for arranging these random snapshots, has broken. But there is another link that may give these pages a semblance of unity. You will have detected in some of the foregoing paragraphs a note of anger . . . youth's righteous indignation. This, I recall, was how I felt as a young man. I used to lie awake at night, clenching my fists about armament makers, about *Punch* being cruel to scullerymaids, about the totally damnable condition of the unemployed, about the slobbering apes who, when they looked at Epstein, were incapable of seeing through the face of the stone to the face of the spirit. Well, there is the link . . . anger. To my surprise, I find the anger persists to this day.

As one recalls all the snarling and snapping which greeted

every sign of youthful exuberance, one is inclined to marvel at the restraint of the younger generation against whom these strictures were directed. It is not as though their elders and betters were setting them such a wonderful example. Even royalty was behaving in rather an odd way. Not British royalty, of course, whose conduct was always impeccable, but foreign royalty, like the late Queen Marie of Roumania.

Although I am a staunch loyalist I am not a great one for royal gossip, and if I saw a royal nursemaid pushing a royal perambulator round the corner I would run a mile rather than listen to what its royal occupant had said, even if I could sell the story to *Life* magazine. But here is a little story about royalty which seems to me to have humour . . . a quality for which royal stories are not usually conspicuous.

On the thirty-first of May, in the year 1925, King George V was extremely angry. He tramped up and down the state apartments at Windsor, waving a Sunday newspaper in his hand, and reading extracts from it to one of his gentlemen-in-waiting.[1] Here are some of these extracts:

MY IDEAL MAN

by

Marie, Queen of Roumania[2]

I, for one, like a man to be a man. I would even like him to be a master, a creature to be looked up to, admired, even obeyed. Oh yes, why not, if he is worth obeying? There is a delicious thrill in obeying something big and strong.

I want to ride through the great wastes with him. I want him to fell trees, swim rivers, climb lonely peaks, watch the setting sun. I want to share his tent, his fire, his food.

Explosion on the part of King George V. I will not invent dialogue, nor make excessive demands on memory, but there is

[1] The Hon. Henry Stonor, who told me this story.
[2] *Weekly Despatch*, 31.5.25.

C

certainly no reason to doubt the reality of that explosion. How could there be? George V was a good man and a family man, with a mind which was constrained not only by nature but by environment. Queen Marie was his cousin. Moreover she had a perfectly good husband living in Roumania. This husband may not have been 'big and strong'—(he was, indeed, rather a dim little creature who was always getting tangled up in his sword on parade)—and he may not have been expert in providing 'delicious thrills', but damn it all, he *was* her husband, and he *was* a king, and here she was, coming out with this stuff about thrills, and riding through the great wastes, and climbing lonely peaks and sharing tents. *Tents.*

More extracts:

I remember a pair of velvety brown eyes, dark, dark, *dark* brown, and it makes me feel all soft inside. I want to sit, in the evening, hand in hand with him and rest. I want to lean my head on his shoulder. I want to hear his strong, faithful heart beat. I want . . .

Really, one begins to wonder what she does want. Owing to the predatory tendencies of a reader in the British Museum Newspaper Library, who has snipped off the end of the article, I am unable to supply the historian with Queen Marie's ultimate desire. But King George V evidently interpreted it unfavourably.

How was it that Queen Marie delivered such hot-making effusions? She was not only a beautiful woman; she had considerable intelligence and a pleasantly astringent taste in literature; on the shelves of her library in Bucharest there were six Aldous Huxleys to one Elinor Glyn. But Glyn at her most voluptuous, when she was writing with a bright purple plume dipped in grocer's *creme de menthe*, never did anything quite as embarrassing as that bit about the 'dark, dark, *dark* brown eyes' that made her feel 'all soft inside'. There is only one retort—in period—to that sort of thing . . . 'Whoops dearie!'

This was a phrase invented by Peter Arno in the *New Yorker*. He attached it to two charming grotesques whom he called 'The Whoops Sisters', and they became so popular that we all went about saying 'Whoops dearie!' to one another, sometimes in the most unsuitable places. And that was yet another reason for our elders and betters to chastise us. When a certain subaltern in a Guards regiment came out with a 'Whoops dearie!' to an outraged colonel on parade, he was required to resign his commission. Nowdays he would have been given a television contract.

As this book is an 'album' I am taking the liberty of sticking bits in here, there and everywhere. And as we have mentioned Elinor Glyn, here is a little snapshot of her. I used to interview her, now and then, which was a rather expensive way of earning a living, because she liked lunching at the Ritz and this was in the days before I had a secretary who understood expense accounts. At one of these luncheons, after she had been served with a huge portion of smoked salmon, she 'drew herself up' and fixed me with a glistening eye and said '*Tell your readers that sex has never touched the hem of my garment!*' It was the most wonderful sentence and it made my luncheon. There was something agonizingly nostalgic about it; it made me think of rich interiors in the nineteen hundreds, and sofas and tiger skins and joss-sticks burning in brass pots, and a gentleman with a moustache—from a Guards regiment, of course—fumbling about in the hopes of reaching the hem, but never quite succeeding.

Another phrase from that luncheon comes back to me. It concerns the Duke of Sutherland, who was then a young man. He was sitting at a near-by table, and Elinor Glyn, swallowing a great dollop of smoked salmon (which I feared would be extra on the bill) leant forward and hissed . . . 'If I were his mother I should make Geordie Sutherland use an electric comb!' I should explain that the Duke's hair was receding. Not enough to worry about, but Elinor, particularly in the matter of dukes, was a perfectionist.

One of the admirable things about Elinor Glyn was her almost fanatical respect for her own body, and for other people's. She once told me a story about going for a bathe with some film star in California. The two ladies, who were both queenly and statuesque, undressed behind some convenient rocks . . . and if any man tells me that he would not have liked to be a Peeping Tom on such an occasion I shall refuse to believe him. Elinor was struck by the beautiful contours of her companion's body and by the flawless quality of her skin. She asked her for her secret. 'A clothes brush, my dear,' replied the lady. 'Just a clothes brush.' So Elinor, ever afterwards, brushed herself heartily after her bath, and she strongly advised me to do the same.

She was a woman of the greatest courage, she was widely read, and she was no mean story-teller. If some of her work today arouses 'the sleeping lions of laughter' . . . well, that may be the fate of more than a few of us. I should have liked to have seen her in the post-henna days, when her hair, which she kept to the end, was frost white. I am told that she never looked more beautiful.

CHAPTER TWO

A LETTER FROM NOEL

I remember I had a lovely time writing a play called 'Ritz Bar' which you, my dear Beverley, most kindly tried to get the Norwegian Ambassador in Paris (why I can't think) to back. Whether he flatly refused or not I have forgotten, but for some reason or other it mercifully never saw the light.

Noel Coward, in a recent letter to the author.

I CAN, and will, refresh Noel's memory. Meanwhile, this might be the place to confess that Noel is for me not only the most entertaining figure of the decade but also, in a sense which few critics would admit, the most significant and the most enduring.

Perhaps I am prejudiced; we have so much in common. We are almost exact contemporaries, we started—economically and socially—from scratch, and at the outset of our careers we both served as an ideal target for the hearty, muscular, hair-on-the-chest type of critic. (When I first went into Fleet Street the chief football correspondent of one of the national dailies was also the dramatic critic. He used the same style for both functions; when one read him on Shakespeare one had a curious feeling that he was describing the tactics of a scrum.) At the time when Noel's first success was being slanged as morbid and degenerate, my own first novel—a little school story called *Prelude*—was being attacked as epicene and decadent. 'Poisonous from cover to cover' was the verdict of a journalist called James Douglas across three columns of the

Sunday Express. In those days I was unfamiliar with the immortal remark of Joseph Conrad, who observed: 'I do not read reviews, I measure them.' To an undergraduate—I was still at Oxford—such onslaughts can be wounding.

However, we both survived. Till late at night we sat over the fire of my tiny flat near the Marble Arch, taking it in turns to put pennies in the meter. We attended our first grand parties in the same variety of cheap dinner jacket . . . my own was so shabby that I used to rub Stephens' ink on to the elbows, with a peculiar effect on my partners' dresses. I remember a party in Grosvenor Square where neither of us knew anybody, though we wandered through the marble halls with glazed smiles directed at all and sundry. I stuck it out to the bitter end, but Noel left at midnight. As he went he said to me: 'In future I shall attend no more parties unless I'm sure of being the star.' The remark was typical . . . and to me, honest and endearing. It was on a par with another remark which he made to me, a year or so later, when we were both staying with Mrs Somerset Maugham at her villa outside Le Touquet. This was a most disastrous week-end in which everybody quarrelled with everybody else. Noel accused a ferocious blonde of cheating at tennis. Lady Plunkett accused an Italian princess—probably rightly—of cheating at backgammon. Liza[1]—Syrie Maugham's small daughter—fell out of a car and bumped her knee and Syrie swore that a fellow guest had pushed her out. A drunken American went to the Casino, won an indecent amount of money and was discovered flat out in the hall under a blanket of mille franc notes. Maugham himself seemed more than faintly bored by it all. These were not his friends, but his wife's; he obviously thought them very small change. Everybody was quite beastly to me, and at five o'clock on Sunday I went to Syrie and said: 'I hate your party and I'm going back to London.'

'You couldn't hate it more than I do,' said Syrie, 'and I'm going back too.'

[1] Now Lady John Hope.

So we ran away and left them all to it, and caught the boat. On the way up to London, in the dining car, Syrie, *a haute voix*, insisted on giving a lurid resume of the sexual peculiarities of her principal guests, to the enthralled attention of the rest of the passengers. On the following day she had a nervous breakdown and retired, for the moment, from the social scene. I did not have a nervous breakdown; I sat down and wrote a fragrant article on *The New Etiquette*.

But this is taking us from our little story about Noel. I was illustrating his perfectionism: 'I won't go to a party unless I'm the star.' It was the same with playing the piano. In one of the few lucid moments at Le Touquet I went into the long white drawing room and began to struggle with one of the easier passages of Rachmaninoff's Second Concerto.

Noel came in. 'You'll never play that concerto,' he snapped.

'No. But I can try. If it comes to that, it wouldn't do you any harm to practise a bit yourself. Why don't you?'

'Because I couldn't be sure of playing like a great artist. And if I couldn't play like a great artist, I'd rather not play at all. I'd rather continue to strum,' he patted me on the shoulder, 'in my own inimitable way.'

This perfectionism can be rather intimidating to the ordinary slap-dash sort of person like myself, who—in music at any rate—is inclined to rush in where Rubinsteins fear to tread. I am glad that Noel, in his maturer years, has tended slightly to relax his standards. Otherwise, surely, he would not have begun to paint. Noel's paintings are remarkable for an amateur, but they remain the paintings of an amateur.

Once Noel kindly asked me to stay at his house in St. Margaret's Bay, on my way to France. When I arrived he was painting in a frenzy—a seascape—and to the framework of an old melody of the twenties he was improvising a number which began . . .

'I'm such a Sisley when the moon comes out.'

He dropped his brushes. 'Beverley, you must learn to paint. At once.'

'But Noel . . .'

The wagging finger interrupted me. 'No prevarications, my dear Beverley. Everybody can paint. Look at Clemence Dane. Look at Ivor. Look at Adele.[1] No, perhaps don't look at darling Adele. But look at Graham.[2] Even Graham is painting. Nudes. They begin as Marie Laurencins but end up as rather dubious Gauguins, because he puts on the paint too thick and makes the sky too dark, so that the clouds run down into the poor darlings' navels. But at least he is painting.'

A pallette was thrust into my hand, brushes were provided, and a number of staccato injunctions were delivered at top speed. Before I realized what was happening Noel had made a brisk exit, slamming the door behind him and turning the key in the lock. From behind the door came the voice of the master informing me that he would be back in an hour to see what I had done.

That hour, for me, was one of mounting panic. What is one to do if suddenly confronted with a blank canvas, without the smallest technical experience, with no vestige of a design in one's head, and with nothing but the knowledge that a ravening genius is prowling about outside, waiting to see what one has accomplished? I decided that the only thing to do was an 'abstract'. Anybody, surely, could do an 'abstract'. So I did one, with trembling fingers. There were some nice little yellow squares and some green blobs and a thing in the corner that looked like a tarantula. I called it 'Crab Salad'.

Footsteps outside. The turn of the key. Entry of the master. He stands in front of the canvas and nods. 'A Klee,' he proclaims. 'A very passable Klee. And now, my dear Beverley, you need a drink.'

I did.

All of this has taken us a long way from Noel's unproduced

[1] Adele Astaire.
[2] Graham Payne.

play *Ritz Bar*, in which I tried to interest the Norwegian Ambassador in Paris. Noel seems to have forgotten the circumstances. I will remind him, not only because any unproduced play of Noel's must have a certain interest, but also because the ambassador was himself, in the twenties, one of the most colourful figures on the international scene.

He was called the Baron Wedel-Jarlsberg, and I asked him to back *Ritz Bar* for two very simple reasons. Firstly because he had a brilliant flair for the theatre—and indeed for all the arts. Secondly because he had a great deal of money. Neither Noel nor I had any, nor were we at that time in a position to command it. All our rich friends were waiting, as it were, in the womb of time.

But the Baron, fortunately, was not in the womb of time; he was in the Rue de Suresne, Numero Vingt Cinq. And he was very rich. So was his wife, who had previously been the Baroness von Arnim. (She was the sister of one of the most civilized statesmen that America has yet produced—Chauncey Depew.) They had the best chef in Paris, and their enormous establishment was almost oppressively elegant; one felt that all the Gobelins had just been whisked off the walls of the Louvre and that the Louis Quinze commodes ought to be under glass cases, and one wondered how many servants would be needed to clean the incredible chandeliers over the gilded staircase. At least, *I* wondered, because I was still in the £10-a-week stage, when it is very important for a good-looking young man to learn how the rich live.

After which, let this be firmly stated. Wedel-Jarlsberg—six foot two, bald-headed, hawk-nosed—was a great man. If he had been born in a German bedroom he would have been a Bismarck; if he had been born in a British bedroom, Churchill would not have had things quite so easy. Even so, with only the tiny state of Norway behind him, he exerted an influence far beyond the power of his country; during the conference of Versailles Clemenceau often sought his counsel, and Venizelos declared that he was the shrewdest diplomat in Europe.

In this opinion the Baron concurred. But though he was *grand seigneur*, with a charming arrogance, he was the kindest of counsellors; and with young artists and writers of talent he showed the most delicate understanding. He understood them so well, indeed, that when he was giving a dinner party which he thought might bore me he would draw me aside and say, in his remarkable English: 'I tink that tonight you must go and be wicked in the Place Pigalle, for there comes to dinner an Ambassador from South America and his wife, who is ogly like my left foot, and Madame X who is ogly like my right foot, and the Duchesse de Y who has a *grosse fortune* but is as stingy as *le diable*; so my dear boy, I tink you go out and find romance.' And he would give me a paternal pat, and push a ten-thousand franc note in my pocket, and out I would waltz through the courtyard, into the Rue de Suresne, with the spring sunshine on the pavements. And of course, I headed for the Ritz Bar, the scene of Noel's play, where romance always began.

The Ritz Bar, in those days, really was something. Perhaps, however, one should say 'bars'; there was a man's bar on the left and a mixed bar on the right, just across the corridor, and never the twain did meet. This did not imply anything sexually sinister; it merely meant, for example, that those two charmers, Eric Sawyer and Barry Dierks, could discuss the chateau they were building for Maxine Elliot in peace, without having Maxine bosoming all over them, suggesting a lot of tiresome alterations. It meant, again, that Cole Porter, looking like a startled leprechaun, could sip a Pernod and cast his dark, syrupy little eyes to the white and gold ceiling, and think out his devastating little rhymes, without the assistance of Tallulah or the Dollies or any of the other energetic ladies who might be around.

(Now I come to think of it, the first rhyme of Cole's that I ever heard was in the Baron's drawing-room. 'There comes

to luncheon a young American called Collporteur,' announced
the Baron. 'I *tink*'—here he wagged his finger—'I *tink* there
is much talent. *Enfin . . . on verra*.' And we saw. We saw Cole
sitting down at the enormous baroque piano, and singing one
of the first numbers he ever wrote, called 'The Babes in the
Wood'. I wonder how many people remember the final
couplet?

> They have found that the fountain of youth
> Is a mixture of gin and vermouth.

I adored the Ritz Bar. Think of it . . . champagne cocktails
at a bob apiece! And the scent of Gaulois cigarettes, and the
echo of Madame Chanel's laughter, and the back view of
Charles B. Cockran's neck, disappearing down the long
gallery lined with *vitrines*, and the sudden flurry of
Mistinguette, wrapped to the hilt in monkey fur, stepping
over the sacred masculine threshold in pursuit of her latest
young man, who is drinking behind a pillar with a rather
dubious Jamaican.

'Never the twain did meet', I seem to have observed, in my
description of the geography of these two institutions. But
in Noel's play they met with a bang. Men who for ten years
had 'never cast their eyes on a white woman'—or for that
matter on a white anything—were suddenly whirled into
terrific intrigues; gigolos were dragged from behind their
pillars and put through the strangest paces. It was all most
enjoyable. To quote Noel himself, from the aforesaid
letter:

> *Ritz Bar* was jagged with sophistication; the characters were
> either *demi-mondaine* or just plain *mondaine*; they shared their
> apartments and their lives with members of the opposite, or the
> same, sex. No wife dreamed for one instant of doing anything
> so banal as living with her husband. It was typical of the phase
> we all went through and, taken by and large, quite harmless:

to call it good, clean fun would perhaps be going too far, but at least it wasn't about the Death Wish and compared with Existentialism it becomes *Rebecca of Sunnybrook Farm*.

But from the point of view of the Norwegian Ambassador, for whose financial assistance I unsuccessfully pleaded, the play had a grave defect. In the last act, one of the young men shot himself. '*Et ça*,' said the Ambassador, leaning back on a *chaise longue* that had once excited the avarice of Queen Mary, '*ça ne ce fait pas au Ritz!*'

So the play remains . . . I hope . . . in the bottom drawer of one of Noel's cabinets in Jamaica. I say 'I hope' because obviously, and rightly, an unpublished manuscript by Noel, even after thirty years, must be worth a lot of money.

Earlier in this chapter I suggested that Noel was not only the most entertaining character of the twenties, but that his work was likely to endure. This suggestion is not shared by all the critics. Time and again, after an evening of delight which he has provided for me in the theatre, I have read, on the following morning, that the play with which he had diverted me, was flimsy, trite, brittle . . . in short a bubble. Sometimes the critics have been rash enough to forecast that so frail a creation was destined for a speedy collapse. This is ill-advised of the critics. These flimsy, trite, brittle bubbles have been floating round the world for the past thirty years and they have obstinately refused to collapse. They float to the backwoods of America, to the boulevards of Paris, to the broadwalks of Tokyo and the dour suburbs of Tunbridge Wells, and they still sparkle and shine. Roles originally created by Gertrude Lawrence in Molyneux dresses are repeated by Winnipeg matrons who buy their blouses at the local drug-store—and they still get across. Naturally, Noel employs stars, when he can get them, but even the brightest star will not draw the town in a bad play. This fact was once brought home to me by old Sir Arthur Pinero. I was in the Garrick Club on the morning

after the premiere of one of my own plays, called *Evensong*.
I was in a state of some irritation because most of the critics
had said that Edith Evans had given an unforgettable performance in a very poor part. Pinero came up behind me.
'Reading your notices?' I nodded. 'I've read 'em, too.' He
smiled. 'Cheer up, young man. They wrote just the same sort
of thing about *The Second Mrs Tanqueray*. And never forget
this: whatever the critics may say, no actress can give a great
performance unless she's got a great part.' In the following
years, whenever *Evensong* was filmed or broadcast or re-
broadcast or televised, I have recalled this remark with a smug
satisfaction.

There is nothing transitory about Noel's impact on the
theatre, indeed on the whole world of entertainment. When
he began to write, the average comedy dialogue was scored,
as it were, *allegro moderato*. Noel rescored it *allegro vivace con
brio*. He emphasized this by his personal direction and interpretation; the verbal speed of a play like *Present Laughter* is
breath-taking; and audiences who have been made accustomed
to this streamlined comedy will never again endure the
longueurs which were common in the pre-Noel theatre. He is
inclined to be pitiless to artists who cannot stand the pace
of his productions. Once, after a matinee of one of his musicals
in which a celebrated couple had slackened the tempo, he went
backstage and informed them that their performance was 'a
triumph of never-mind over doesn't-matter'. Before they had
time to recover from this observation he added darkly: 'And
remember, my dears, that nobody . . . but *nobody*, is indis-
pensable.' Exit.

Again, to the art of lyric-writing he gave a polish and a
sparkle which is comparable, and in some cases superior, to the
art of Gilbert. A quartette such as *The Stately Homes of England*
. . . another of those 'bubbles' . . . is a minor masterpiece. Not
only are the words wedded to the music with a perfection that
is only possible when the author is also the composer, but the
'bubble' itself is composed of very sturdy ingredients; the

whole lyric is a very penetrating piece of social satire of which
Sheridan, if he had ever written lyrics, would not have been
ashamed.

Noel can be a headache, on occasion a splitting one, but he
can never be a bore. Even if the Last Trump were to sound he
would have something apposite to say about it . . . probably
that it was flat. Which reminds me of the story of Noel's
arrival in heaven. The news of his decease naturally causes a
stir of pleasurable anticipation in the celestial regions; special
efforts are made to ensure that all shall be worthy of the
occasion; and as he approaches the pearly gates a vast assembly
of angels and archangels, suitably lit and dramatically disposed,
are ranged in serried ranks to greet him—rather in the manner
of a charity matinee of *Cavalcade*. The gates swing open; Noel
steps forward; the heavens are hushed, waiting for his first
words. His eyes sweep the arena from stalls to gallery, pausing
for a moment at the Royal Box. Then comes the celebrated
clipped accent which has so often echoed from the world
below. 'Which'—(pause for effect)—'which . . . is God?'

Noel, as we observed, can be a headache, even to his best
friends. He adored Gertrude Lawrence, and theirs was on the
whole an enchanting relationship. But it was not always idyllic;
there were occasions when the master gave full rein to his
powers of vituperation. Gertie herself told me of one of these
occasions. It was in the very early days; she had just been taken
for her first trip to the Riviera; and she came back bronzed and
delicious . . . but also rather grand. When she saw Noel there
were stories of parties and yachts and a great many titles. Noel
listened in silence, looking more and more Chinese. Then
Gertie, with an elaborate sigh, observed: 'Of course, I shall be
going again in the winter. I really don't think I could stand the
English winter.'

Noel nodded. 'No, darling. I don't think you could. Not
after all those years in sun-drenched Peckham.'

One forgives a great many headaches . . . at least I do . . . for
gusts of comedy such as that.

But there was one Noel headache—or rather, a whole trio of headaches—which is still faintly throbbing in the recollection of those who were the victims of it. And that is the cue for the entry of the Sitwells.

CHAPTER THREE

THE BATTLE OF THE POETS

A FEW years ago in New York, shortly after a performance of *Façade*, I saw Dame Edith Sitwell sailing through a crowd of American reporters. Sailing was indeed the word; she was like a proud ship, braving the winds of criticism. Her skirts billowed, her beautifully carved face—like a figurehead—was held erect; in the hiss and babble of tongues around her you could almost hear the echo of the spray.

Here, I thought, is a woman who is completely *réussie*, not because she has won world fame but because of the manner in which she has won it, and the odds against which she had to fight. She has always been completely true to herself; she has never written a syllable for effect nor composed an empty cadence. If compromise is indeed 'the grave of the soul' Dame Edith is among the immortals. One can see this even in her appearance. The finely but faintly drawn figure of the twenties —like a sketch in which the artist's hand has faltered, hovering uncertainly over the significance of certain lines and shadows— has matured into a figure which the eye contemplates with delight. It is a tribute to the flair of Cecil Beaton that he was among the first to see her beauty. When he took her photograph he laid her flat on the floor, in the manner of a monumental statue on a medieval tomb. This photograph gave rise to a great deal of acid comment in Mayfair. Lady Oxford observed, in my hearing, that it was 'sheer blasphemy'. In those days ladies were not accustomed to being laid flat on the

B. N. looking earnest

Edith: the quintessence of the exquisite

floor—at least not for the purposes of photography. They preferred to sit bolt upright against balustrades, with ancestral mansions in the background.

Edith has, of course, in private life, an enormous mansion in the background, and enough ancestors to fill a book. And that was her problem . . . to step out of the background into the light of day. Those who have read Sir Osbert Sitwell's monumental autobiography will need no introduction to the great house of Renishaw, which is its background. Renishaw was, to me, a frightening house. I remember lunching there in the early twenties. It was midsummer, but I could not rid myself of the impression that I was in the depths of winter; not because the day was cold but because the whole vast pile seemed to be overshadowed by . . . something. This impression was apparently shared by John Piper, who illustrated the book; all his drawings look as though they had been done in a thunderstorm. Which reminds me of a story about John Piper and King George VI. Piper was commissioned to execute a series of drawings of Windsor. They were apparently superb, but they all had Piper's familiar background of sombre skies and lowering clouds. 'What a pity, Mr Piper,' the King is supposed to have said, 'that you had *such* bad weather when you were down there.' If that story is not true, it ought to be.

Sir George—Osbert's father, who plays so large a part in the book—was also, to me, extremely alarming. (Osbert used to call him 'Ginger'.) When he came in to luncheon he glared at me as though I were an intruder, and when Osbert introduced me he merely sniffed and went away to sit by himself in a corner. He only uttered one remark during luncheon. He suddenly looked up at me and said 'I never know anybody in this house.' This was perhaps hardly surprising. Osbert's mother, Lady Ida, sat with two Greek ladies whom nobody else seemed to know. Sacheverell sat with a young man who, if anybody knew him, was not introduced. Osbert and I sat together. There was, in short, an atmosphere of some strain. This atmosphere pervaded the youth of this brilliant trio, and it was entirely due to the

D

strange, twisted personality of their father. Osbert's unforgettable picture of him in the autobiography has been sometimes
criticized for lack of taste; 'a son should not write like that
about his father'. This seems to me a ludicrous doctrine. If
one's father is a tyrant what is one expected to do? I am not suggesting that Sir George was always a tyrant, but he was not an
easy man, and in some respects the Sitwells would have been
better off if they had been born in a less stately home.

In spite of this strange background, and the perverse, aloof
and totally unpredictable parent who dominated it, the Sitwells conquered London in the very early twenties. Their
impact was sharp and immediate. Edith's early poems shot up
in the literary sky like fireworks; Osbert's epigrams echoed
round the town . . . rather, one imagines, as Wilde's must have
done, thirty years before. They had an astonishing flair for
spotting talent. If Lord Duveen had employed Osbert as a
buyer of modern pictures he would have made another fortune.

To the gossip writers of the period there was something not
quite nice about their conduct. After all, their social position
was impeccable or should have been; there were all sorts of
earls in the background, and even dukes; there was Eton, there
was the Coldstream Guards, or the Grenadiers, or one of those
things. There was money, and vast estates, and . . . horses. But
Osbert showed none of the right feelings about horses. The
sort of horses he liked were large and shaggy and docile, with
gentle mouths demanding sugar . . . the sort of horses who
pose, rather self-consciously, by rustic gates, as though they
were aware that Constable was about to paint them. Sleek,
professional horses, as portrayed by Sir Alfred Munnings, left
him cold. They left Edith and Sachy cold, too. And so this
regrettable trio, who might have been having a wonderful
time, going to delicious dances and riding to hounds, preferred
to spend their youth in the studios of really rather odd artists,
like that man Walter Sickert, or in the company of really rather
uncouth young men who played the piano like . . . what was
his name? Oh yes . . . William Walton.

So the press attacked them. And the Sitwells hit back. Here is an interview with Edith Sitwell, dated November, 1926.

WHO ARE THE SITWELLS? AND WHY DO THEY DO IT?
by Edith Sitwell

I wish people would stop saying we jeer at things. We never jeer. We hate cruelty and meanness and say so. We hate hypocrisy and say so. We are bored by snobbishness and say so. Do you want us to do otherwise?

Then there is the trouble about our view of natural objects. One gentleman complained because Mr Sacheverell Sitwell wrote:

Such are the clouds—
They float with white coolness and snowy shade
Sometimes preening their flightless feathers.
Float, proud swans, on the calm lake
And wave your clipped wings in the azure air.
Then arch your neck and look into the deep for pearls.
Now can you drink dew from tall trees and sloping fields
    of Heaven,
Gather new coolness for tomorrow's heat
And sleep through the soft night with folded wing.

The gentleman said he had never thought of clouds like that. Knowing him, I was not surprised.

It was inevitable that so vital and aggressive a trio should catch, sooner or later, the roving eye of Noel Coward. Noel in those days—the actual year was 1923—was writing his first revues. And revues are, in a sense, the journalism of the theatre, as anyone who has ever tried to write one is well aware. When you are writing a revue your ear must be sharpened to catch the echoes of every aspect of the contemporary scene. The ideal revue is dramatized *rapportage*.

So Noel's eye lit upon the Sitwells. He did not recognize their genius, he saw only the flamboyant cloaks in which they sometimes chose to disguise themselves. It was rather as though a young reporter, hurrying through a gallery of early works by Piccasso—whom the Sitwells, by the way, were among the first to champion—had dismissed these masterpieces with an airy epigram.

The result was devastating. One night in the autumn of 1923 the populace of London flocked to the Duke of York's Theatre to attend the premiere of a new revue by Noel Coward —*London Calling*. This was a brilliantly sweet and sour entertainment, with a number of haunting tunes, and plenty of expert dashes of vinegar. The vinegar bottle was in the hands of a plump, red-faced, middle-aged comedienne called Maisie Gay, who was an angel in private life but a demon on the stage, when satire was in the air. It was very much in the air on this occasion. For the peak comedy number of the second part of the revue was called 'The Swiss Family Whittlebot', and it was a savage parody of the Sitwells. The very names were wounding; Osbert was called Gob, Sacheverell was called Sago, and Edith . . . this was the unforgiveable word . . . Edith was called Hernia.

The curtain rose on Miss Whittlebot dressed in undraped green sacking with a necklet of uncut amber beads. Gob wore cycling breeches with a big bow and a green velvet coat, Sago a morning coat. By their side was a collection of rather peculiar musical instruments, to one of which Noel gave the name of the cophutican. Suddenly Miss Whittlebot—who had a little clump of fruit below each ear—burst into the following doggerel, accompanied by fitful gusts on the cophutican from Gob and Sago :

> Beloved, it is Dawn, I rise
> To smell the roses sweet
> Emphatic are my hips and thighs
> Phlegmatic are my feet . . .

The house rocked, and went on rocking. This was the sort of satire for which the British Theatre had been waiting. On a different note she gaily intoned . . .

> Rain, rain, pebbles and pain
> Tuckle and truckle and do it again,
> Houpla, houpla, dickery dee,
> Trolderol, trolderol, fancy me!

The programme ended with the Stage Manager frenziedly endeavouring to get Miss Whittlebot off the stage, and finally ordering the orchestra to strike up the next number.

If I had been sitting next to the Sitwells on this historic occasion I should have had this to say to them: 'Yes, Noel should be slapped; but darlings, if you ask for it in *la vie de Boheme* you get it, and you *have* asked for it . . . with the same delightfully arrogant assurance as Oscar, in the nineties, when he announced that he was "trying to live up to his blue china". Oscar had the impudence of genius and so have you, and these little episodes are part of the rough and tumble of the artist's life, and you should all rise above it.'

But it took them a very long time to rise above it. Though there was no actual duel, there were coolnesses which swept down the corridors of a great many country houses. In Noel's own words:

> It was on account of the 'Whittletot' sketch in this Revue that I unwittingly offended Osbert and Edith Sitwell. Some acrimonious letters were exchanged between Osbert Sitwell and myself, which we both enjoyed writing and reading, and the whole thing degenerated into a tiresome feud which continued convulsively for a few years, during which time we cut each other ostentatiously on every possible occasion and subjected many of our hostesses to delighted inconvenience.
>
> A few years ago I met Osbert Sitwell in New York, and he was extremely nice about the whole affair and persuaded his sister by cable to forgive me, so the feud finally evaporated, for which I was exceedingly glad, as I should hate my whole-hearted admiration for the Sitwell family to be impaired by a personal matter of such small account.

Before I leave this subject, in justice to Noel, the slap-worthy, and to make sure that both parties are offended, I feel justified in reminding the reader that the Sitwells were themselves not entirely unskilled in the art of holding people up to ridicule and contempt. I remember one occasion—(later than the twenties)—when they borrowed Lady Crewe's house in Chelsea for one afternoon in order to award prizes for The Worst Book of the Year, The Worst Poem of the Year, several other Worst Somethings or Others. Osbert and Edith received us dressed in deep black, with solemn faces, looking like literary undertakers. The 'prizes' were very repulsive, and consisted mostly of things like stuffed, glazed fish in glass cases. One of them—a curiously mangy stuffed cat, playing with some diseased mice and surmounted by a huge dome of glass —was dispatched to Harold Nicolson at the House of Commons. Harold Nicolson might have been justified in taking a dim view of this episode. If he did, he kept his feelings to himself.

CHAPTER FOUR

STITCHES IN TIME

TIME is the great caricaturist; the sharpest parodies are created merely by the passing of the years. Time has already drawn unkindly lines round many of the famous literary faces of the twenties, swelling the cheeks of the beer-drinking poets to grotesque proportions, fading the purple of G. K. Chesterton's waistcoat to a shoddy mauve, narrowing the lips of the Bloomsbury school till their prose sounds often pinched and thin. I was never 'received' by the members of the Bloomsbury school; I wrote with too coarse a nib in the wrong coloured ink, and I was more interested in life than in literature. On the very few occasions when I met Virginia Woolf I thought her lacking in kindness and not overloaded with humour.

Although she was regarded as an aspen of sensibility she was, in fact, capable of astonishing lapses in taste. One example will suffice. During the early years of the war, when the Royal Air Force was making its first sorties over Germany, the public became accustomed to a routine announcement of tragic significance . . . 'one of our aircraft has failed to return.' Night after night the quiet voice of the announcer ended his bulletin with these words—sometimes, of course, there were many more than one—and each time the words spelled tragedy, for somebody. The trite, official sentence acquired the sinister dignity of a tocsin. This was the phrase which Virginia Woolf chose to mock by applying it to a work of her own . . . the biography of Roger Fry. This appeared in the late summer of

1940, at the height of the Battle of Britain. As always, when a new book of hers was published, time halted for Virginia Woolf until she had learned the verdict of the critics; the pages of her diary flutter in agitation. . . . What will *The Times* say? How will the *Manchester Guardian* react? And the popular papers? Not that *they* really matter!

As it happened, on this occasion, when the very existence of the British people, and indeed of European civilization, lay in the tired hands of a few dogged young fliers, the biography of Roger Fry did not create quite the furore that its author had hoped. Eagerly she scanned the papers, flicking aside the tiresome news about the war, but the press ignored her. Finally, on August 2nd she opened her diary and wrote these appalling words: 'Complete silence surrounds my book; it might have sailed into the blue and been lost. *One of our books did not return* as the BBC puts it.'

To me, that is one of the most damning sentences in the whole of literature. True, Virginia Woolf was a pathological egocentric; she not only spent her life looking in the mirror but she pressed the glass so closely to her face that it bruised her features. But there should be limits even to pathological eccentricity; and she exceeded them.

II

Bloomsbury, in the twenties, was very sure of the immortality of those whom it admitted to its circle, and equally sure of the imminent literary demise of those whom it excluded. Time, however, has ruled otherwise. Somerset Maugham was never 'in', but his stature lengthens with his shadow. (A great many eyebrows were raised in Bloomsbury when Desmond McCarthy, who *was* in, published an article suggesting that though Maugham wrote for the popular magazines, he wrote extremely well). Arnold Bennett, needless to say, was not 'in', nor Hugh Walpole, nor—in the true sense of the word— the Sitwells. Rebecca West was neither 'in' nor 'out'; I fancy that Bloomsbury was a little afraid of her. There was a 'don't-give-a-damn' air about Rebecca in those days. She had a matchless critical intelligence, and she could out-write nearly all of her contemporaries, when she chose; but her lust for life was stronger than her love of letters. She was quite capable of breaking up a literary discussion—in the most charming way, of course—and suggesting that everybody went out for a drink at the nearest pub.

P. G. Wodehouse, oddly enough, was 'in', though one had a feeling that he had been admitted by the servants' entrance. He was a sort of licensed buffoon, and it was quite permissible to wander round Bedford Square with a portfolio of Braque drawings, a volume of Lytton Strachey's essays, a copy of *The Times Literary Supplement* and . . . the latest Jeeves. (I must pause a moment to tell my favourite Wodehouse story. Once we went to the Zoo together. After a while we found ourselves in the monkey house. A large and ferocious-looking monkey stalked towards us, and stared. Plum Wodehouse stared back. Then the monkey got bored, turned round, and walked away, disclosing the fact that it was one of those monkeys with very bright behinds. This was, indeed, a behind to end all behinds, scarlet and purple and orange. Plum sighed and shook his head. 'That monkey,' he said, 'is wearing its club colours in the wrong place.')

Wodehouse, as we have seen, was 'in', Evelyn Waugh was not. This may seem surprising; but it may be explained by the fact that humour was not, to put it mildly, the distinguishing feature of the Bloomsbury school. Even Lytton Strachey's humour, with the passage of time, has a thin and peevish ring, as though he were writing on a slate.

And yet humour, surely, is the preserving salt of the novelist; it is an essential quality without which his work turns stale and unpalatable with the passage of time. That is why there is already such a musty flavour to the pages of D. H. Lawrence, who was one of the literary giants of the decade. Lawrence was devoid of humour; as a result he constantly produced—in all seriousness—lines which are apt to tie the average man up in knots. Nothing in the literature of parody is funnier than his tribute to the cow which he bought in his last days, when he was living in New Mexico. Lawrence could not buy a bicycle without investing it with a dark, mystic, sexual significance, so when he bought a cow, one feared the worst. One was not disappointed. After milking the amiable creature, in an ecstasy of devotion, he sat down and wrote: *The queer cowy mystery of her is her changeless cowy desirableness.* After reading such a sentence one is inclined to view Lawrence's heroines in a new light.

Maybe it is too early for *Lady Chatterly's Lover* to assume its place as one of the masterpieces of comic literature, but the time will come. This piece of nonsense was printed in Florence in 1928, and was immediately banned. Hugh Walpole gave me a private reading of it during luncheon in Piccadilly. He was no great admirer of Lawrence, either as a man or as a writer. He told me that during the first World War, when the Lawrences were in Cornwall, Mrs Lawrence used to wander about the cliffs alone, reciting poetry with a great wealth of gesture, spreading out her arms, invoking the sun and all that sort of thing. As she happened to be a German, this conduct aroused suspicion among the locals, who concluded that she must be semaphoring to submarines. The Lawrences took this very badly, as yet another proof of the general brutishness of the British.

III

Time has not only a pencil but an india-rubber, a fact which some contemporary novelists, with inflated ideas of their own importance, might do well to remember.

Consider the remarkable phenomenon of Sir Hall Caine. In the literature of the twenties he loomed very large indeed, today he has sunk into total oblivion. Let me fish him up for a moment. Hall Caine was a pompous little gnome of a man,

with a gigantic forehead, a small white beard, and a pronounced
stoop. He looked like somebody who had dressed up as
Shakespeare in a charade, which was hardly surprising, for he
was somebody who had dressed up as Shakespeare in a charade
. . . the charade being the literary parade of the day.

He resided—perhaps it would be more apt to say that he
'reigned'—in the Isle of Man, and people used to make pil-
grimages [*sic*] to see him there. When he came to London he
stayed at the Savoy, where he always spent a great deal of time
in the hall, prowling round in a long black cloak, basking in the
recognition of the public. I once tried to interview him there,
without success; he would never keep still, he was constantly
popping up from the sofa and sweeping across the hall to show
himself off. If I had known the word in those days, I should
have diagnosed him as an advanced case of paranoia.

He sold enormously—but enormously; one used to feel
quite sickened by the publisher's announcements. 'First edition
of fifty thousand copies exhausted before publication, second
edition of fifty thousand copies almost exhausted' etc., etc.
His novels were very long and he attached embarrassing titles
to them, such as *The Woman Thou Gavest Me*. I read *The
Woman Thou Gavest Me* at school, where I kept it in my desk
under a copy of Borchardt's Arithmetic. What a book! Such
goings-on! Somebody in it, I recall, went to bed with a nun,
or rather, thought of going to bed with a nun; nobody seemed
quite certain about it, least of all the nun. But England discussed
it with bated breath, and clergymen leapt into their pulpits to
denounce it all over Britain.

Strange as it may seem—or is it so strange?—this third-rate
novelist was held in some esteem by Bernard Shaw. Among
Shaw's lesser-known contributions to the drama is a scene in a
play called *The Wild Oat* by Sydney Blow. In this play Shaw
and Hall Caine were both satirized, and Shaw, whose mania for
self-advertisement was pathological, took the trouble to write
his own dialogue for the scene with Hall Caine. This is what
he wrote:

Shaw: When you open your lips, Hall, I seem to hear the immortal bard himself.

Caine (surprised): Ho ho! This from *you*, George!

Shaw: You deserve it, Hall. There are not two men living who admire themselves and one another more sincerely than you and I.

Here is a postscript. Turning over the files of an old magazine I found a photograph of Sir Hall Caine setting out to a very grand dinner that was being given to him by some of the leading members of the House of Commons, to celebrate the publication of his latest novel by Heinemann's. So I wrote to Heinemann's to find out if they still sold any of his books. No, they said, they didn't. Hall Caine left them at some time in the twenties to go to Cassell's. (Apparently there was a coolness because his name had appeared in an advertisement below that of John Galsworthy.)

So then I wrote to Cassell's. Did *they* sell any of his books today? Sir Newman Flower, the literary director of Cassell's replied in a tone of courteous regret. No, he said, they certainly had no Hall Caine titles in print today. Cassell's stopped publishing him in the 1940's. But there was a note in their ledgers to say that Heinemann's had taken over the stock. Perhaps they might help?

Well, every dog has his day.

Shaw, as we have seen, admired Hall Caine, or was willing to pose as doing so. Shaw's poses are sometimes difficult to detach from his principles.

At the beginning of the twenties Shaw, for the bulk of the respectable middle class, was still *persona non grata*. They had not forgotten his war record. Many years were to elapse before he was finally accepted as a major prophet. This worried Shaw not at all, and he went on his way prophecying. I have a personal reason for regretting one of those prophecies, because it cost me five pounds. This was the first of a series of disillusionments which were to continue over the years.

The occasion of the disillusionment was the Carpentier-Dempsey fight in July 1921, which roused the populations of England and America to frenzies of hysteria. People who would normally never have glanced at the result of a boxing match found themselves suddenly caught up in the general excitement, largely, one suspects, because of the considerable physical attractions of the young Frenchman. From such snares Shaw was no doubt immune; nevertheless he jumped up on to his rostrum and announced to the world, in terms as emphatic as he could command, that Carpentier was going to win.

The article appeared in the *Daily News* for June 30th. Its effect on me was so great that I backed Carpentier. How could any disciple of Shaw have done otherwise? Never was such a spate of invective aimed at those who dared to suggest that the Frenchman could conceivably lose. Such people were 'ignorant dupes'—'British greenhorns'—'jackasses'—'total incompetents'—'not fit to be trusted with money'. As a contribution to Shaviana this outburst seems to me of interest.

CARPENTIER AND DEMPSEY

A Warning to Betting Men

by G. Bernard Shaw

The time is evidently very near when journalists will have to obtain certificates of competence, like navigating officers.

I hope they will be examined just as strictly in pugilism as in political economy when that time comes. And by pugilism I mean not only the art of boxing, but the art of living by betting on prize-fights.

I affirm, *on my reputation for knowing what I write about*, that if all the reporters who have been contributing articles about the coming contest in New Jersey, had been put through twelve rounds with a competent professional, ninety per cent of those articles would not have been written, and nine-point-nine of them would have been contemptuously rejected as bookmakers' advertisements.

The last article of the kind at which I have glanced declares that the odds against Carpentier are four to one. How has this result been brought about in face of the fact that *the real odds are fifty to one against Dempsey?*

Why do the pugilists and the reporters go on like this? Georges is the most formidable boxer in the world; he is ideally built for his profession; another pound weight would be no use to him; he is game to his last breath, he has brains, style, character, consummate skill, and everything that a champion can have.

The explanation is simple. All these people who are running down Carpentier are so certain that he will win that they mean to put their shirts on him when they have humbugged all good American patriots into offering ridiculous odds against him.

If any British greenhorn doubts this, I ask him to recollect the precisely similar ramp that was rigged against Carpentier before his fight with Beckett. Why do I write this article, when there are so many other more momentous subjects to occupy me? Sheer compassion, nothing else.

I know nothing of Mr Dempsey; I have never seen him; and he may, for all I know, have every quality his admirers claim for him. But what I do know, absolutely and positively, is that they are talking arrant nonsense about Carpentier, and that they must know it if they know anything about boxing.

It is simply not humanly possible for any boxer to be superior enough to Carpentier to justify the odds at present announced; and, whatever the result may be, the people who are betting against Carpentier at those odds are being grossly duped. All the probabilities are that the French genius will win, and any man who bets on the contrary assumption is not fit to be trusted with money.

In conclusion, I solemnly declare that I am not waiting for the effect of this article to back Dempsey. Betting on boxing matches is not risky enough to excite me. I prefer writing plays about Creative Evolution.

Five days later Carpentier, who never had the ghost of a chance from the outset, was knocked out in the fourth round.

As I said, this was my first shock of disillusionment about Shaw. To me, personally, whenever I met him, he was always the soul of courtesy. I used sometimes to go to see him at Whitehall Court, as a reporter; it was a refreshing experience, for he treated reporters as equals. This was not one's invariable experience in reporting. Any journalist who had the ill-fortune to interview Lord Curzon, for example, was treated as though he had come to tune the piano. But then, of course, Lord Curzon was a very common man; if he had any of the instincts of a gentleman he was at pains to conceal them. Shaw, on the contrary, had exquisite manners, and he was always prompt to perform small acts of kindness. Thus, one day over a cup of tea, the conversation turned to his habit of writing postcards, and I asked him if there was any truth in the story of the postcard which he had sent to the OUDS. Apparently the President had written to ask if the society could produce Candida, and Shaw was supposed to have replied with a card bearing the words 'You can't but you may. G.B.S.'

'Yes,' said Shaw. 'I sent that card.' Then he added: 'Most of the important things about life can be put on a postcard.'

'And death?'

'Certainly.'

'A postcard from you on that subject would be worth a lot of money.'

'In that case I'll give you one.'

Whereupon he rose and went to his desk. A few moments later he came back with the card in his hand. On it he had written:

Combine my advice with Dogberry's: die like a gentleman and thank God you are rid of a knave. Tennyson told us to 'rise on stepping-stones of our dead selves to higher things.' I tell people the same. But no; we want our dead selves to be kept as my grandmother used to keep old wax candle-ends. I have no patience with such conceit.

I learned afterwards that this passage was not written on the spur of the moment; it was an extract from an article which he was writing for a Sunday newspaper. It was none the less precious to me.

In this article there is another characteristic passage: 'All the people I know who look forward to an eternity of themselves stipulate that they shall be angels in the next world. As in that case they certainly will not recognize themselves, nor be recognized by any of their friends, they might just as well go the way of all flesh without murmuring.'

How will Time deal with Shaw? That question would be easier to answer if it were not for Shaw's hagiographers, of whom the most fervent is Mr Sean O'Casey, once of Dublin, now of Torquay. (The change of locale does not seem to have improved the quality of Mr O'Casey's work.) One can understand O'Casey's genuflections but one is puzzled by those of Mr Colin Wilson, the author of that volume of elegant extracts *The Outsider*. He assures us that Shaw is at the moment at the nadir of his fame; he looks forward to a future in which the range of his works will tower lofty and secure, snowy-capped against infinity. This seems to me nonsense. Apart from *Saint Joan*, Shaw never wrote a line of great poetry, nor in the whole of his plays did he create a single character who lives when he steps off the stage. Men like Micawber and Pecksniff are always with us, and we may meet Becky Sharp at any party, but Shaw's characters only come to life in the limelight . . . and not always even then.

I remembered the postcard which Shaw had written for me, so long ago, when I paid a visit to his home at Ayot St Lawrence after his death. I went down as a tripper, and wandered through the hideous little house, asking myself, in growing bewilderment, how he could have lived in such a place, where almost every object was an affront to the eyes. How could he have endured such pictures and such ornaments? How could he have walked in such a garden, with its ghastly little triangular beds of golden rod?

The final shock was in the bedroom in which he died. 'Die

Melba. A rare picture, for she detested photographers—particularly in the open air

Inset

1. Melba's Low C.
Note mathematical regularity of vibrations
2. Top G.
3. Melba's trill

At bottom the modes owed little to nature

like a gentleman, and thank God you are rid of a knave,' Shaw
had written. He certainly died like a gentleman, with patience
and good humour, but he was not rid of a knave. For there,
grinning from the mantelpiece, was a signed portrait of Stalin.
The manner of a man's death is his own affair, and doubtless
Shaw, if he had lived to see the dethronement of his idol, would
have been ready with plenty of ingenious arguments to excuse
himself. As it was, he left the world with a smile from Stalin. I
could not help wondering how he would explain that to Saint
Joan.

E

CHAPTER FIVE

CAUSE CELÈBRE

Darling Peidi Mia,

Tonight was impulse—natural—I couldn't resist—I had to hold you darling little sweetheart of mine—darlint I was afraid—I thought you were going to refuse to kiss me—darlint little girl —I love you so much and the only way I can control myself is by not seeing you and I'm not going to do that. Darlint Peidi Mia—I must have you—I love you darlint—logic and what others call reason do not enter into our lives, and where two halves are concerned. I had no intention darlint of doing that— it just happened that's all—I'm glad now chere—darlint when you suggested the occupied carriage, I didn't want to go in it—did you think that perhaps I did—so that there would have been no opportunity for me, to break the conditions that I had stipulated —darlint I felt quite confident that I would be able to keep my feelings down—I was wrong Peidi. I was reckoning on will power over ordinary forces—but I was fighting what? not ordinary forces. Peidi you are my magnet—I cannot resist darlint—you draw me to you now and always, I shall never be able to see you and remain impassive. Darlint Peidi Mia Idol mine—I love you—always—always Ma Chere.

If I were ever to compile an anthology of love letters, this letter would be given a place of honour. The accent is common but the emotion is explosive. It hits the paper like the blow of a fist . . . the clenched fist of a man who is taut with sexual passion. A rather frightening letter, I think, a letter with rape in it . . . which was, of course, why it so greatly appealed to the lady to whom it was addressed.

The letter was written by a young ship's steward called Frederick Bywaters to a woman some nine years his senior called Edith Thompson. The pent-up passion in it led, at last, to murder, and the most celebrated case of the decade. Let us clothe these people, without any more ado, in flesh and blood; a murder trial is boring if one does not know what the principals looked like.

Edith Thompson had lovely eyes, fluffy brown hair, and . . . a very beautiful neck. It was white and supple and slender, and when you were close to her at the Old Bailey, and when there was a very tense piece of cross-examination, you could see the throbbing of the veins. Edith Thompson's neck was probably the physical symbol which set the seal on my hatred of capital punishment. I could not keep my mind off it. I could see the shadow of the rope closing in, drawing tighter, tighter.

Her lover, Freddy Bywaters, was square-chinned, square-shouldered, and rigid with sex. Like most over-sexed youths he was probably a violent sentimentalist; he was certainly a very mixed-up person; an amiable ape with the occasional instincts of a Lochinvar.

The judge was my least favourite sort of judge. His name was Shearman; he had a repulsively hard moustache which must have been torture for any female who came in contact with it; his voice sounded as though it had been kept for years in a rather cheap refrigerator. He was physically and spiritually thin-lipped. His son, Monty Shearman, was a very good friend of mine and an unlikely chip to come from such a block. Monty was quite a figure of the twenties. He lived in Adams Street—an exquisite façade which has since been destroyed. He had a great many charmingly disreputable artist friends who sponged on him. He drank too much, and told bawdy stories in a whisper, with a sly, secret smile. He did not care for his father overmuch.

Those are the dramatis personae. The suburban syren, with

the lovely neck, in a frenzy of physical passion over the lusty young sailor. Hovering over them, mercilessly scrutinizing them, the square, arid figure of a judge from whom all passion had long since departed. And in the background a dull, dark figure, slumped to the pavement in a pool of blood, the murdered husband . . . a figure whom most people, in the heat of the moment, tended to forget.

The story, as they say, 'had everything'. And I was destined to report it.

The Thompson-Bywaters murder case was the first piece of reporting which made me feel ashamed of being a journalist. And, I believe, the last.

The shame did not come till the last act, after Edith Thompson had been sentenced to death, when I was given the job of trying to persuade her father to give me her life story. This task was so utterly distasteful that it nearly made me quit Fleet Street for good. At the beginning, however, like everyone else, I was swept away by the sheer force and impact of the tragedy.

The facts were simple. At midnight on October 3rd, 1922, Edith Thompson and her husband alighted from the last train at Ilford, a dreary suburb in the North of London, and proceeded to walk down the long and equally dreary Belgrave Road, in the direction of their home. They were, presumably, tired. Both of them had been working all day—he as a shipping clerk, she as a book-keeper in a milliner's shop. At the end of the day's work they had spent an evening at the theatre. Now they were trudging home, alone with their thoughts.

The road was almost, but not quite, deserted. Following them, in the shadows, was a tough, lithe young man—Freddy Bywaters. He came at great speed, keeping close to the wall. There was a knife in his pocket. He caught up with them under the lamplight. He swung Thompson round, hurled a few insults at him, and stabbed him to death. Whereupon he ran away. From Mrs Thompson there were moans of distraction and despair. Then she heard other footsteps in the distance . . . a trio of late revellers returning from the station. She ran in their direction, and she cried 'Oh my God! Will you help me? My husband is ill; he is bleeding.'

Next day Bywaters was arrested, and in due course the two of them were charged with murder. Those are the bare, the very bare facts of the case.

Not a very extraordinary case, one would have thought. It was all excessively suburban—the locale, the characters, even the dialogue. Perhaps the dagger could hardly be described as suburban; even so, it was a weapon which had been used before.

Why then did this case sweep the world?

There is one very simple answer to that . . . sex. True, sexual crimes are committed every day of the year, murders of jealousy, of lust, of naked pathological aberration; but they are seldom, from the dramatic point of view, well cast. Only too often the murderer proves to be a little man with a weak chest, and his mistress a woman with thick ankles; and if they have been rash enough to write to one another, their communications are singularly flat and uninspiring.

But in the Thompson-Bywaters case the characters were perfectly cast. Both of them vibrated with sex. Moreover, the woman had been mad enough to pour out her desires on paper. And her desires—though the vast majority of British womanhood would have been outraged if you suggested it— were the desires of Everywoman. She longed to be hurt, to be dominated, to be subdued, to be trampled upon. These same desires, at the time of the trial, were being profitably exploited by a number of female novelists who, when they wished their heroines to have a really good time, always provided the hero with a whip. (If Rudolf Valentino had ever lost his whip, he would have lost nine-tenths of his income. One hopes that it was insured.)

Was this female masochism exceptionally developed in the twenties? Were women, after the horrors of the 1914–18 war, more inclined to surrender, to lie back, to cry, 'Do as you will, as long as it hurts?' This question could only be answered by an historian who was a combination of Freud, Gibbon and Taine . . . a monster who has, perhaps fortunately, not yet made his appearance.

'You must do with me as you please—you are my master . . . my love will endure any suffering you administer.' That is the theme of the letters which she poured out month after month.

For example: 'I am wax in your hands, to do with *as you will* and I feel that if you do as *you* wish I shall be happy. It's purely physical, but you will understand, won't you darlint?'

She constantly uses the word 'bully' as a term of endearment. And—a common psychological quirk in such cases—she betrays a secret desire by pretending to repel it. At the end of an especially passionate paragraph she writes, in ecstasy, 'I won't, I won't, I *won't* let you bully me !' Here is the eternal spectacle of the female who flies in order to experience the delight of being pursued.

'When it is something you want'—this is a recurrent note —'you must do it—I want to give it—I want to *stifle* all my own feelings.' This is the familiar 'slave and master' motif.

The word 'hurt' is used again and again, always with a shudder of pleasure. 'Even the looking forward to your return *hurts* me . . . my inside keeps turning over and over—all my nerves seem like wires continually quivering.'

She buys a book called *The Slave* and writes long passages about it, always identifying herself—and enjoying it—with the heroine and her humiliations. All the novels which she discusses in her letters have strongly sadistic heroes, to whom she is obviously attracted.

One passage is a quite unabashed confession of her desire to be taken by force, and her determination to satisfy this desire, even if Bywaters had no desire to co-operate. 'Darlinest boy, you said to me "Say no Peidi, say No" didn't you? But you didn't wish me to say "No", did you? You felt you wanted all of me in exchange for all you, didn't you? I knew this—felt this

instinctively. I wouldn't say "No" for this very reason.' A
moment later she cries 'Oh it hurts—terribly hard—how much
I love you!'

Constantly there are these curious, groping questions, from
the shadows of her ultra-feminine little brain. For example,
after referring to a night of ecstasy—('I'm glad you held me
tightly')—she inquires: 'Darlingest, what would have happened
if I had refused when you asked me to kiss? *I want to know.*'
One does not have to be an advanced student of morbid
psychology to recognize in this another rape fantasy.

The effect of such torrid epistles on an over-sexed young
man, cooped up on board a ship sailing through tropical
waters, may well be imagined. He took his mistress's cue and
responded in kind. Most of his letters were destroyed, but those
few which survived were erotic to the point of obscenity.

Meanwhile, Edith Thompson was already toying with the
idea of murdering her husband. The idea soon became an
obsession, which she communicated to Bywaters. Whatever
one's opinion about capital punishment, or about the comparative guilt of the two parties, there can be no doubt whatever that Edith Thompson continually incited Bywaters to the
act of murder, and continually—though in a crude and fumbling fashion—attempted it herself. If the setting were not so
sinister there would be, at times, a macabre humour in the
spectacle of the unfortunate Mr Thompson serving as a long-
suffering guinea-pig for the deadly but amateurish experiments
of his wife. She uses anything that comes to hand, such as
broken glass. 'I'm going to try the glass again occasionally—
when it is safe—I've got an electric light globe this time.' She
finds a bottle of aromatic tincture of opium and writes to ask
him about its possibilities. 'I shall keep it till I hear from you.'
In one letter there is a startling postscript: 'Have you studied
bichloride of mercury?' This was a curious question to address
to a young ship's steward. She asks him: 'Darlint, how can one

get ptomaine poisoning from a tin of salmon? One of our boy's mothers has just died of it.' She nags and nags him to buy some poison abroad and send it to her. 'Darlint, why can't you send me *something* . . . quickly?' She refers to making small pills coated with soap and dipped in liquorice powder. She experiments with overdoses of quinine. 'It was enough for an elephant, but the bitter taste allows only a small quantity.' She reverts to the broken glass. 'I was buoyed up with the hope of the light bulb and I used a lot—big pieces too—not powdered. But it had no effect.'

Greedily she scans the newspapers for reports of mysterious deaths, and sends him the cuttings to ask if they suggest any possibilities. A curate dies of hyacine poisoning, there is no evidence to show how it was administered. Would that be any use? The Vice-Chancellor of Oxford receives an anonymous box of chocolates filled with 'an insidious form of Indian poison'. Any comments? A woman dispenser makes an error in calculation and kills a patient by an overdose. Might there be a hint in that? She sends him Robert Hichens' novel *Bella Donna* with the comment: 'You may learn something from this book to help us.' And she quotes a significant extract from it: 'It must be remembered that digitalin is a cumulative poison and that the same dose, harmless if taken once, becomes deadly if frequently repeated.'

The effect of these letters, of course, was damning, and not even the shoddy brilliance of Sir Henry Curtis Bennett could save her. True, she had not struck the blow which killed her husband, but she had very clearly directed it. She was sentenced to be hanged by the neck.

Criminals have this in common with actors; some have 'star quality' and some have not. This is why some crimes seem to colour a whole decade, while others—more brutal, more cunning, more destructive—fade into oblivion. Thus, the 'crime' of Oscar Wilde—if in these days it is to be so classified

—seemed to give a special tinge to the nineties; it floated like a sickly perfume over the whole era.

The period of the nineties was in fact a pioneering decade, politically and economically, and there was nothing in the least *fin de siècle* about it except its date. Thanks, however, to Wilde, and his dazzling star quality, there has floated over it this aura of historical decay; it is almost as though one were reading about the Boer War 'to the sound of flutes'. When we step over the border into the twentieth century—the century of the little man—we find our ideal felon in Crippen, who was even so obliging as to emphasize the new fashion in criminals by being the first murderer to be caught by wireless. I was eight years old, and violently anti-capital punishment, when Crippen was sentenced to death. I had been taken by my mother to a singular entertainment called 'Poole's Mirrorama' at the Bath Saloons, Torquay. This was a glorified magic lantern show, accompanied by sea-lions. When the news of Crippen's sentence was made known it was flashed on to the screen, and the entire audience, including the sea-lions, cheered themselves hoarse. But I had hysterics and was carried out kicking. Perhaps this is why the Edwardian era, to me, is coloured by the personality of this little doctor, who cut up his fat music-hall wife and distributed her in such neatly carved portions in the cellar.

Perhaps, also, it was because of my own part in the Thompson Bywaters affairs that it seemed to me the crime *par excellence* of the decade, with its throbbing under-current of masochism, which so aptly illustrated a theory which was beginning to be expounded by the psycho-analysts—the theory of the Death Wish. At times during the trial I certainly wished that I were dead myself, but never so much as after Edith Thompson had been sentenced to be hanged.

The telephone rang one night in my little flat in Bryanston Street—(£2 a week and no major disturbances except when the ladies of the Church Army opposite were in a particularly militant mood.) I lifted the receiver and heard the voice of

Bernard Falk, my editor. Falk was one of the great Fleet Street personalities of the twenties. He had an enormous nose, a broad Lancashire accent, and a hawk's eye for news. He posed as a vulgarian; he was in fact a most discerning critic of literature and the arts. After 'seeing the paper to bed' in the small hours of Sunday morning he would read a page of Addison or Swift before retiring, to get the taste of journalism out of his mouth. As a hobby he bought miniatures and gradually built up a collection of minor masterpieces which is sometimes shown to the public.

On this occasion, however, it was the editor speaking, and not the connoisseur. And as an editor he was compelled to answer the public clamour for news—a clamour which was increasing, hour by hour. Edith Thompson was to die, so we had to get her life story, and I was the one to get it. But from whom? From Mr Graydon, her father, of course. But how? That was up to me. But what was I expected to do? If the worst came to the worst I could 'rely on the Oxford manner'. This was the only concrete phrase I could remember in his whole instructions. When he rang off I did not even know where Mr Graydon lived. A cub reporter is supposed to find out these things for himself.

The morning was grey when I set out for North London on this hateful mission, and nowhere was it greyer than in the road called Manor Park. It was a very long road, and after I had been walking down it for some minutes I saw in the distance a group of men clustered round the front door of one of the houses. They were ringing the bell and banging the knocker. As I came closer I realized that they were reporters. Among them were some of the toughest types in Fleet Street.

My heart sank. What chance was there against such competition? This was an occasion when money would do the talking, and I had no definite authority to offer any sum at all. If it were not money it would be another kind of talk—loud, blustering, bullying talk. 'Come on, Mr Graydon, you'd better give us the facts; we'll get 'em sooner or later.' I was not good at that sort of thing.

I stood there, on the far side of the road, and stared. So this was the point at which one had arrived, as the result of being the bright boy at school! This was one's academic accolade; this was the reward for burning the midnight oil at Balliol, editing the *Isis* and becoming President of the Oxford Union. One had become a Fleet Street scavenger, and not even a very efficient scavenger—a minor vulture who hovered on the edge, hesitating to go in for the kill. That was how those reporters seemed to me. Which was all, of course, very young and tiresome. Those reporters were honest men, doing a difficult and highly technical job. Moreover, they were supplying a public demand. That is a fact which the sensitive newspaper reader might bear in mind, when he declaims against the revelations of some enterprising journal. 'These damned reporters should be shot!' he snorts. 'Listen to this! And look at this!' And then he gets out his glasses to scan the photographs more closely.

However, in those days I was on the side of the sensitive newspaper reader rather than the brash reporter. I was temperamentally softer than the average Fleet Street man, and my background was different. So I stood there and stared, and shivered, and felt utterly miserable.

And then I walked away.

The rest of the day passed in a sort of daze. I did not go back to my flat because I knew that the telephone would be ringing. I did not go back to the office because I knew that I should be blown up. Indeed, I suspected that I should never return to the office at all; my brief Fleet Street career was ended. I wandered about in the Park; I went to a cinema; and I have a vague memory of sending the Graydons a telegram. Then I went to a pub called the Argyll, near Oxford Circus, with the firm intention of getting drunk.

I did not get drunk . . . at least, not very drunk. But I had just enough to make me suddenly get up and put down my glass and walk across to the tube station and take the tube back to Manor Park. It was then about nine o'clock at night.

Once again I set out down the long dreary road. This time Manor Park was deserted. There was no light in the Graydon's house, and when I rang the bell there was no reply. Perhaps they had gone—perhaps they had fled—perhaps I could be rid of the whole wretched business. Then there were footsteps. A light was switched on; the door opened, and I found myself staring into the face of a man who was weeping. There was some muttered conversation, and then, to my bewilderment, I found myself admitted into a little room which was lit by a glaring white globe hanging from the middle of the ceiling. I shall always remember that ruthless globe in the tiny room. Tragedy should be dimly lit; this globe was pitiless; it even gave a harsh sparkle to the tears on the old man's cheeks.

I might write a touching dialogue about what transpired in that little room. I will not do so—though it would probably be reasonably accurate—because there are only two sentences which I remember, down the years, with absolute clarity, and they tell the whole story.

I spoke the first sentence. I said: 'I only came to tell you that I am so terribly sorry.' Nothing could have been more trite, but it happened, at that moment, to be true. Standing there under that ghastly light, with those pathetic masculine sniffs punctuating the silence, I had ceased to be a journalist, and had become a human being. I didn't want a 'story', I only wanted in some fumbling way to help, and if that sounds priggish it is just too bad. Sometimes one has decent instincts, and though one need not make a parade of them, it is false modesty to deny them when they are apposite. On this occasion they were very apposite indeed. Precisely because I *had* ceased to be a journalist, and because I really was distressed, and . . . for the time being at any rate . . . entirely disinterested, the Graydons trusted me, felt that they could work with me, and eventually agreed to give the story which they had refused to everybody else.

The second sentence was spoken by Mr Graydon, and it was a sentence that was to echo round the world. He threw out his arms in a clumsy gesture and he cried: 'That this should happen to *people like us!*'

'People like us.' People who had neat little houses in dreary suburban crescents. People who had a pair of Staffordshire dogs, very brightly polished, on each side of a clock with a glass case over it. People who had an upright piano with a piece of beaded silk on the top, and a pile of songs which included *Because* and *Friend of Mine*. People with shiny linoleum on the stairs and heavy Victorian armoires in which the breast pockets of the Sunday suits were stuffed with lavender. People who were low church, and deeply interested in the royal family. People, above all, for whom respectability was a passion.

'People like us.'

That phrase, as I said, was to echo round the world. Some years later I was telling this story to a brilliant young dramatist called Frank Vosper. (His death at sea, in mysterious circumstances, was not only a tragedy for his friends but a very great loss to the theatre.) When I came to the phrase 'People like us,' he said: 'Stop! I must write a play about this and that must be the title. May I use it? Or do you want to use it yourself?' As it happened, I had rather wanted to use it myself; some titles are not merely 'labels' but have a life of their own with which they invigorate and sustain the whole work. However, at that time the title was still only brooding in my mind; it had gathered to itself neither characters nor design; so I gallantly handed it to Frank who—being a most charming scoundrel in such matters—would certainly have used it in any case. In due course *People Like Us* was produced . . . with *éclat*. I write *éclat* because the first of many productions was in Paris, on account of the usual ludicrous contortions of the British censorship.

So I got my story after all. It was probably one of the few

occasions when any journalist has 'pulled off a world scoop' by endeavouring to behave like a gentleman. For the next few weeks I was to see a lot of the Graydons, and always in circumstances of the most hideous vulgarity and squalor . . . outside Holloway Prison on Saturday afternoons. That was the time when they were allowed to see their daughter, and I used to meet them at the gate and ask them questions. How was she? How did she look? Had she hopes that her appeal would succeed? The noise of the traffic was so loud that I had to shout to make myself heard, and sometimes I could not understand their replies because they were usually crying.

The other day an old journalist said to me: 'What we want is another Thompson-Bywaters case, with somebody like you to report it.' I thanked him, but suggested that I no longer had the flair for that sort of thing. Which, I sincerely hope, is true.

CHAPTER SIX

RED CARPETS

THE hostesses of the twenties were like great galleons, sailing the social seas with all flags flying and all guns manned, relentlessly pursuing their charted course—and not above indulging in a little piracy if the occasion demanded it. Those were days when women really did ensnare each other's chefs and kidnap each other's head gardeners, and offer the most shameless bribes to each other's 'treasures'. (The word 'treasure' is charmingly period. In the upper classes it implied the perfect Jeeves or the ideal nanny. In the middle classes it usually referred to a housemaid or a cook.)

One of the greatest of all the hostesses was the Honorable Mrs Ronald Greville, who was called Mrs Ronnie by her acquaintances and Maggie by her friends. She was a short, stout, grey-haired woman of no great beauty, though she had pretty hands and feet and a good complexion, on which she used nothing but soap and water. Once when I was staying with her she walked by mistake into the bedroom of one of her guests, Mrs Sacheverell Sitwell, and saw that the dressing-table was covered with cosmetics. We heard a lot about *that*, afterwards. 'Why does darling Georgia have to put all that rubbish on her pretty face? By the time she is my age, she will be an old woman.' The prophecy, I am happy to say, has not been fulfilled.

Maggie was enormously rich, having inherited the fortune of her father, John McEwen, who made a great deal of beer in

Scotland. Judging from the picture of him which used to hang in the dining-room of her country house, he must have been a formidable old gentleman. Maggie was childless and I never heard her speak of her husband, Ronald Greville, who had died some years before I met her. Indeed, now I come to think of it, I hardly ever heard anybody else speak of him. Not because there was any scandal nor lack of affection nor because he was in any way deficient, but because he was obscured by the overwhelming personality of his wife.

Maggie never made any effort to conceal the origins of her fortune. 'I would rather be a beeress,' she used to say, 'than a peeress.' As a beeress she certainly made her mark. One of the reasons why she fascinated me was because she was fundamentally an Edwardian . . . a period which was before even my time. Through her eyes I could look back into a richer and more opulent age, and at her parties I had a glimpse of a fabulous world which would otherwise have been closed.

'One uses up so many red carpets in a season,' she once complained to me. We were sitting in the drawing-room of her huge house in Charles Street, waiting for the Queen of Spain to come to dinner. The remark, again, is charmingly period, and typically Maggie. Red carpets were reserved for royals, and there were enchanted nights in the twenties when the people around Grosvenor Square were giving so many grand parties that the pavements were as bright as a sunset.

Maggie had need of her red carpets, for royalty doted on her. At Polesden Lacey—the big Georgian house which she lent to King George VI and Queen Elizabeth for their honeymoon, when they were Duke and Duchess of York—she never knew whether Queen Mary might suddenly telephone and announce herself for tea. These were the only occasions when Maggie, who was fundamentally a very honest woman, would allow herself a little feminine conceit. She would pretend to be annoyed. '*Dear* Queen Mary,' she would sigh. 'Such a wonderful woman! But always such short notice! And I *cannot* imagine what she will have in common with His Excellency.'

(There always seemed to be an ambassador of some sort, wandering about Polesden at week-ends.) After which she would ring the bell for Bowles the butler, and give him his instructions. Maggie's teas were terrific, with great Georgian silver tea-pots, and Indian *or* China, and muffins and cream cakes and silver kettles sending up their steam, and Queen Mary saying 'Indian, if you please, and no sugar'. Today, Polesden belongs to the 'nation', and a stream of tourists flows past Maggie's tea-table. I wonder if any of them ever senses that the room is filled with ghosts.

Maggie was an extraordinary mixture of Scottish cautiousness and golden-hearted generosity. Here are examples of both. Towards every Christmas she used to promise a number of her friends a case of a certain beer which used to be specially brewed for her friend King Edward VII. It was apparently of fabulous potency, and we longed for the beer to materialize, but it never did. Indeed, the only Christmas present I ever had from her was rather dim. The occasion was after dinner on Christmas Eve; Maggie had gone to bed, and the rest of the party were sitting about the huge gilded drawing-room reading or playing bridge. Suddenly a footman came in with a small parcel on a silver salver. He advanced towards me. 'With Mrs Greville's compliments,' he said. I opened the parcel and found a small jade paper-knife in a satin-lined case. The satin looked far from new, and I was not surprised when Lady Chamberlain leaned over my shoulder and said: 'Really, that's the paper knife I gave her three years ago!'

Now for an example of her generosity. I was once trying to raise some money for a cancer hospital. The appeal took the form of a letter in my own handwriting, which the authorities caused to be printed and sent to various possible contributors. When next I saw Maggie she said: 'Thank you for your letter, my dear. It would have melted a heart of stone.' I was taken aback. I had no idea that the hospital had sent her the appeal,

F

and told her so. 'Never mind, my dear. Here is a little cheque, on one condition. My name must *not* be mentioned. I *never* allow my name to be mentioned. That is why I have a reputation for meanness, which gives me the *greatest* pleasure.' Whereupon she gave me a cheque for a hundred guineas.

Maggie was always doing things like that. I cannot give a list of her benefactions, because they were never proclaimed to the world. 'I am not like Lord X,' she used to say, 'who blows a trumpet every time he puts a shilling into the collection bag.' She certainly wasn't; Maggie would have been more likely to blow a trumpet if she had taken a shilling out. She had an impish delight in shocking people. Once at a luncheon party I heard her turn to a bishop and say, in the little cooing voice:

'I know that we *ought* to leave our money to the poor.'

'Yes, Mrs Greville?' replied the bishop hopefully.

'But *I*, my dear bishop, am going to leave *my* money to the rich.'

And she did. She left money, for example, to Sir Osbert Sitwell. Well, nobody would quarrel with that. Osbert was a devoted friend, his home at Renishaw needs a great deal of keeping up, and anyway, the Sitwell family is not as rich as all that. Some of her other bequests were not perhaps so admirably disposed.

Perhaps Maggie was so rich that she did not quite realize what money meant to most of us. That seems difficult to believe, in so shrewd a woman. And yet, on no other basis can I explain the following conversation.

We were sitting alone in the drawing-room at Polesden Lacey. This was a room of quite exceptional hideousness, smothered in gilt and crimson velvet; it looked like the salon of an exceptionally luxurious *bordel* in Edwardian Paris.

'Do you know, my dear Twenty-five, what I should do if I lost all my money?' (Maggie always called me 'Twenty-five', after reading a book of that title which I published in the mid-twenties.)

'No, Maggie. What?'

'If I were suddenly ruined . . . well, not *absolutely* ruined, but if I were reduced to, say, ten thousand a year?'

I gulped and waited.

'I think I should leave the country and take a tiny apartment in Paris.' There was a timbre of melancholy resignation in her voice that almost brought tears to my eyes. 'I hope my maid would come with me. Indeed, I am sure that she would. And though, naturally, I should not be able to entertain, I could have a few people to tea, once a week. And perhaps . . . though one cannot be sure . . . perhaps some of the people whom I have entertained in the past would invite me back, and then . . .'

At which point the door opened, and Bowles the butler announced the first guest, who was, of course, an ambassador, but which one I forget.

But I shall never forget Maggie and the Ford. She was walking down Regent Street one day and she saw a Ford van in the window. 'Such a pretty little affair, my dear Twenty-five, and I always admired Mr Ford, even though he trod on one's feet when he made one do those extraordinary square dances. I always carry a little loose money in my bag'—(the Ford, in those days, was about £600)—'so I went in and bought it for cash.' She put her hand on my arm. '*Always* pay cash, my dear Twenty-five. It always pays.'

Once Maggie offered me cash . . . a great deal of cash . . . but I refused. It was when Duff Cooper was standing as Tory candidate for Westminster. For some reason Maggie did not like Duff Cooper. She was certainly blind to the radiance of Lady Diana, who—I suspect—was hardly dazzled by Maggie herself. ('My dear,' Maggie would say, 'what *is* the world coming to? Violet Rutland's daughter going on the stage as a *nun*!') One day Maggie telephoned to me and asked me to see her. She was in bed, but the matter was urgent. When I arrived she had an extraordinary proposition to make; she wanted me to stand as an independent candidate against Duff Cooper in the Westminster bye-election.

'But Maggie, I couldn't possibly afford it.'

'I will pay all your expenses.' A pause. 'And a great deal more.'

'And in any case, I shouldn't get in.'

'Perhaps not. But at least you would split the vote and keep him out.'

I began to see the reason for this unexpected gesture. After some more discussion, in which Maggie brought all her big guns to bear, I told her that I would think it over. So I went home and did precisely that. Here, it seemed, was the chance of a lifetime—all the money in the world and spectacular publicity. But it was not the sort of chance I wanted, and the more I thought about it the less I liked it. I had the greatest admiration for Duff Cooper. He had a first-class brain and a wide experience. He was a scholar, a fighter, and in the best sense of the word, an aristocrat. To range myself against him, merely to appease the whims of a rich old lady, would be an act which I should regret for the rest of my life, even if it were to set me on the road to fortune. So I wrote and refused Maggie's offer. She took it very well, but I am sure she thought me a fool. 'Dear Twenty-five,' she used to coo, 'so unworldly.'

Nobody could accuse Maggie of being unworldly herself. She loved power, and she used it. I do not know the secret history of the intrigues which prevented Lord Lloyd from becoming Viceroy of India—a post for which he was superbly equipped—but Maggie was the animating spirit. In the presence of Lord Reading—himself an ex-Viceroy—she turned to me and said: 'That dreadful Lord Lloyd had the impudence to think he might be Viceroy, but I soon put a stop to *that*!'

She did not like to think that other women might also have a certain influence in political affairs. When Lady Chamberlain went to Rome and saw Mussolini, and came back with a great many stories about her interviews and how co-operative the Duce had been, Maggie sighed deeply and shook her head and said: 'Dear Ivy Chamberlain! It would not be the first time that Rome had been saved by a goose!' Nor did she care greatly for ladies whose jewels were more spectacular than hers. I shall never forget an occasion after dinner, when a very rich and famous American lady suddenly discovered that the principal diamond had dropped from her necklace. It must have been about the size of a broad-bean. We all got on our knees and routed around, and then Maggie's voice was heard, speaking to a footman. 'Perhaps *this*,' she was saying, 'might be of some assistance.' She was handing him a large magnifying glass.

Yet she was not really malicious. 'I do not follow people into their bedrooms,' was one of her stock phrases. And though she loved power, she was not really a snob. This was proved by her relationship with her personal maid, whom she always called 'The Archduchess'. The title was apt; the Archduchess, who was deeply devoted to her mistress, had a natural distinction. One day I walked into the ground floor of the Café Royal and saw Maggie, in a plain black dress, sitting in a corner dining with the Archduchess. There was nothing incongruous or embarrassing about it. Why should there be? The two women were not only mistress and maid, they were friends.

Once, when I was staying at Polesden, Maggie took me aside and led me down the long corridor towards the drawing-room. Half-way down she paused, in front of a dubious Ruysdael. (Her taste in pictures was by no means impeccable.) She put her finger to her lips. 'My dear,' she said, in a stage whisper, 'do you know what I have just been told? I have been told that Gracie Vanderbilt has an extraordinary notion that she might be able to entice away the Archduchess! And I don't believe she has ever even spoken to her. It's simply jealousy.'

I expressed suitable astonishment.

'She may be rich,' continued Maggie, with a snort of indignation, 'but she is not as rich as *that*!' Then a softer note came into her voice. 'And in any case, it is not a question of money.

I don't believe the Archduchess would leave me even if Gracie were to offer her a million dollars. Poor Gracie! Such a snob. And like all Americans, no sense of proportion.'

As she spoke, I recalled another occasion on which the fabulous Mrs Vanderbilt, who was the last of the gallant old hulks of New York society, had displayed a similar lack of proportion. Shortly after the first World War Maggie and Gracie . . . who even in those days could hardly be described as chickens . . . found themselves together in Paris. One day they went out to luncheon at Fontainebleu. They came home by a minor road, which was very bumpy, and suddenly the back axle broke. The chauffeur, Pierre, was stunned, and the two ladies, replete with lobster cardinale and Chateau Yquem, were landed in the ditch.

'Heavens!' wailed Gracie. 'What shall we do?'

'We shall stop the first driver that comes along and take Pierre to hospital,' retorted Maggie.

'But supposing we were to be taken for two cocottes?'

Maggie, stout, flushed, filled with lobster cardinale and Chateau Yquem, drew herself up in the ditch, and disentangled a nettle from her rubies.

'I think, my dear, that we may take that risk.'

An imaginary episode? The nettles and the rubies, maybe. But I can still hear Maggie's voice, telling me all the rest of it.

Indeed, I can hear her voice all through the twenties . . . and far beyond, through the thirties and into the days of the war. Perhaps the reader will forgive me for retelling a story which I have told before,[1] about my last meeting with her.

It was during the days of some of the worst bombing. Maggie, who could never bear to be out of things, had come up to London to live at the Dorchester—not on the ground floor, like the nervous ones, but high up, overlooking Hyde Park, in a large suite of rooms whose safety value was considerably less than many other parts of the hotel. And here, during raids, she would issue little crooning invitations to some

[1] In a book called *All I Could Never Be*.

of her friends—particularly if she disapproved of their war record—asking them to come up and keep her company. They very seldom had the courage to refuse; it was easier to brave the Luftwaffe than to incur Maggie's displeasure.

The sirens had just sounded for the third time that night as I entered the hotel, and I expected to find her in her usual chair, with the telephone by her side, calling up her friends. ('But my dear Lord X, you really *must* come up. I'm sure the air in that shelter is very bad, and I know you have a weak chest!')

This time, however, she was in bed, and it needed no second glance to inform one that Maggie's world, in every sense of the word, was drawing rapidly to an end. She looked frail and shrunken, and yet indomitably *mondaine*. All the apparatus of luxury surrounded her. By her bedside was a bowl of yellow orchids. On her hands the fabulous diamonds still sparkled, though she was now so thin that she had to clench her fingers to prevent them from slipping off.

'Dear Twenty-five,' she murmured, 'coming all this way to see an old woman on a night like this. Not like Lord X, who will not even come upstairs. But then, of course, the X's were always cowards. I remember . . .'

And she proceeded to remember. And for a little while the memories had the same subtle malice that had always enchanted me. But not for long. The malice flickered lower, like a lamp going out, and now and then there was even a faint glow of that Christian charity that so often hovers round the scenes of death.

Soon after dinner I rose to go, for she was very weak.

'Au revoir, Maggie.'

She shook her head. 'I think not, my dear Twenty-five. I think it is good-bye.'

Suddenly the windows rattled as a bomb fell unpleasantly near, in Hyde Park.

'That damned Ribbentrop,' she whispered. 'Thank God I told him what I thought of him when he came to Polesden.'

'What was that, Maggie?'

'I told him that if ever there was a war, he might beat the English, but he would never beat the Scots.'

Her eyes closed, and she fell asleep. I had heard the last of Maggie's reminiscences.

CHAPTER SEVEN

THE HOSTESS WITH THE MOSTEST

To compare Lady Cunard with Mrs Ronnie Greville would be like comparing a butterfly with a bison.

These two great social rivals—who, needless to say, detested one another—had nothing whatever in common. Everything about Maggie Greville was solid, everything about Emerald Cunard was insubstantial. It was the difference between a monumental Gainsborough and a delicate sketch by Fragonard.

Maggie was square, heavy, and down to earth, and she used nothing but soap and water. Emerald was wispy, ethereal, and always indulging in fantasy, and what she used on her face was nobody's business. There were rumours that she had a beauty specialist who rolled her about in a barrel, and that she used a face lotion of such potency that it stung like nettles and could only be applied with the cooling aid of an electric fan. The effect, if not beautiful, was startling, like a brightly painted budgerigar.

Maggie's social circle was so respectable that it was awe-inspiring. Perhaps this may best be illustrated by their respective contacts with royalty. Maggie's nearest royal friends were the Duke and Duchess of York, who were afterwards, of course, to reign as George VI and Queen Elizabeth. (We have already recalled that she lent them her country house for their honeymoon.) To say that this was indeed a true friendship is no example of royal sycophancy; one of the nicest things about Maggie was her unaffected love of the lady who is now the

Queen-Mother . . . a love which is not difficult to understand. She once said to me that if she had ever had a daughter she would have wished her to be like the Queen-Mother. And that reminds me of the only time I ever saw Maggie cry. There had been a royal visit to Paris . . . I think, but am not certain, that it was when Queen Elizabeth was actually on the throne. On the following day Maggie, who was ill in bed, telephoned to ask me to go and see her. She told me how, within a few hours of her return to England, the Queen, hearing she was ill, had come round to Charles Street and sat by her bedside and told her all about the wonderful, fairy-like time she had spent in Paris . . . and then Maggie broke off and began to cry, and said, 'Oh, my dear Twenty-five, what it would be to have a daughter like that!' After which, ashamed of her display of emotion—for it was her policy to emphasize her worldliness— she sat up abruptly and ordered half a bottle of champagne, and was very rude to the footman who brought it.

Emerald Cunard's royal contacts, on the other hand, were largely confined to the Duke of Windsor, or—as he then was— the Prince of Wales. Nobody would have been more astonished than herself if, as at Polesden, Queen Mary had suddenly rung up and proposed herself for tea. There would have been exhilaration, of course, but there would also have been con-sternation. (What shall we show her? What shall we talk about? And where shall we hide that peculiar young artist who drank too much at luncheon?) Moreover, in spite of the glitter and brilliance of her parties, there was always a curious feeling, even when the room was thick with duchesses and ambassadors, that this was not really 'society' but 'café society'. I am not socially qualified to judge; I am merely giving the impressions of a reporter.

Perhaps the root of the real difference between the two ladies was economic. About the prosperity of Maggie's breweries there could be no argument. But in what, precisely, did Emerald's fortune consist? When she died there was little left. Presumably, through all those sparkling days of the twenties she was living on capital, and perhaps that is why one had this feeling of instability, of insecurity . . . which was enhanced by the fact that she was born an American.

Let me put it like this. The huge house at the corner of Grosvenor Square—she had no country house because she hated the country and even preferred to spend her Sundays in London—was really a pack of cards sustained by only one thing—talk—Emerald's talk, swift, bird-like, inconsequential and totally impossible to reproduce. Without that talk the whole apparatus would have crumbled. The Windsors would have stayed away, the ambassadors would have absented themselves, and even the shadow of Sir Thomas Beecham might not have fallen so often over the steps. Grosvenor Square was not really a home at all, it was a stage set for talk. There was not even anything very precious or interesting in it. There were some Marie Laurencin pictures for which she had paid about £800 apiece—the usual anaemic floosies in pastel shades which, to me, look like portraits fashioned from Turkish delight. (Once, when she wanted another one to fill in a gap, her talented friend Volkoff painted it for her. She hung it up and nobody noticed the difference.) There was some passable Louis Seize and one or two good rugs and a Houdin bust, and the curtains were quite pretty. But if there was anything that would have interested Lord Duveen or caused a sensation at Sotheby's, it escaped my attention.

It was all talk, talk, talk—echoing through the upper strata of the social atmosphere of the twenties, and seeming, in its curious way, to colour the whole period. 'But my dear Winston, what are we to do about Mrs Baldwin's *hats*? Have you seen Mrs Baldwin's hats? They upset the atmosphere of the entire budget.' Or . . . 'But my dear Lord Linlithgow, we should *all* dress like Mr Gandhi. Look at Mabel Corrigan. *She* dresses like Mr Gandhi and what happens? Monsieur Clemenceau comes to luncheon the very next day.' But no, it will not do. Such gossamer stuff cannot be recaptured. And yet, for those who heard it, Emerald's talk was unforgettable, a fabulous sort of cabaret act. And although it was gossamer, there was sometimes a tougher substance to it. She had an unusually copious vocabulary; her choice of adjectives was dainty and precise, and her quotations were by no means always familiar. I only once went to her bedroom, when she had laryngitis—a suitable complaint for so tireless a word-spinner. The little French table by her bedside was piled high with Gilbert Murray's translations of the Greek classics. The pages were thumbed and dog-eared and there was a notebook filled with pencilled scribblings. No doubt these would come in handy at the next luncheon. 'But my dear ambassador, is it really true that Madame X is going to have a baby? Are you sure? I seem to remember something that Aristophanes said in a similar connection . . . about a woman who pretended that she was going to have a baby and it turned out to be . . . what was it? . . . ah yes! A "wind-egg". I wish I could remember the original Greek.'

Yes, she was very like E. F. Benson's immortal Lucia, who indulged in similar deceits. You may say that she was ridiculous. And yet . . . how many hostesses are there today who would go to the trouble of sitting up late at night, burning the midnight oil in Grosvenor Square, in order to give a classic flavour to their conversational performance on the following day . . . merely because the Regius Professor of Greek was coming down from Oxford for luncheon?

One begins to think that the twenties, even as represented by their hostesses, were tough.

Emerald terrified me. Whenever I was asked to eat at 4 Grosvenor Square, I used to arrive early and spend ten minutes walking round the square, summoning up the courage to ring the bell. (Somerset Maugham, in the days when he was afflicted by a stutter, was another pre-luncheon square-walker.) Usually it was about twenty minutes to two before I took the plunge, after I had observed, with increasing dismay, an incredibly grand collection of people ascending the marble steps.

Even then, after one had been ushered into the white and gold drawing room, the worst moment was yet to come . . . Emerald herself was never there. She had invented a social technique by which she was always the last to put in an appearance at her own parties. We would stand around waiting —ambassadors, cabinet ministers, famous artists—making desultory conversation, watching the clock. A quarter to two, ten to two . . . really, Emerald was going too far.

And then, just before two o'clock the door would burst open and in would hurry Emerald, with her arms outstretched, burbling absurd apologies. It was an old-fashioned star entrance, and on several occasions I noticed, with amusement, that as she swept in, the footman at the doorway switched on the lights of the chandelier.

Then the introductions began. These, to me, were sheer horror. One never knew what label she would attach to one, nor to anybody else. I shall always remember a supper party where, for once in a way, I was the last arrival. Nearly everybody was a star with the possible exception of a charming young woman who in those days was called Mrs von Hofmannsthal. The monologue, as I was conducted round the room, went something like this. 'Here is Lady Diana Cooper, who is the most beautiful woman in the world, and here is Mr Winston Churchill, who is the greatest orator since Bright, and here is Mr George Moore, who is an immortal, and here is Madame Pavlova who is another immortal, and here is the Duke of Westminster, who owns the whole of Grosvenor Square, and there, my dear Beverley, in the corner, are several ambassadors, and here . . .' We had arrived at Mrs von Hofmannsthal. Dead silence. 'And here,' piped Emerald, 'is darling Alice von Hofmannsthal, *who came by tube*!'

The remark was not as cruel as it may seem. Alice was a good deal richer than Emerald. (She was an Astor, and her mother later married Lord Ribblesdale, who was painted by Sargent in that very vulgar picture 'The Aristocrat'.) She had probably come in a Rolls-Royce. At the same time, that sort of thing is rather drying-up. And Emerald was always doing it. She would lean across, rap her small talons on the table, commanding silence, and say, 'And now dear Beverley is going to tell us what he really thinks of Sir Thomas Beecham.' You have to be on your toes to make the right sort of riposte on such an occasion, particularly if Sir Thomas is sitting immediately opposite you. The only man I ever saw defeat Emerald was George Moore. She had chosen him as her target for the moment, and had thrown him some challenge about *The Brook Kerith*. Moore did not answer her. He rose from the table and walked to the window in silence. He stayed there for a moment, tapping the glass. Then he turned round, and said, in his sad, Irish voice, 'You foolish woman, chattering and chattering, while the fountain is running dry.'

The word 'fountain' was constantly on George Moore's lips when he talked of Lady Cunard. The beautiful dedication of *Ulick and Soracha* runs:

> Dear Lady of my thoughts, dear Lady Cunard, time turns all things into analogues and symbols, and in the course of the years I have come to think of you as an evening fountain under embosoming trees. The fountain murmurs, sings, exults; it welcomes every coming minute; and when the dusk deepens in the garden and the gallants enfold their ladies in scarves and veils and the rout disperses, the fountain sings alone the sorrow of the water-lilies to the moon.

'You were enchanting last night' he wrote to her, shortly afterwards, 'so alert, so witty, so enveigling; never were you brighter or more wonderful, more like a fountain.'

Once, after lunching at Grosvenor Square, I walked home with him to his house in Ebury Street, and all the way, through the Park, through the bustle of Grosvenor Place and Belgravia, he elaborated on the simile of the fountain, the glitter of the words, the flutter of the hands, the sparkle of the eyes. It is a wonder that we were not run over.

The unkindest thing that was ever said about Moore may

well have had reference to Emerald. 'Most men kiss and never
tell; George Moore told and never kissed.' He certainly told.
In the famous 'suppressed chapter' of *Memoirs of my Dead Life*
there is the following passage, which beyond any question
refers to Emerald:

> Her courage, independence, her intellectual audacity, no doubt
> captured my imagination . . . I admired her cold sensuality, cold
> because it was divorced from tenderness and passion. . . . Her
> sensuality was so serene that it never seemed to become trivial or
> foolish. While walking in the woods with one, she would say:
> 'Let us sit here', and after looking steadily at one for a few
> seconds, her pale marmoreal eyes glowing, she would say, 'You
> can make love to me now, if you like.'

And again:

> The air seemed ominous, and there was sadness in her and a
> shroud of evil on the night. What did we do but sink into love
> of each other's bodies, seeking forgetfulness of the fate about to
> take us apart.

This certainly seems to indicate an intimate relationship,
but somehow—to me—it does not ring quite true. Perhaps this
is because at the time when I knew them they were both rather
beyond that sort of thing . . . if people ever get beyond that sort
of thing, which one is sometimes inclined to doubt.

Emerald's most constant companion and associate, in those
days, was Sir Thomas Beecham. It would be an overstatement
to say that theirs was a 'marriage of true minds', for no woman,
and precious few men, could claim an intellectual parity with
Sit Thomas; it was rather a happy partnership between artistic
genius and social flair. Sir Thomas concerned himself with the
music; Emerald was like a tiny, jewelled herald, trumpeting
the glories of his work to the rich ranks of the Philistines.
Whether she gained more pleasure from the opera, or from the

glitter which the opera entailed, is a question which need not concern us. Certainly she 'dragged 'em in'. She bludgeoned the Philistines into taking boxes, and if she encountered a likely customer she summoned her to luncheon, and subjected her to a barrage of charm and intimidation.

As a result, some rather peculiar people were swept into Emerald's circle—people for whom there was no explanation but the fact that they might support the opera. Such a one was an American lady, of whom there is told a very agreeable story. She had undergone a facial operation, which for some months afterwards caused her to have the appearance of pouting. Indeed, her lips always looked rather odd and protuberant. During her convalescence, so the story goes, she went to a village near Chartres in order to recuperate, and one day she paid a visit to the cathedral. As she was contemplating the glories of the scene around her, a priest approached and tapped her gently on the arm. '*Madame*,' he said, '*il est défendu de siffler dans l'église.*'

I wish that I had collected Beecham stories; there were dozens of them floating round London in those days. Has this one ever been published? It concerns Madame Sadowa, who was singing Dulcinea in Massenet's *Don Quixote*. The part of the Don was played by Chaliapin. At the end of the last act there are some very difficult passages between the soprano and the bass, and in spite of constant repetition Madame Sadowa could not synchronize them. At last, in desperation, she appealed to Sir Thomas. 'It is not my fault,' she protested. 'Monsieur Chaliapin always dies too soon.' To which Sir Thomas replied: 'No opera star has yet died soon enough for *me*!' In spite of such caustic comments, his players adore him. He was even forgiven by an absent-minded oboe player whom he reproved by saying, very gently: 'My dear sir, we cannot expect your attention *all* the time, but perhaps you would keep in touch with us occasionally?'

The best Beecham story I ever heard concerns a fellow conductor, and although it is out of period, it is so charming

Fashions. And nobody even smiled!

Bathing Belle (Note the deep distress of the lady in the black hat behind the model's arm)

Lily Elsie and Jack Buchanan: even Lily's enchantment was dimmed by such costumes

Fred and Adele Astaire. 'I wonder if *anybody* in London is going to like us just a little bit?' (Fred to B.N. just before this picture was taken)

that I cannot resist telling it. During the war this conductor, who must be nameless, played a distinguished role in entertaining the troops. On one occasion he found himself leading a scratch orchestra uncomfortably near the front lines. So near, indeed, that after the concert his car was riddled by bullets from skirmishing Arabs. When Sir Thomas heard his story he listened with the greatest attention. But when he came to the bit about the Arabs trying to shoot him, Sir Thomas's eyebrows rose in polite astonishment. 'Dear me!' he said. 'I had no idea that the Arabs were so musical.'

Will there ever again be such a partnership as that which existed between Sir Thomas and Emerald Cunard? I doubt it. The conditions no longer exist. Emerald's house in Grosvenor Square no longer echoes to the laughter of the bold and the rich and the beautiful; God knows what it does echo to in these days; it is probably filled with the sound of typewriters and good intentions. As for Sir Thomas, music still flows through him, like a crystal spring through the mouth of some exquisite fountain of the Renaissance. But the day, alas, will come when he will feel that somebody else must take from him the baton which, for so long, he has used like a sword in the service of British music. All of us, no doubt, have our theories as to whom this man will be. I certainly have mine. But where will be his Emerald? And is it conceivable that he will be able to play the role, not only of a musician but of a *grand seigneur*? Sir Thomas, even when he is floating to heaven on a melody by Mozart, has always been *grand seigneur*; there is always a glitter of gold on the tip of his baton. He is one of the last great Englishmen who makes one feel that it is as proper to dress up for Covent Garden as to put on a hat for church.

In a moment we will replace on its shelf the figure of this singular woman, who during her life-time was often compared to a piece of Dresden china. This image was inept, and always made Emerald angry; once, when she found herself so described in an expensive volume of modern photography, she hurled the book into the fire, and held it down with a poker till it was

G

burned to ashes. There was nothing frail about Emerald; she was as tough as they come. This was proved by her relationship with her daughter, Nancy.

Just after the end of the decade, a strange and explosive booklet burst upon London. It contained only eleven pages, but there was enough in them to make society rub its eyes. Even the title made people sit up . . .

BLACK MAN AND WHITE LADYSHIP
by
Nancy Cunard
Privately printed, not for sale

In the first lines of this booklet a painful and dramatic situation is exposed. Nancy Cunard announces that she has a negro friend—'a very close friend', who has often accompanied her to London. She then introduces her mother, under the title of 'Her Ladyship'. She explains that though she is on amiable, though distant, terms with 'Her Ladyship', she has always sedulously avoided the social glitter of Grosvenor Square.

And then, in the next line, she brings a third character on to the scene, in the shape of Margot Asquith, Lady Oxford. This is when the fireworks begin. For she tells how Lady Oxford, hearing of the negro friend, burst into one of 'Her Ladyship's' grandest luncheon parties and loudly inquired 'Hello Emerald —what is it now . . . drink, drugs, or niggers?'

The resultant confusion may be imagined. Before tea-time the scandal was all over London, or rather, that part of London which acknowledged Emerald's sway. In the few faded copies of *Black Man and White Ladyship* which still exist in the desks of ageing dowagers, it is there for all to read. I do not propose to retell the story of this booklet. But I do feel that this might be an opportunity to pay a belated tribute to its author.

Nancy Cunard was one of the most gifted of all the young

women of the twenties; she was a fine poet, a sensitive critic of the arts, and—at her best—an inspired conversationalist, who held the attention and commanded the respect of the best brains of the decade. She was *une originale*, not because she desired to draw attention to herself but because she was cursed with an implacable honesty. It was inevitable that such a personality should be ill at ease in her mother's drawing-room; the old phrase—'a bird in a gilded cage'—might have been coined expressly to describe her plight; she was a wild bird herself, and Emerald's drawing-room was to her little more than a baroque aviary, with ormulu embellishments, which resounded perpetually to the chatter of parakeets.

Such was the author of *Black Man and White Ladyship*. This strange, tortured tract of the times was dragged from her in a convulsive spasm of indignation. If it created a scandal, that was unfortunate but—so she might argue—the scandal was none of her making, it was there already for all to see, the scandal of that spiritual cancer which is smugly fobbed off as 'the colour problem'. Confronted by this fundamental human injustice her indignation flamed so fiercely that her pen burned into the paper, and sometimes her arguments were blurred. (Wordsworth's 'emotion remembered in tranquillity' has as much force for the pamphleteer as for the poet.) In spite of this, the second section of *Black Man and White Ladyship* is superb. In this section she leaves Mayfair and draws a bitterly etched picture of the world landscape in relation to its coloured peoples. This is one of the most powerful polemics I have ever read, and—tragically enough—it is as apposite today as when it was first written.

All this has taken us a long way from the white and gold of Emerald's drawing-room. But I can never recall that room without seeing the shadow of a black man slowly stealing across the walls.

Emerald somehow survived the war, and kept her flags flying and her toy guns crackling from such strategic outposts as the Ritz Hotel in New York. When she died, a great many people thought they were going to get a lot of money, for she had often, in her conversation, distributed bequests to her friends. But they proved to be ghostly legacies, for there was little money left, and the emeralds, the celebrated emeralds, proved to be made of glass.

CHAPTER EIGHT

SEX—AND A SONG

'I THOUGHT men like that shot themselves.'

The speaker was King George V, the place was Buckingham Palace. The man to whom he was referring was one of the great noblemen of England—a man whom he had loaded with the highest honours. I will not enumerate those honours, for they would certainly identify him. We will call him Lord X.

There was only one thing, allegedly, wrong with Lord X. He was rumoured to be a homosexual, and the King had just found this out.

I think that this story is to be accepted, because it was told to me, under the stress of great emotion, by one of his nearest relatives. He described how the King stared straight in front of him, repeating the words *shot themselves . . . shot themselves* in his thick, guttural voice. Lord X did not shoot himself; maybe it would have been better if he had. He resigned honour after honour—each resignation was gloatingly recorded in the popular press—and finally he left the country, never to return.

No, that is wrong, he *did* return . . . once, for a single hour. He had a last ambition to see again the home of his ancestors. It was indeed one of the loveliest houses in England with its terraced walks and its fabulous rose gardens, which had been planted in the reign of Henry VIII. Somehow or other he fulfilled that ambition . . . how, I do not know. Some say that the authorities relented or turned a blind eye, others that he arrived in a yacht at dead of night and motored through the sleeping country-side. All that matters is that he arrived at ... I nearly wrote the name of the house . . . just before dawn. It was still too dark to see very much, but he knew every inch of the gardens. He groped his way round the balustrades, shining a torch, from time to time, on a favourite rose or a bed of lilies. He picked a rose. Then he went away, and a few months later he died. He was a fairly young man and he still had foreign honours of which even the King could not deprive him; but the newspapers, which had found plenty of space to chronicle his misfortunes, spared hardly an inch for his decease.

Yes, it might indeed have been better if he had shot himself.

I tell that sad little story because it affords a striking illustration of the total change in public opinion—regarding at least one aspect of sex—that has come about in the past thirty years. Today it is hardly conceivable that any adult person should still cherish the illusion that 'men like that' shoot themselves. He may wish that they did, but that is another matter.

The twenties, in such matters, were comparatively naïve. True, they have acquired a great reputation for naughtiness and general licentiousness, and from some accounts one would think that Noel Coward and Oliver Messel and Evelyn Waugh and Cecil Beaton and Graham Sutherland and all the rest of us spent one half of our lives rollicking in licentiousness and the other half dead drunk on the linoleum. If we did, we must have had remarkable constitutions.

In fact, outside 'Mayfair'—a charming title that was tarnished by Michael Arlen, who gave it a vulgar gloss—there was a strongly puritan element in the country, particularly in the press. Whatever posterity may decide about my prose, I can claim one distinction . . . I was the first British journalist to get the word 'syphilis' published in a national newspaper. 'Syphilis' is not a pleasant word; it hisses and undulates like a snake; which was precisely the reason why I wanted to use it.

Until my modest gesture 'syphilis' had always been described as 'a certain disease', just as an attempt at rape had been described as 'a certain suggestion', and the result of the rape on the lady was described as leaving her in 'a certain condition'.

This seemed to me not only bad prose but bad principle; ugly things should not be covered in genteel packages; spades —when they are busy at the muck heap—should be called spades.

So I said to the editor: 'I am bored with men with certain complaints who made certain suggestions to certain women who became in a certain condition; it gets me all muddled up. There may be lots of nice little dewy-eyed housemaids who read this stuff and think it is all about toadstools.' Or words to that effect.

So 'syphilis', for probably the first time since the days of John Wilkes, duly made its verbal debut in Fleet Street.

But we were talking about Lord X and homosexuality.

As we have seen, there were still a large number of people— particularly in high places—to whom the whole of this problem was so dark, so difficult, and so innately poisonous, that they instinctively shut their eyes to it. If they thought of it at all, they shared the views of George V. The sexually divergent should be condemned to the firing squad—a fate that was really too good for them, since they should have been strangled at birth.

How about the offenders themselves? Was this, in actual fact, a particularly 'abnormal' decade? The question, although I have asked it myself, is not a very intelligent one. The proportion of homosexuality in any nation, at any period of history, is probably fairly static; if there had been psychoanalysts in the time of Cromwell they would have discovered an equal percentage of psychological aberrations in the nation as a whole—though the homosexual element might have been more noticeable among the Cavaliers than the Roundheads.

To quote the popular song, homosexuals may be headaches, but they are very seldom bores.

What is quite certain is that the word 'homosexual', in the twenties, was unknown by the man-in-the-street. By the 'man-in-the-street' I need hardly say that I do not mean the man in Harley Street—nor, if it comes to that, the average intelligent undergraduate. I mean . . . well, the man-in-the-street. Today the word is so common that one would hardly be surprised to see it over the entrance to one of the departments in a general store. But in the twenties it was taboo, and I think it is correct to say that the first time it began to come into general circulation was during the case of *The Well of Loneliness*, by Radclyffe Hall.

This book—though not as fine a novel as *Adam's Breed*, for which she was awarded the Femina Vie Heureuse prize—is one of the most austerely moral works ever written. And yet, fate has ordained that it should be stocked in shady Parisian bookshops cheek by jowl with such erotica as *The Harems of Harlem* and *Pleasures of the Rod*. It is placed there, of course, with the idea that young persons who have heard of its reputation may purchase it in the hope of finding passages of lurid vice. In fact, it is about as vicious as *Pride and Prejudice*, and its powers of corruption are hardly equal to those of a grocer's catalogue.

And yet . . . what an uproar it made! Such a hullaballoo is unthinkable in the fifties, and for this reason it may perhaps be instructive to recall some of the personalities in a case which though it was an *affaire de scandale* was not without its humour.

Radclyffe Hall was a very virtuous woman. She was brave, honourable, and deeply religious, and had it not been for that unfortunate accident of nature she might have ended up as a bishop or a field marshal.

But she was embarrassing to meet in public. She used to attend many first nights wearing a black military cape, with a high stiff collar and a man's stock. Her grey hair was cut and parted like a man's. Her entry into the theatre always caused a minor sensation, and whenever I saw her striding towards me I used to beat a rapid retreat into the one place where, ironically enough, she was unable to follow me.

At home, it was a different matter. She had a pretty house at Rye, where she was accepted by the locals as an amiable eccentric. Rye is an almost hysterically picturesque town in Sussex. When you walk down its narrow streets you feel that at any moment a horde of Morris dancers may burst through the doors of one of the oldy-worldly cafés. Sometimes, to your alarm, they do. The *bonne bouche* of Rye is Henry James's old house at the top of the High Street. It was later occupied by the Edwardian novelist, E. F. Benson, who made it the setting for the Lucia novels, which are among the minor neglected masterpieces of English comic literature. They are worthy of a shelf not so very much lower than the novels of Jane herself, but most of them, alas, are out of print.

At home, Radclyffe Hall impressed one as a person of passionate integrity and almost overwhelming moral rectitude . . . provided that one did not regard her as a woman. How *could* one regard her as a woman? There was nothing in the least feminine about her. I can see her now, standing in front of the fireplace at Rye, doing what some of us called her 'British policeman act'. This is the symbolic gesture associated with the conventional music-hall cop . . . hands clasped behind the back, chin thrust up, knees bent and jerked outward in a springy, aggressive motion. While indulging in these callisthenics she would discourse intelligently about the latest novel. It was her boast that she knew nothing about housekeeping. She must have regarded this ignorance as a sign of virility, because she so often referred to it. 'Couldn't boil an egg,' she would proclaim gruffly, jerking out her knees with extra gusto. 'Couldn't light a fire, couldn't dust a chimneypiece.'

The man who chose to drag the name of this eccentric but honourable woman in the mud, and whose 'revelations' were responsible for banishing her book to the shelves of shady libraries in Paris, was called James Douglas. He wrote a weekly column in a Sunday newspaper with a bombastic fervour that marked him as the spiritual heir to Horatio Bottomley. He had a turgidly rhetorical style, in which he made a farcical use of the apt aid of alliteration. He was unctuously moral and a great champion of the muscular Christian.

This was the man who launched his attack on *The Well of Loneliness* . . . a novel which had already been soberly and generously reviewed in such journals as *The Times*, and had been received without a flutter of protest by the majority of the subscription libraries. If anybody were ever to compile an Anthology of Overstatement, one sentence in Douglas's article would deserve a page to itself. Here it is:

'*I would rather give a healthy boy or girl a phial of prussic acid than this novel.*'

The young reader of today may well ask himself 'But what was all the fuss about? Was there really anything in the book that might cause anybody any harm?' I can answer that question with precision. On the day after the storm burst I happened to be lunching in Fleet Street with a young journalist whose editor had given him the not very elevating task of going through *The Well of Loneliness* and extracting what he was pleased to call 'the juicy bits', in order that they might be relayed to a larger public. He was in a state of great depression.

'There just aren't any juicy bits,' he said sadly.

'But surely,' I said—for my ears were still stinging from the assaults of James Douglas's article—'there must be some?'

He shook his head. 'There's a lot about a girl reading bits of Freud in the library of a country house, but that could all be published in the *Church Times*. Then there's a lot of rather starry-eyed talk about the girl friend. That could go straight into the *Methodist Recorder*. There's only one solitary sentence of seven words in the whole book which could possibly be regarded as objectionable.'

'Yes?' I listened breathlessly.

'It's at the end of a chapter where they go away together, and walk about in a field. The daylight fades, the moon rises, and they talk interminably . . . it couldn't be more starry-eyed, till those seven words.'

'But what *are* they?'

'I'll show you.' He opened the book and pointed to a sentence that he had underlined. I read it . . .

'*And that night they were not divided.*'

The *Well of Loneliness* scandal was one of those deplorable examples of mob hysteria which periodically make the British people so ridiculous in the eyes of the rest of the world. Such an episode would be scarcely possible today. To that extent, we have progressed.

On the other hand, in the theatre we have stood still. Thirty years have passed since the squalid and farcical history of the banning of *Young Woodley*, but I make no apology for reviving the story. It affords one of the grossest examples of censorial stupidity which can be provided even by the Lord Chamberlain's office.

Young Woodley, a delicate play with the bloom of adolescence on it, was written in the spring of 1925 by John Van Druten, who can hardly need any introduction to the civilized theatregoer. John, in those days, was a struggling twenty-four-year-old teacher in Wales, and this was his first major work. He wrote it for a brilliant young actor called Tom Douglas, and sent it to Basil Dean, who accepted it. Rapture in Wales . . . dreams of fame and fortune . . . all the wonderful thrills that come to a young dramatist on these occasions. Shall we sit in a box with mum on the first night? Or shall we prowl round at the back of the dress circle? Shall we make a speech? What shall we buy for mum with the first royalties? Shall we be able to retire and take to play-writing for the rest of our lives?

The answer to all these questions was in the negative. We

should be able to do none of these things, for the simple reason that the Censor banned the play.

Here is John's own account of the episode, which he wrote for me just before his untimely death.

> The official reason for banning the play was that it might be regarded as hostile to the Public School system, and that it might therefore 'cause grief and anxiety to parents'. There was no appeal from this at all. My own mother had foreseen it, and had warned me that '*they* will never let it be done'. So that was that. My Professor in Wales thought that I ought to bring a libel action against them for hinting that I had written a dirty play. But I didn't because . . . well, you know what happened.

What happened, of course, was that the play was promptly produced in America, where it was a triumphant success. (Nobody was so dirty-minded as to suggest that it would harm a susceptible child of eight.) What also happened was that three years later it was allowed to tiptoe into London, via the Arts Theatre Club, where it was shown to club members for a week. The reviews of the play were so rapturous that the Lord Chamberlain was obliged to go and see it for himself. Having seen it . . . he proceeded to reverse his ban!

Was the Lord Chamberlain promptly sacked? Did he recompense the author for the material loss and mental anxiety that he had caused him? Did an indignant public march in force to burn down the Censor's office, as a bloody-minded instrument of tyranny that ought to have gone with the Star Chamber? No. None of these things happened. For this is Britain, and if there is one thing certain about the British public it is that in the theatre they enjoy being dragooned, bludgeoned, and ordered about by amateurs who tell them what they may or may not admire. The latest proof of this, which would be funny if it were not exasperating, is the banning of Arthur Miller's *A View From the Bridge*. America had acclaimed it, half the capitals of Europe had cheered it, but London . . . oh dear me no! It could not possibly be shown to

Londoners except through the medium of a private club; it was far too strong meat for the citizens of the greatest capital of the world. Why? Because in the second act a man kisses another man. The embrace is decidedly brusque; neither of them appears—or is indeed intended by the dramatist—to enjoy it; and any episode less calculated to advertise the lures of homosexuality could hardly be imagined. In spite of this, the Censor banned the play.

So we seem to have reached the conclusion that the twenties' reputation for naughtiness was ill deserved. It was a journalistic reputation, conceived in printers' ink and moulded with the compositor's fingers. By and large, no age is 'naughtier' than any other; the sexual impulse is as regular and rhythmical as the surge of the tides; its ripples and variations are merely a sort of social spray, dependent upon external circumstances.

One comparison, however, we may legitimately draw between this brightly painted period and our own decade. Whether people were more, or less, promiscuous, they certainly were more elegant in these matters. A dinner-jacket was folded over the back of a chair and a brightly beaded dress was hung on a hook. It wasn't a question of an old pair of jeans tossed into a corner and a drab jumper pushed into the linen basket.

Moreover they approached the culmination of their romance, as it were, by more graceful avenues. Those were days when a young couple in evening clothes could still walk home after the theatre, through theatreland, without being stared at as though they were nudists. They could converse with each other quietly and gently, without being interrupted by street fights, intoxicated Americans and hordes of coloured prostitutes. London's theatreland was never a monastic retreat nor an architect's dream, but in the early twenties it was a quiet little paradise compared with the shambles of today. There were, for example, no milk bars. In passing, one may ask why the persons who frequent these institutions so often look so far more degenerate than the persons who go to pubs? If Hogarth were reincarnated he would make straight for the nearest milk bar, and the result would be more alarming than the crudest passages in Gin Alley. Another who might have found inspiration in the modern milk bar is Aubrey Beardsley. His wasp-tipped pencil would have delighted to trace the spindly hips of the Teddy Boys and he would have lingered lovingly over the monstrous shapes of their female companions, all the more repulsive because they are created, not from flesh, but from plastic.

This is ugly writing but one is dealing with ugly things. Let us retrace our steps. There we were, boy and girl, walking home, and there was comparative quiet and leisure. And though we were not particularly rich, we were dressed in some style. Every young man with some pretensions to gentility possessed not only a dinner jacket but a tail coat. When a modern hostess writes the words 'black tie' on her invitation cards she means that it is a comparatively formal party; when a hostess of the twenties wrote those words, she meant that it wasn't. Young men wore tails and white ties as a matter of course. The scruffy ones bought their things in Oxford Street and the Strand and such places, the others went to Hanover Square, Savile Row, Dover Street and Jermyn Street. The people for white waistcoats were called—and still are—Messrs Hawes and Curtis, who flourished at the end of the Piccadilly Arcade. I once interviewed Michael Arlen there. (Does *anybody* but Tallulah remember *The Green Hat*?) I was being tried on for some white waistcoats and so was he, and I thought I might pay for at least one of the waistcoats by an article about him. The interview was conducted through a velvet curtain.

'What is your real name, Michael?' I asked.

I can't remember what he told me his real name was, but it sounded pretty sinister.

Then he added: 'I'm an Armenian Jew, could anything be lower?'

Which I thought was endearing.

Michael did all the correct Mayfair things . . . whatever they may be . . . but he did them rather too well. I believe it was Rebecca West who described him as every other inch a gentleman. He even made Messrs Hawes and Curtis's waistcoats look somehow wrong. They had a nice line in piqués, which matched one's shirts, and they had very good piqué white ties, too. An ordinary casual young man would choose his various piqués at random, but Michael had them all to match, waistcoats, shirts and ties, and the resulting whiteness was a bit overpowering, like something out of Moby Dick, particularly as he tied his bows with such Armenian competence that they always looked made up. There was once a scuffle on the steps of White's Club because young Lord Alington accused him of wearing a made-up bow.

Yes, there was more style about the young men of the twenties, and I mourn its passing. I mourn the little crystal links on the cuffs, and the single pearls in the shirt, and the gold cigarette cases in the hip pockets. However hard up we were, we all seemed to have gold cigarette cases, even if they were quite small, and nine carat, and purchased in Regent Street. I regret the red carnations for the dinner jackets and the white carnations for the tails. (The aforesaid Lord Alington had a standing order with a flower shop in Piccadilly to send him a red and a white carnation every evening throughout the season. I even did the same thing myself, but I gave it up because I don't like wires stuck into the stalks of flowers. Also, the carnations never seemed to die, but lingered on for weeks in tumblers in the bathroom.)

But there is one minor sartorial detail that I regret most of all. The other day, rummaging through a trunk in an attic, I came across a flat, black object which, for the moment, I could not identify. I fished it out, dusted it, and recognized it as my old opera hat. Bought at Messrs Scotts in Piccadilly in 1926 . . . for about a guinea. Whereupon I did something which I had not done for thirty years. Holding the brim firmly between the thumb and forefinger of the right hand, I tapped the hat sharply on my left forearm and—hey presto, the charming thing snapped open, releasing a cloud of dust and a host of memories. The very sound of it was nostalgic . . . the muffled snap of the springs and the little whisper of braided silk.

Most of the memories that flocked from that old hat would be of small interest to anybody but myself. It had accompanied me to many enchanting parties, such as Mrs Somerset Maugham's 'all white' ball, with the girls in white dresses and the young men with white carnations and the menservants in white jackets and drifts of regale lilies against white screens. Always remember the importance of white when you are trying to form a mental picture of the twenties. It did not dominate, but it provided many delightful passages . . . largely thanks to Syrie Maugham. She used it in the prettiest ways, with huge armchairs in white leather and carpets made out of clipped sheep-skin and white pots of china camellias in the hall.

One of the memories evoked by the opera hat is of Melba's 'Farewell' at Covent Garden. I can pass that by; I have written about it elsewhere. But here is another Melba memory that is worth recalling, for it gives practical substance to the legend of her supremely beautiful voice—a legend that is only dimly sustained by her gramophone records.

Melba, when I met her in the early twenties, had installed herself in a large Adam house in Mansfield Street. By that time —she was about sixty-four—she had acquired a certain degree of taste, largely through the tuition of the Marquis Boni de Castellane. (He was a tiny pomaded creature who reminded me of a scented meringue; he married a Gould and wrote some rather dreadful memoirs.) Boni had persuaded her to discard the bows, the gold stuffed divans and the second-rate Louis Seize and invest in good solid Chippendale. The change in the furniture was accompanied by a change in her appearance; her hair was dyed a softer black, and she had her jewels reset. The voice was still of miraculous beauty.

One of my Fleet Street friends was a brilliant young scientist

They called this a traffic jam!

The owner of this motor car was Owen Nares, one of the foremost matinée idols of the twenties. He conquered London in a play called *Romance* with Doris Keane

'Ivor was very beautiful . . .'

called Professor A. M. Low. Among his many inventions was an apparatus called the audiometer, for photographing sound. I was fanatical about Melba's voice, and everything connected with it, and I tried to persuade her to sing into the audiometer. At first I was unsuccessful.

'How can you possibly photograph sound?' demanded the diva.

'I don't know, but you can.' And I told her how, a few days before, Professor Low had gone down to the Cenotaph to photograph the effect of the new rubber composition which they had sprayed on the road to deaden the sound of the traffic.

The use of the word Cenotaph was unfortunate. 'I don't want to get mixed up with the Cenotaph,' snorted Melba. Her reactions were not always very logical. 'The Cenotaph is the last sort of publicity one wants. It makes people think of gravestones.'

I assured her that the Cenotaph would play no part in the experiment; it was merely a question of photographing her voice. I told her that it was a duty she owed to posterity, and I suggested, rather rashly, that the British Museum would no doubt wish to have a copy of the film. That did the trick. Melba loved official recognition and rightly regarded herself as of the blood royal. (When she was in Australia one of her most characteristic gestures was to design a form of royal warrant, beautifully engraved and framed with a gold 'M', which she presented to various tradesmen in Melbourne.) So the British Museum was just her cup of tea. Patti had never got into the British Museum, nor Tettrazini, but *she* would get in. She never did, of course, but I had gained my point.

The following day Professor Low arrived after luncheon, and at first Melba was all charm, as well she might be, for the Professor in those days was a very handsome young man. He also looked like everybody's idea of a professor; he had a shock of untidy black hair, keen sensitive features, and beautiful fingers, with which he constantly made notes of ideas which

H

occurred to him during conversation. This habit used to embarrass people, who concluded that he was taking down their
thoughts. They flattered themselves; he was not.

Melba asked what should she sing? Where should she stand?
Did he like her dress, or would something simpler be better.for
the public? The Professor had difficulty in persuading her that
this was not an audition for the movies but a scientific experiment. He fused the lights, and rucked up the carpets, and got
very hot and bothered, and one of the footmen, the tall pale
one, tripped over a cable and hurt his ankle. Melba retired in
dudgeon, and I fancy that I heard her mutter the word 'Cenotaph' as she left the room. But at last all was ready, and she
came back to sing.

She sang middle E. Then she sang a scale, rather grumpily.
Then she sang top A flat. She was flicking her fingers restlessly
and staring at the machine as if it were a hostile audience.

I was sitting at the big Mason and Hamlin piano giving her
the notes. I said: 'I think you ought to sing a trill.'

'Why should I sing a trill?' she snapped. 'It wouldn't come
out.' She turned to the Professor. 'Or would it?'

The Professor assured her that it would 'come out'.

'*My* trills . . .' began Melba. And then she stopped, as well
she might. How could she, or anybody else, describe the
incredible delicacy and precision of her trills? They did not
flutter or wobble or wander from the notes, like the trills of an
ordinary soprano. They were as true as the trills of Kreisler on
his Stradivarius. Sometimes, when I felt I had earned a present,
I used to say to Melba, 'Please do a trill for me.' And usually she
would smile, and do a trill, and I would sit in ecstasy. Once I
asked her to do a trill when we were driving in the little motor-
car she used in London. It was a conveyance of the greatest chic,
like a jewel box in black enamel. On this occasion she trilled
all the way up Regent Street, and astonished passers-by, who
turned round and stared as though they had heard the voice of a
truant angel.

So now I said to her again: 'Please do a trill for me.'

She shrugged her shoulders. 'Very well.' And she trilled, and that was that.

Now for the sequel. A few days later the Professor came round with the photographs. He had, in the meantime, taken photographs of the voices of several other celebrated sopranos who had better be nameless, and had put them through the same tests. The results were astonishing, and to my mind conclusive. Melba's top A flat, for example, was far richer and more complicated in design than any of the other singers. I suppose one would call these 'overtones'. But the most remarkable proof was afforded by the trill. All the other singers' trills had strayed all over the film, varying in line and shape; they suggested haphazard patterns traced by an aneroid barometer. But Melba's trill might have been drawn by a geometrician, it was uniform and parallel and flawless.

Melba was greatly impressed and observed that science was a wonderful thing. She also expressed the hope that her perfect trill might be reproduced across three columns of the *Daily Mail*, accompanied by the inferior trills of her rivals. '*That* would show them,' she said. Indeed it would, I agreed, but it would also lead to several whacking libel actions. So the trill remained unpublished.

When the Professor died, a few months ago, his secretary sent me a little parcel, with a note to say that he had specially asked for it to be delivered to me. I stood there for a moment before I opened it, recalling his many kindnesses and the delight I had always felt in his company, ever since the first time I went to interview him. He had startled me, on that occasion, by suddenly asking, 'Why should a wheel be round?' He had the most original mind I ever met, and though I knew nothing of science he sometimes allowed me, as it were, to look at life through a scientist's eyes. Now that he is dead there seems no harm in confessing that he was the prototype of The Professor in *Down the Garden Path* and its sequels. Whenever I was unhappy about a piece of dialogue in which he appeared I used to telephone to him, and he would talk, and in a few moments all would be well. I still get letters from all over the world, in many languages, asking if he was a real person. He was indeed, a very real person.

Then I opened the parcel. Out of it fluttered the film that we had made on that sunny afternoon in Mansfield Street so many years ago. I felt deeply moved. I walked to the window and looked out on to the garden in all its spring beauty. It was a perfect morning, the sky was very blue, and somewhere in the distance a lark was singing.

CHAPTER NINE

HOME OF LOST CAUSES

By about the middle of the decade Oxford had given me up as a bad job. The bright young editor of *The Isis* had blotted his copybook by reporting crime in the Sunday newspapers; the bright young President of the Union had refused to go into politics; and the bright young author of *Prelude* had produced a really shocking novel called *Self*. To this last stricture I had no reply. *Self* is—in the humble opinion of its author—about the worst novel that was ever written. It was not about me, as its title would suggest, but about a red-haired hussy who went to bed with the vicar. There is a tremendously 'powerful' chapter in it about her having a baby. I really ached with enthusiasm when I wrote that chapter. The last sentence, as I recall it, was, 'And through the dark, storm-tossed night there came to Walter's ears the faint cry of a new-born child.' I cannot be quite sure about the 'storm-tossed' because my only copy of *Self* was blown up, and rightly, in the blitz.

Shortly after the publication of *Self* Michael Arlen had severe stomach trouble at the Mayfair Hotel. (There was no connection between these two events.) I went round with a dear friend of mine called Barbara Back to see him, and found him lying in bed, having a baby too . . . on paper. He told us all about it. I do not know if his baby ever saw the light—I fancy that it was struck out in the proofs—but I do remember saying, rather hotly, that having a baby was not at all like that. 'Oh yes it is,' said Michael, 'it is precisely like that.' To which

I retorted that I had myself had a baby, at the highest pressure, only a few months before. 'We all know about that,' said Michael. 'And it's a bastard.' Barbara gently interrupted us by suggesting that as she happened to have had a real baby as opposed to a paper one she might perhaps be able to offer both of us a few hints. We waved her aside with scorn; she knew nothing about it; she was only a woman. If Michael had not been in a certain condition we should probably have come to blows.

Oxford, as I was saying, had given me up as a bad job. All that brightness gone to dust. And all one's contemporaries being earnest and sensible, like David Maxwell Fyffe, who had a sort of aura of Lord Chancellorship about him even when he was an undergraduate. Which is more than one could say for Bob Boothby. The twinkling, grey-haired, avuncular Sir Robert Boothby was a charming undergraduate, as slim as a straw, as dark as a gypsy, and up to no end of tricks. Once, after a dinner in which pink champagne had flowed as copiously as cocoa flows today, a number of us chased Sir Robert down the moonlit High Street in an endeavour to debag him. What a very macabre cavalcade such a spectacle would present today.

For a time I toyed with the idea of a legal career; I even joined the Inner Temple—if 'joined' is the right word—and lunched there once or twice, dutifully munching plum cake with my mutton. But after Fleet Street I found that most of the young men around me were quite startling bores. Apart from that, I had rather strong feelings about quite a number of the laws which I should be called upon to uphold; I thought that the divorce laws were a sorry mess and many of the sex laws medieval; and on my few visits to the Bankruptcy Courts my sympathies had been in the dock. I was not much of a moralist nor a particularly original thinker, but I had already formulated a philosophy that I was to hold for the rest of my life—namely, that the essence of all sin was cruelty. If an act was cruel it was sinful, if it was not cruel it was not sinful—and therefore should not be illegal. To me it seemed, and still seems, as simple as that. Holding such views it would have been difficult to argue, with any conviction, in favour of the conditions of—let us say—the Criminal Amendment Act.

So I went my wicked way. However, Oxford still called, though in less seductive accents, and from time to time I went down to speak at the Union. In the early twenties the Union was a far more representative body than it is today. There really was some justification for calling it a Parliament of Youth, and for regarding its decisions as representative of the average intelligent young man's point of view. For this reason I have thought it worth while to examine the records of the debates, to extract those decisions which seem significant and—since statistics bore me—to marshal the facts in the form of a dialogue.

Q. What was the Union's attitude towards the League of Nations?

A. We never stopped talking about it, and we never stopped voting for it.

Q. For example?

A. Right at the beginning of the decade[1] we gave it the biggest majority in the history of the Union. The motion was 'That this house desires the immediate and actual establishment of a League of Nations'.

Q. What was the majority?

A. 825 to 99.

Q. Any particular reason for such figures?

A. Well, old Lord Robert Cecil helped. He was the proposer. I suppose he wasn't so old, really, but you know how antediluvian people look when you're nineteen. And he had a terrific stoop and a big nose and he drank a lot of cold water before his peroration . . . all of which is pretty ageing, don't you think? Anyway, we lapped him up.

[1] The actual date was October 30th, 1919.

Q. Did you debate about the female sex? And if so what was the general attitude?

A. We were agin' it.

Q. How do you mean?

A. Nothing sinister. Just that we didn't want women around too much.

Q. For example?

A. Don't let's get too serious about this. But in November 1926 we passed a motion that 'Women's Colleges should be levelled to the ground'.

Q. A big majority?

A. Much of a muchness. 223 to 198. But it caused an absolute stinkaroo in the women's colleges. There was a rumour that they were all lining up on the ramparts of Balliol waiting to scald us with molten cocoa.

Q. Communism?

A. We doted on it.

Q. Meaning?

A. Well, it was all rather gay, to begin with. There was a shop in the High which sold a lovely line in cherry-coloured velvet ties. If you were a healthy young man you had to have one of those. Then there was a man called Rothstein[1] at Balliol who was pretty persuasive. He went about telling people that if only they joined the party they'd feel like St Francis on Monday and Joan of Arc on Tuesday and the Duke of Norfolk all the week, which you must admit is a pretty good selling line.

Q. Examples?

A. Certainly. Date 1925. Motion: 'This house calls upon the Government to take active measures to suppress Communist sedition in this country.' Result . . . defeated. I forget the majority, but it was pretty hefty.

Q. What about social conditions in general?

A. We were pretty liberal on the whole. For instance, we passed a motion that 'immediate and drastic reforms are

[1] Andrew Rothstein.

needed in our public schools'. There was a chap called Evelyn
Waugh who spoke in favour . . . which is funny, when you
come to think of it. He was quoted in the Oxford Magazine as
saying how sorry he was that all the speakers, so far, had been
so bad. To which the Oxford Magazine retorted 'Mr Waugh
was certainly no better'.

Q. What about Europe?

A. We decided that Mussolini was 'a menace to the well-
being of Europe'. That was as early as 1923. We came out for
official recognition of Russia in 1925. We were pretty hot
against the colour bar.

Q. What about America?

A. Well, we were pretty sore when America backed out of
the League of Nations. We felt that we'd been left holding the
baby . . . which indeed we had. There was a motion 'that this
house approves of American non-intervention in European
affairs'. It was beaten by a majority of 160. You ought to
remember that, because you were the official opposer.

After 1926 . . . possibly because of a reaction from the
general strike and possibly because already, in the distance,
could be heard the faint thunders of the economic crash of 1929
. . . Oxford was seized with a hectic gaiety. There was a feeling
of *après moi le deluge*. The dreaming spires were floodlit with a
curious flickering glare. Attendance at such sober institutions
as the Union fell to an all-time low, and in order to attract the
reluctant undergraduates the subjects for debate became more
and more sensational. In 1928 the Union, by a large majority,
registered its approval of birth control as a national policy.
This decision caused rivers of dirty ink to swirl down the
Fleet Street gutters. Side by side with these subjects, which
were at least adult, there were nights of pure tomfoolery.
Typical of these was one which proclaimed 'That this house
dislikes Amy Johnson, Adolf Hitler, and Oxford Journalism'.
Why poor Amy Johnson should have been chosen for attack it

is difficult to conceive. She was the bravest woman who ever piloted an aeroplane. Maybe it was because she was what we would nowadays call 'non-U'. She had a peculiar accent, agonizingly refined, with echoes of pure Wapping. All the same, I think that Oxford should have let her alone. There are a great many sharks in the Timor Sea, and Amy crossed it solo, flying the sort of aeroplane in which most people nowadays would hesitate to fly the Channel.

But then, as we have observed, the mood was one of deliberate, almost desperate gaiety. Communities of people, especially of young people, are not so very different from herds of animals; they can scent danger in the air. And there was plenty of danger ahead, in those last years of the decade. Economic empires were toppling, armies were lining up to march to unknown destinations, under new and ugly flags. And so . . . while the sap was still lively in his blood, while there was still a little money in the bank, the undergraduate said to himself, 'To hell with it. Let's dance. Let's go crazy. Let's *épater* the whole world.'

That is why those three years, 1926 to 1929, were probably the last in which Oxford was—to decadent people like myself —really Oxford. They were years in which somehow—don't ask me why—there was still a certain elegance in owing money to one's tailor. Years in which young men who had scarcely started to shave had already acquired a sound taste in vintage claret. Years in which one could really dress up—the last years of the dandy.

Flick over the pages of the *Isis* and you will find echoes of this charming insouciance.

'Refrain from striking your tutor'—so begins one editorial —'or if you must, be on the safe side and kill him.'

Advice to freshmen included solemn injunctions such as, 'never go on playing bridge after four a.m., or you will be late for your morning golf'.

As for the Union . . . 'The Union has two billard tables and no other features of importance.'

And of course—as we used to say in those days—sex was 'rearing its ugly head'. (One wonders who invented that music-hall metaphor?) As expressed in contemporary anthologies of 'Oxford Poetry' sex was indeed rather ugly, finding vent in such couplets as

> He walks the streets and winks at women
> In the night, the slimy night.

or again . . .

> A man would rejoice to play with her
> Because of the muscularity of her sunburnt arms.

Fond fathers, reading such effusions, were naturally disturbed. Perhaps, they asked themselves, their sons were not getting enough exercise? This was certainly the opinion of a gentleman called Judge Radcliffe. Reminiscing in *The Oxford Magazine*, he deeply regretted that rowing was no longer a duty as in his day, and inveighed against 'fleets of punts mounting the Cherwell whose occupants spend the afternoon lying on cushions and reading a novel . . . this is a most disquieting sight; it means the demise of the College spirit . . . fills me with some apprehension for the subsequent virility in the world of this generation'.

Maybe, after all, it *had* been a mistake to admit women to Oxford? Maybe the *Isis* had been right when it announced that 'the cream of our country's youth will be distracted, if not enmeshed'? (This is surely one of the most endearing examples of the mixed metaphor ever to be printed.) The Principal of Lady Margaret Hall evidently shared these misgivings. Here is an extract from the College Regulations:

> Mixed theatre parties must include at least two women in the party. A woman undergraduate may not go for walks, bicycle-rides or motor rides with men (other than her brother) unless permission previously obtained from her Principal before hand, and there must be at least two women in the party.

CHAPTER TEN

A SPLASH OF COLOUR

I am a great colour thinker, if you know what that means, and I see the 1920's in light shades of pink, and the 1930's as a complete change to dark blue and purple.

Sandy Wilson, in a letter to the author.

SANDY WILSON, for the benefit of those few people who have been marooned on desert islands for the past five years, is the author of that artful little piece *The Boy Friend* . . . a musical comedy which is a loving skit on the twenties. How so subtle and delicate a conceit managed to defeat the concerted stupidities of Broadway and St Martin's Lane is one of the many unsolved mysteries of the theatre. The plot of *The Boy Friend* has the frail perfection of an essay by Max Beerbohm, and it is set to music which is nothing in itself but everything in its context. You would think that it would have been puffed off the stage by the first adverse wind, but it has run and run, and its audiences are largely composed of teenagers. This suggests that the charm of the twenties is not only apparent to the middle-aged.

Sandy Wilson may be right about his 'dark blues and purples of the thirties'—there is certainly some psychological justification for dressing that menacing decade in sombre hues. But he is wrong about his 'light pinks' of the twenties. There was very little light pink about, except when the Beaton sisters were

making their entrances and their exits. The distinctive colours
—even the names are dated—were:

> Jade Green
> Tango Orange
> Cerise

If the middle-aged would close their eyes for a moment they
would probably see these colours flickering on the backcloth of
their memory. They might remember an actress in a skin-tight
jade green dress, walking into the Savoy Grill, and flicking
a cigarette into the face of a dramatic critic called Hannen
Swaffer, and then giving him a resounding slap on the jaw.
Swaffer, who wrote two pages of superb theatrical gossip—one
could hardly call it criticism—thrived on slaps, and he was
never happier than when an outraged management closed the
doors of a theatre to him.

Cerise and tango! Cerise was the colour Gertie Lawrence
was wearing when I first met her with Noel Coward. I remember this because she came into the room exclaiming 'cherry
roipe, cherry roipe' in a Cockney accent. As for 'tango', it
really meant what it said. Women really did dress up of an
afternoon in orange—or burnt sienna or chrome or whatever
particular shade was in the mode—and they really did take
themselves off to expensive little *boites* in Mayfair and proceed
to go through the motions of what they fondly imagined to
be the tango. This dance, as performed in those days, gave the
illusion that the participants were threading their way along
the ledges of dangerous precipices; on the faces of the dancers
there was a look of acute apprehension, as though they were
well aware of the dizzy depths below, and the arms were
spread out stiffly, groping, as it were, at the walls of imaginary
cliffs. The effect was painful in the extreme, but at least it was
dancing—in the sense that certain definite steps were learned
and executed. The last time I saw a tango danced in a London
ballroom there were no definite steps at all, the movements
were fluid and formless, and the look of fascinated terror on

the faces of the dancers had been replaced by one of amiable vacuity.

Jade green, cerise, tango . . . surely there is a colour lacking? Yes, there is. We have left out beige. This was definitely an invention of the twenties; the first time that beige stockings were worn, with any *éclat*, was in the summer of 1922. Two young ladies called the Trix Sisters appeared in them for luncheon at the Ritz, and a number of elderly ladies felt that the country had taken another step towards the Pit. And indeed, the first beige stockings had a startling impact on even the sophisticated; until the Trix Sisters stockings had been white, or black, or dyed to match the dress. Beige suggested the nude, and the nude—then as now—was not quite nice. One doubts if it ever will be.

So much for the general 'colour' of the twenties, from the feminine point of view. What about the shape?

Perhaps this can be most crisply summed up by a remark which was made to me by Norman Hartnell, the Queen's dressmaker. He said:

'If Sabrina[1] had lived in those days, she would have been obliged to stay indoors.'

We had been looking through some of his old albums, and as we turned the pages, encountering one tube-shaped female after another, I asked him if women had indeed changed their shapes in the last thirty years—if there had been, so to speak, a sort of mass swelling and puffing out. No, said Norman, women had not changed their shapes, they had merely changed their minds. And very glad he was that they had done so, for apart from their innate hideousness, the dresses of the twenties involved the designers in an arduous and exhausting struggle against nature. It was the battle of the brassiere in reverse; and half the dressmaker's time was spent in making intricate

[1] For the benefit of readers abroad it should be explained that Sabrina is a young lady in 'show business' who has a highly developed chest.

MANNERS AND MODES.

TYPICAL VOTARIES OF TERPSICHORE, MOST GRACEFUL OF THE MUSES

contraptions of canvas and elastic to be fitted tightly over any busts that showed signs of intransigence.

'To own a bust in the twenties,' said Norman, 'was extremely *déclassée.*'

Yes, but there was one glorious exception to this rule—one great woman, and one great bust, whose figure looms large over the period. Here is a story about her.

One day, for reasons which I have forgotten, I found myself in Norman Hartnell's pleasantly regal establishment in Bruton Street. Norman was busy but he said that I could wander round. I did so, and opening a great many doors which should not have been opened, I found myself in a large deserted workroom filled with busts. On each bust was a label: 'The Countess of X', 'Madame de P', 'The Hon Mrs Q'.

I realized that I was in the most rarified atmosphere of *la haute couture*. Here, in a sort of waxless, headless Madame Tussauds, were the corporeal likenesses of the great ladies of the town. The Countess of X, Madame de P, and the Hon Mrs Q were all far, far too busy to come and be fitted in person; they were all roaring off to Ascot, or—much smarter—standing in a queue outside the Café de Paris to see the latest pantry-boy banging a biscuit tin at £100 a night. So these ladies had their busts copied, and kept at Norman's, and when they wanted a new frock they just rang up and the bust got all the boredom and the pin-pricks. There may be minor errors in this piece of rapportage but that is the rough idea, and if I were very rich I should have a permanent model of my hips, preferably in marble, in the basement of Messrs Kilgour and French.

Now for the climax of our tale. My eyes wandered round the room and lit upon a bust standing all by itself in the corner. Or rather, on the vague outlines of a bust, for it was reverently wrapped up in a lot of brown paper. Even so, there was something about this truncated object that seemed vaguely familiar. It looked the sort of bust that would stand no nonsense. It had an aura—yes—an aura of majesty.

Then Norman came into the room. And suddenly I realized who the bust was.

I turned to him. 'That bust in the parcel,' I began, 'is it Queen Ma . . . ?'

But the second syllable froze on my lips. It was, of course. But Norman never discusses his royal clients. Which is one of the reasons why they gave him the CMG.

'To own a bust,' said Norman, 'was extremely *déclassé*.' In the jargon of today—or yesterday—there was nothing so non-U as a bust; it was worse than a mirror or a mantlepiece, and nearly as bad as a lounge.

One wonders, in passing, if there is anything of psychological significance in this startling change of fashion? Or is it merely a proof of the general idiocy of women in the matter of their own appearance? Whatever the reason, it is interesting to note that in the age of the Bright Young People, which has so often been painted as an era of licentiousness, quite an important portion of the female body was hedged and wired in and barricaded with as much care as if it had been composed of radio-active substances.

Sabrina is not the only young lady who would have caused a sensation if she had walked down Berkeley Square in those days . . . days when the nightingales were really singing there, and the owls hooting into the bargain. Almost any female film-star would have stopped the traffic, with her mouth. The cavernous, scarlet mouths of the modern stars, mouths that suggest the slaughter-house, mouths that make no concession to the exquisite lines drawn by human lips . . . these obscenities had not yet been invented. However vigorously the young ladies of the twenties might constrain the curves of their busts, they accentuated the curves of their lips. Cupid's bow was still the ideal, and a mouth could still be compared with a rosebud. Today a more fitting simile would be provided by a rhododendron. The technique of the lipstick was elaborate, and often required two lipsticks . . . one, the more vivid, to outline the bow of the upper lip, the other, in a softer shade, to modify the

I

curve of the lower. Perhaps it is for this reason that so many photographs of the beauties of the twenties give them a rather prim expression.

Sandy Wilson, whose letter started me off on these random reflections, added . . . 'Writing *The Boy Friend* has been rather like unlocking that old trunk in the attic, which your parents said you weren't to touch and had nothing in it anyway, although you knew very well that it was full of romantic treasures.'

So it has been in this chapter, which is really only a rummaging through an old trunk. Let us dip into it and see what we can find. What is this curious object? But of course . . . it is a piece of monkey fur. This starts a whole train of memories. Very few women wear monkey fur today; in the twenties it was 'terribly smart'. I remember it on people like Baba Lucinge,[1] who was as thin as a rake, with antennae eyebrows and a face like a small, beautiful wasp. The Dolly Sisters used to wear a great deal of it too.

Fur fashions have altered radically. If you were rich, and if you had no aversion to advertising the fact, you wore sables, just as in the Edwardian days you would have worn ermine. (The ermine cloaks of the Edwardian ladies really were the most barbaric garments, fit only for savages, with all the tails of those nice little animals hanging round their necks like so many scalps. The day will come, one hopes, when a civilized woman will regard a coat made from the skins of animals with the same horror as she would regard a lampshade made from the skins of men, but that is not likely to be in my time.)

Then, as the final fur de luxe, there was chinchilla, but this was so expensive and wore so badly that only the very richest women went in for it. But there was one woman who actually had chinchilla rugs on the floor, and not only trod on them but laid on them and generally bounced about on them from morning till night. Her name was Gaby Deslys.

Gaby was a sort of Mistinguette, who was reputed to be the

[1] Princesse Faucigny-Lucinge.

mistress of King Manoel of Portugal. She wore gigantic head-dresses and carried vast fans and spent most of her stage career stalking up and down staircases, in the traditional manner. She was in my opinion an all-enveloping bore but she had a remarkable effect on the gentlemen, including—of all people—Sir James Barrie, who wrote a play for her with the horrid title *Rosy Rapture*. Her partner was a very good-looking young man called Harry Pilcer, whose talents were far superior to her own. One of the many admirers of Pilcer's art was the fabulous young novelist Ronald Firbank. (It is good to know that the works of Firbank—particularly *Valmouth* and *The Flower Beneath the Foot* are enjoying a sudden unexpected renaissance in America. He was like a moth who had fluttered from be-tween the pages of Beardsley's *Sous La Colline* to land on Norman Douglas's shoulder.) When Firbank first saw Harry Pilcer dance—he was chasing Gaby Deslys up one of her stair-cases at the time—he was so overwhelmed that he rushed out and bought a huge bunch of orchids which he sent to Pilcer's dressing-room, accompanied by an invitation to supper. Whether Pilcer ever got the flowers we shall never know; he certainly returned no answer. Whereupon Firbank, with tears streaming down his face, returned to the theatre, which was just filling up for the last act. Still sobbing, he advanced to the front row and walked slowly along by the side of the orchestra pit, tossing cypripediums and odontoglossums with tragic gestures to the astonished musicians. This, for Firbank, was proof of a violent emotional disturbance; he was the shyest of men; when he was receiving guests at Oxford he used fre-quently to dart behind a large screen as soon as he heard them coming upstairs, and remain behind it, carrying on a desultory conversation, until he felt sufficiently confident to emerge.

How this long dissertation developed from a piece of monkey fur, you may well inquire. My excuse must be that we were rummaging in an old treasure chest. Let us have another dip into it. What are all these things in this bundle? We lift them out and find a pile of coloured glass bangles, and we remember that women used to wear them up to the elbow. And here is a whole box full of cigarette holders. Very smart, those were. They came in all colours, some of them were a foot long, and the girls stuck 'Russian' cigarettes in them, which were firmly Virginian except for the paper, which was black. The long cigarette holder served the same coquettish purpose for the girl of the twenties as the fan for the girl of the nineties; but it was not so easy to manipulate and at times was a positive menace. Several of the lustier members of White's Club were constantly appearing at luncheon with their eyes nearly gouged out.

And here is a whole dress. If we hold it up to the light we shall probable agree that it represents an all-time low in the history of female costume. The reason for this is not far to seek. Throughout the ages women have been committing the wildest extravagances in dress, but they have always held true to the principle of emphasizing their physical features rather than denying them. Thus the bustle, if we are being frank, was merely an extension of the female bottom, for which there is much to be said, particularly when it is painted by Velasquez. Again, the Elizabethan stomacher was based on the wasp waist, and there is much to be said for that too. And the 'Winterhalter line' of the upper bosom, which has persisted in various degrees throughout the ages, is in no way a refutation of nature; rather is it a graceful caress which enhances nature's design.

But in the twenties this admirable principle was suddenly and violently rejected, for the first and one hopes for the last time in history. Busts, in any shape or form, became taboo overnight, which was bad enough. Even worse, waists plummetted nine inches, to remain suspended somewhere below the navel, decorated with as many beads as a bamboo curtain. As if this were not enough, skirts shot up so high that when the ladies were agitated, which was quite often, their knees were displayed, and there is nothing, but nothing, to be said for the female knee. It is the one part of the female anatomy that has left the poets cold since the days of Sappho. Ears, yes, and necks and eyes and ankles and nostrils and teeth and chins and finger-nails and even toes . . . all these have been celebrated. But when confronted by that small patch of skin which conceals the semilunar cartilege, the poets have always been struck dumb. Not until the twenties did knees come into their own.

In spite of the hideousness of the dominant designs, a few dressmakers managed to rise above them. One of these was Edward Molyneux, a young British soldier who suddenly stormed the hitherto impregnable citadel of Paris and—to everybody's astonishment—established himself firmly as an arbiter of elegance. Now that Edward is, one hopes, a million-aire, with a European reputation as an important artist in his own right, it is difficult to appreciate the almost foolhardy courage of that Parisian adventure. Another dressmaker who flouted the conventions was Lucile . . . a pseudonym for Lady Duff-Gordon. She was a rather tiresome woman who used to trail around in mauve tulle talking about the 'dress of tempera-ment'. If she had dressed to match her own temperament she would have worn sateen shorts. And then of course there was our own Norman Hartnell, in whose launching I played a minor role. I met him at a party in Cambridge and was so impressed by his designs that I whisked him off to the house of a lady called Gracie Ansell, who was herself an unforgettable figure of the twenties. She was really an Edwardian, with all that goes with that word. 'My dear,' she would hiss in her curious, throaty voice, 'I used to be able to sit on my hair. And when I know you better, my dear, I shall tell you what King Edward said about *that* at Goodwood!' But she was still gay and beautiful and eager for the latest craze, and so it was not surprising when we arrived at her house to find a game of mah-jong in progress, with Lady Diana Cooper and 'Oggie' Lynn and Tallulah Bankhead and Gracie herself. One day, before I am ninety, I hope that somebody will make mah-jong fashionable again. It was so terribly pretty, with those ivory counters, engraved with the green 'bamboos' and the delicate black 'characters' and the 'flowers' and the 'winds' and the 'dragons'. I can hear an echo of the dialogue to this day.

Oggie: Oh dear! That wretched Tallulah's got my flower.

Tallulah: Well, dahling, you've got my wind.

Gracie: Diana's made a gong of the prevailing wind and *I* haven't got any winds or dragons or anything.

Lady Diana: It isn't the prevailing wind, darling. East's prevailing.

Tallulah: No dahling. West. (Suddenly.) *Pong!*

This, to the modern generation, must sound like double Dutch. They must take my word for it that mah-jong was an enchanting diversion. They must also take my word for it that the beautiful Lady Diana Cooper was of the variety celebrated by Poe in the verses 'To Helen'. My acquaintance with her was of the slightest, and it was not furthered by the fact that whenever I met her I was tongue-tied by the sheer impact of loveliness. Mrs Patrick Campbell once said to me: 'One should never meet Lady Diana socially; as soon as she comes into a room one should be allowed to retire behind the curtains, and peer through, and *gloat.*' That was how I felt about her, and still feel . . . for the radiance is scarcely dimmed today.

So the game of mah-jong rattled on, and young Norman Hartnell sat in a corner, clutching his portfolio of sketches with trembling fingers, and nobody—least of all himself—suspected that one day those same fingers would be drawing the design for a dress that was to play its part in the pageant of history—the Coronation dress of Queen Elizabeth the Second. But when the game was over, they gathered round, and they said the designs were marvellous—(pronounced 'mahvlz')—and Tallulah said, 'Dahling, you'll go to the top," and—well, he did.

CHAPTER ELEVEN

PLUS ÇA CHANGE

FEMALE hair, throughout the ages, has always excited the fiercest of passions. Even St Paul lost all sense of proportion about it. If one goes back to the epistles with an open mind one is bewildered and indeed somewhat shocked to find so great a spiritual leader working himself up into such a frenzy of indignation about women who do not wear a hat to church . . . for that is really all it amounted to. This must surely be one of the strangest passages in the Bible, or indeed in any of the great spiritual treasuries of mankind.

What St Paul would have said in the twenties one trembles to think, for it was then that women began to cut their hair *en masse*. Two new words made their appearance in the newspaper, 'bobbing' and 'shingling',[1] and both these words were used as clubs with which to batter the heads of the younger generation. When one reads the spate of impassioned prose which was directed against these two styles of *coiffure* by the clergy of all denominations, one would think that 'bobbing and shingling' were pseudonyms for the penchants of Sodom and Gomorrah.

Even nice old ladies like Lady Bland-Sutton fell over backwards in their efforts to stop the menace of the encroaching scissors. Lady Bland-Sutton was one of the people for whom I used to 'ghost' articles. Her husband was President of the Royal

[1] 'Bobbing', in fact, was not a new word. The Oxford Dictionary dates it from 1822. 'Shingling' is dated 1924.

College of Surgeons, and they had a house next to Claridges with an extraordinary Egyptian dining-room which was supposed to be modelled on the discoveries of Tutankhamen. Whenever she felt strongly about a social problem, Lady Bland-Sutton used to telephone and ask me to luncheon 'to discuss an article' . . . and since she was not only a darling but had an excellent cook, and since I could write the article under her name and get three guineas for it, I was delighted to accept.

How strongly Lady Bland-Sutton felt about 'bobbing and shingling' may be judged from the following extract from an article under her name in *The Weekly Dispatch* for January 18th, 1925.

'I wish it were possible' she writes, 'to collect statistics of marriage proposals, giving the exact number of offers which each type of woman is receiving. I believe that the figures would be more instructive today than at any time I can remember, and would probably read something like this:

The girl who keeps her hair, 90 per cent; the girl who has compromised with a bob, 70 per cent; the girl who has shingled, 25 per cent.'

How Lady Bland-Sutton arrived at these alarming statistics it would be impossible to say. But it is certain that her views were shared by the vast majority of her contemporaries . . . particularly in the paragraph that follows:

'And have you noticed that, in some cases, shingling seems to have a psychological effect, and that just as Samson lost his strength when inveigled by Delilah, so do the modern Delilahs lose something of their restraint when they cut off their hair?'

Fiercer and fiercer waxed the controversy. Only a few weeks after Lady Bland-Sutton's article, an even more awful prophecy was published in the same paper . . .

BALD WOMEN . . . A WARNING

There is nothing actually unhealthy about shingling, although there have been cases where its devotees have caught cold or suffered for a week or so from stiff necks.

But shingling, according to every medical man with whom I have discussed the matter, though not unhealthy, *is bound to make women, sooner or later, as bald as men.*

But the *comble* came in August 1925. Admittedly it was the silly season, but the facts, as reported on the leader page of *The Weekly Dispatch*, were not so silly. Here they are:

BOBBED TO DEATH

Many women have spoken lightly of the bobbed hair vogue. But in every comedy there is an element of tragedy. So it is with bobbing. It has found a victim in a twenty-two-years-old Preston mill girl. This poor girl adopted the new fashion some three weeks ago. When she had got her locks duly shorn, she was displeased with the result. She gazed at herself in the mirror and concluded that her appearance had suffered much under the hairdresser's remorseless scissors. She talked to her sweetheart on the subject, and he endeavoured to console her. But she refused to be comforted. She thought she had made herself not merely ill-favoured but also ridiculous. People laughed at her. They did not, but that was what she fancied, and the thought preyed on her mind, so that finally she went out and drowned herself in the canal.

'Bobbing and shingling' were two of the signs by which 'the modern girl' was recognized, and a very large section of the older generation regarded them as signs of the devil. 'What is a modern girl?' This question was put by a reporter to a woman called Lady Walpole. Drawing herself up to her full height and taking a deep breath, her ladyship retorted: 'She is an inane, insane, Eton-cropped, useless, idle, mannish young woman who smokes doped cigarettes, uses bad language, wears practically no clothes, and is an abomination to her fellow creatures.' Which was fairly inclusive.

Nor did the 'modern young man' receive much kinder treatment at the hands of his elders and betters, particularly when he began to brighten up his wardrobe. His most spectacular method of doing so was by wearing Oxford trousers, a sartorial curiosity which first crept into the news at the beginning of the decade . . .

'Flannel trousers twenty inches broad at the base have become the rage at Oxford. These are made in shades varying from canary yellow to wisteria blue.' This announcement was followed by a symposium of opinions from the sort of people who always contribute to symposiums—a bishop, a general, an elderly actress, and an 'eminent Harley Street surgeon'. (The latter is usually one of the junior crime reporters.) All these persons, without exception, tied themselves into knots about Oxford trousers, and hinted that they were somehow connected with atheism, effeminacy, the decline of the English theatre and chills on the liver. I rather liked Oxford trousers myself, and wrote a poem about them when I was editor of *The Isis*—a position I occupied for one extremely hectic term. The poem was about a young man who went much too far and had his trousers made from a cubist material. They were removed from him, and hoisted on top of the Martyr's Memorial by a group of hearties from Brazenose College. The piece had no value, even as a parody, but the 'lay-out' may have a period interest. When young men had nothing to say in those days they found that they could say it more effectively by cutting their words in half. Thus:

'I will wear Cu
        Bist trousers' he
    said.
        But the Philis-
            Tines who were
            Not beautif
            ul
                De
                bagged
                him.
                    'We do not like Cu
                    Bist
                    Trous
                        Ers' they said. Etc., etc.

Oxford trousers and the Teddy Boys; the 'modern girl' of the twenties and the 'modern girl' of the fifties; the Charleston and Rock 'n Roll; is there so much difference after all? I doubt it. To the elderly and pompous all these were, and are, symbols of going to the devil. You pay your money and take your choice. The only difference between the twenties and the fifties —if it is a question of going to the devil—is that in the fifties you can go to the devil in a faster car.

You can also go to the devil with comparative safety. In these days venereal disease is as easy to cure as a cold in the head; in the twenties it was still a scourge, involving long and painful treatment.

One method in which a woman went to the devil—in the opinion of the older generation—was by having her face lifted. Today this seems difficult to believe. A modern woman who is going to have her face lifted will announce the fact as carelessly as if she were telling you that she is going to the dentist. But in the twenties the whole science of facial surgery was still invested with the mystery of a black art. To recapture youth by this means, it was felt, must involve some sacrifice of the soul; one newspaper dramatically summed up the views of the woman-in-the-street by an article entitled 'Faust in Harley Street'.

Perhaps the reason for this reaction was partly due to the very odd appearance of some of the ladies who had been treated in this manner; the art was still in its infancy; the holocaust of the Second World War and the tortured faces of thousands of young men, scarred in battle, were needed to bring it to perfection. It is an ironical thought that the dramas of the hospital ward should be re-enacted in the beauty parlour.

The woman who did more than any other to put face-lifting on the map was an American actress called Fanny Ward. One used often to see her having supper at the Savoy Grill. Her appearance was spectacular and slightly alarming. Although she admitted to over sixty, she had the face of a little girl—pink, flawless, and totally devoid of expression. As the years went by, her fluffy hair—or perhaps it was a wig—was dressed further and further forward, in order to hide her scars. The only tell-tale features were her hands; in those primitive days hands could not be lifted; now, I am told, they can, which must be a great comfort.

Fanny Ward, and her face, provided the material for an endless repertoire of stories, most of them—particularly the one about the navel—unprintable. One story, however, I believe is true. This concerned her husband, on whom she is said to have experimented with various devices before she tried them out herself. The treatment involved the use of paraffin wax, which was injected under the eyes to remove pouches. The unfortunate man, having acted as a guinea-pig—so the story goes—went and sat too near the fire, so that the wax melted, ran down his cheeks and gathered under his chin, giving him the appearance of a turkey cock. After that, he sported a beard.

For me, Fanny Ward had a fascination verging on the morbid. I could not keep my eyes off her. It was a great moment when, in New York, at a Cole Porter first night, I suddenly found myself sitting in the stall immediately behind her, and when, by a happy chance, her cloak slipped, revealing a battle-ground of scars round her neck. No lover ever gazed on his mistress with more delight, and when I returned to my hotel after the performance, I sat down and scribbled the first draft of a poem to her. This was a parody of Kipling's *If*, beginning:

> If you can keep your chin, when all the rest
> Are losing theirs, and wondering how you do it,
> If you can sleep in a reducing vest
> And breakfast off a lemon and some suet . . .

Lord knows how it went on, but I remember the final couplet:

> And what is more, the world will think that you
> Are sixty-one, instead of sixty-two.

There is an amusing footnote to this piece of nonsense. In 1929, Cochran commissioned me to write his next revue. I was desperately in need of those most precious of all items to the revue writer, the 'front-cloth numbers', which can be played without props or scenery. It occurred to me that the Fanny Ward verse might form one of a series of literary parodies, to be played in costume by an enchantingly vulgar comedian called Douglas Byng. I read it to Cochran, who was enthusiastic. Then he frowned. 'But we'll have to get her permission,' he said, 'and I can't see any woman in her senses allowing herself to be made to look such a fool. All the same, it's worth a shot.'

He rang the bell for his secretary. 'Take this telegram: "Miss Fanny Ward, St Regis Hotel, New York City. My dear Fanny may I have your permission to make a little gentle fun of you in my next revue Charles Cochran".'

Within a few hours the reply came back: 'Regret cannot give permission must think of position of Lord Plunket Fanny Ward.'

This mysterious message needs interpretation. Fanny Ward's daughter—who was a dancing angel of a girl—had married a nice young man called Lord Plunket. They were as charming a couple as you ever met—destined for a tragic end—but that is neither here nor there.

The sketch seemed to be doomed. But Cochran never gave in without a fight. 'Write out the whole poem for me,' he said, 'and I'll cable it to her. It's just possible that she mayn't see the point.'

So I wrote out the whole poem, with very little hope. As I said before, I can't remember it, but it was—or was intended to be—vitriolic. There were dreadful references to surgeons' masks and knives, and I had even managed to find a rhyme for 'chloroform'. (Which reminds me of a time when I met a distracted Cole Porter wandering round the Ritz in Paris trying to find a rhyme for 'duck-billed platypus'. One could write a book about rhyming. How many of the young generation, in a quiz game, could give the correct answer to the rhyme which Browning, in a wager, invented for 'ranunculus'?)

We digress and digress. Here is the end of this silly story. On the following morning Cochran greeted me with a broad grin. He had in his hand a cablegram: 'Have read poem delighted to give permission Fanny Ward.'

What was one to make of it? Had she suddenly forgotten about 'the position of Lord Plunket'? Had she swallowed the venom and mistaken it for milk? One did not know. All one knew was that when a month later Douglas Byng declaimed it, in an orange wig and a *poitrine à outrance*, it brought down the house.

Were the twenties, then, one long, silly season? Sometimes one is tempted to think so. Consider the case of Rudolf Valentino. Some day a competent psychologist should write a serious treatise on the Valentino phenomenon. Here is an actor whose film revivals arouse gales of laughter. True, for technical reasons they are usually played a few degrees faster than their original versions, so that some of the gestures appear unnecessarily abrupt, but the difference in tempo is not as marked as all that. The essence of the performance gets through; the facial expressions, the flashing of the eyes, the curling of the lips, the juttings of the chin . . . all these are presented to us much as they were presented to the audiences of the twenties. Those audiences, by and large, were enraptured. British women, in those days, left home for Valentino, quite literally. They took the rent money out of the ornaments on the mantlepieces, and got into ships and sailed to America, just to be near him. When he died there were scenes of mass hysteria on both sides of the Atlantic. All for a figure who today is a Number One Comic in the Saturday night Palladium show.

Here, surely, is a mystery. How can the passage of a mere thirty years have made so much difference? The answer cannot

be found in any external accident such as dress; Magda, played
in a costume of the twenties, might arouse derision, but
Valentino's classic roles—such as the Sheikh—were played in
costumes that do not date. Nor is it due to any weakness in his
scripts. The plays in which he appeared were silly, but no sillier
than many of the plays today. They all had the same fundamental theme of sadism. He strode through reel after reel,
hurling women about as though they were sacks of potatoes,
snarling at them, smacking them on the bottom. The women
of the twenties lapped it up, and came out of the theatre
mentally black and blue. Perhaps that is the heart of the
mystery; perhaps they were experiencing on the screen
the same masochistic excitement which they had found in the
case of Edith Thompson. If so, we are confronted once more
with our old friend the Death Wish. I imagine that it is both
bad history and bad psychiatry to attempt to label a whole
decade with a human psychological characteristic. And yet the
facts need explanation. The women of the twenties thrilled to
the crack of Valentino's whip; the women of the fifties hoot
with laughter. Why?

Incidentally Valentino, when I interviewed him, was a sad
disappointment. He was very short, with a sallow complexion,
and he looked as though he ought to have been carrying a
tray in Soho. The only woman of my acquaintance who had
any personal experience of his romantic talents informed me,
rather tersely, that he snored.

But though there are many reasons for regarding the twenties
as a long silly season, this does not imply that they were any
sillier than the fifties. Today it seems almost impossible to
believe that in 1922—a year when the stage of Europe was
being rapidly reset for a revival of the tragedy on which the
curtain had scarcely fallen—Mr Winston Churchill was soundly
defeated at Dundee, by an eccentric teetotaller called Edwin
Scrimgeour. This person had gained, among the British people,

the affectionate nickname of 'Pussyfoot', and they drank his health, in beer, when he informed them that they need not worry about the Bolsheviks; all they need think about was the pub next door. So Winston was sent packing, Mr Scrimgeour went to Parliament, and the lunatic stage-hands hurried on, preparing for the next bloody melodrama. That seems strange to us today. But in thirty years time—should this globe remain still unshattered—will it not seem equally strange that Mr Churchill was sent packing at the end of the last war, by the people whom he had most certainly saved from destruction?

Memories are mercifully short. When the Italian mob tied the rope round Mussolini's neck before they strung him up on that lamp-post in Lereto, how many people were aware that this same neck had been honoured with a ribbon from the hands of the King of England? Yes, in 1922 Mussolini was made a GCB by King George V. Lazlo painted a flashy, oily picture of the Duce, as spicy as an Italian salad, which was hung in the French Gallery in Pall Mall. And quantities of nice tweedy gentlemen, whose sons were later to die on the slopes of Monte Cassino, filed past it and said: ' *That's* the sort of chap we ought to have over here!'

Curioser and curioser it all seems, as one looks back, and yet so strangely familiar! In international relationships the pattern repeats itself with sickening monotony. Listen to this:

> I have told the American people that I would do my best to unite America behind a plan for an Association of Nations, which we may join with safety, honour and good conscience, but without selling our birthright for a mess of military pottage.

That has a familiar ring, has it not? You can hear the American twang, sniff the cigar smoke, visualize the long, over-heated marble corridors of Washington. I have heard this sort of thing at American press conferences for the past thirty years. These particular words, which of course mean—and were

Gertrude Lawrence once looked at herself in the glass, turned to me and said, 'Not beautiful, but glamorous, don't you think?' To me she was both

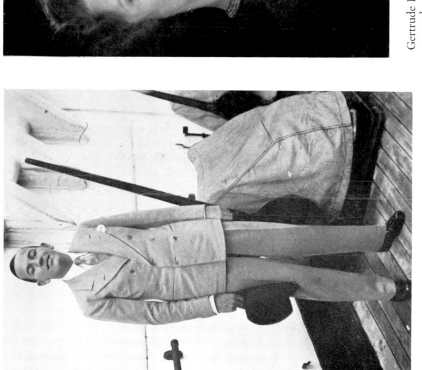

Noel: setting out to conquer the New World

Cecil, going just a little too far?

intended to mean—nothing at all, were spoken when Warren
Harding was elected President of the United States in November 1920. Harding was a hardfaced provincial politician, of
quite exceptional ignorance. Few people would deny that
since those days the standard of American leadership has improved, but the white sheet of righteousness is still very much
in evidence. And nothing—not even the Ku-Klux-Klan, nor
racial segregation nor the final horror of Hiroshima—seems
likely to persuade the Americans that they are not entitled to
wear it exclusively. For those of us who believe, with some
reason, that all the members of all the nations are only a lot of
miserable sinners, this is apt to be irritating.

President Harding, by the way, proceeded to implement his
desire for international fraternity by letting off quite a number
of painful explosions. In 1923 the first white phosphorus air
bomb, weighing twenty-five pounds, was exploded from
the top of a ninety-foot tower in Texas, with—for those
days— shattering results. Observers noticed, with interest,
that it produced a cloud shaped like a mushroom. Wall
Street was buoyant the next morning. 'That would teach
'em!'

One startling difference between the twenties and the
fifties is the extent to which the Americans have extended their
cultural conquest of Britain, if 'cultural' is the right word.
The change has come about so gradually that few people are
conscious of its extent. Here is G. K. Chesterton, writing in
1922. 'I have just read an American story called The Waffle
Iron. Does any English reader know what a waffle is?' Such a
question today could only be asked by the traditional ignor-
amus of the Bench. In the twenties, chewing gum was an
exotic, today it is British as butterscotch. Even British clothes
have 'gone American'. Savile Row and Jermyn Street have
not yet succumbed, but the Charing Cross Road is flooded
with cheap editions of lumber jackets, cowboy hats, jeans, and
Broadway ties. And the Cockney chatter of the passing crowds
has been reorchestrated with many new and strident notes . . .

K

Oh yeah . . . sez you . . . O.K. Only the middle-aged and the elderly are fully aware of what has happened. They are not likely to welcome it, for most of them are too old to learn an American accent.

But though these have been changed, the theme is still . . . *plus ça change.* Consider the realm of medicine. It is possible that the future historian may decide that one of the most vital chapters in the history of mankind was being written in the 1950's—not in the Middle East nor in the atomic experimental stations, but in the studies of a few doctors who are making the first, hesitant steps into the uncharted science of radiaesthesia, and in the sanctuaries of a few spiritualists who are beginning to tap the healing resources of the spirit world. Pain, after all, is the ultimate arbiter, and the object of the ideal legislator should be not only to give the greatest happiness to the greatest number, but to save the greatest number from the greatest pain.

The twenties were ignorant of radiaesthesia, but they had their own mental healers, one of whom was a charming, dumpy little Frenchman called Monsieur Coué, who became a national figure, though whether as a hero or a buffoon it would be difficult to decide. Coué's philosophy stemmed from Mesmer via Mary Baker Eddy, and was summed up in a phrase that rang round the world . . . 'Every day in every way I am getting better and better and better.' One was supposed to repeat this twenty times, on rising and retiring, in a monotonous voice, at the same time counting a string tied with twenty knots.

Coué used to give lectures at Grosvenor Gardens, which were thronged by eager crowds. The only one which I attended was somewhat disturbed by Lord Berners. We had gone there together, and though Gerald Berners was normally very abstemious, he had consumed two side-car cocktails at luncheon, which had disagreed with him. Through the chorus of 'better and better and better'—for we all had to intone the slogan together—came his hollow tones—'worse and WORSE and WORSE.'

Plus ça change . . . every folly of today can be matched with a folly of the twenties. When Aneurin Bevan, not so long ago, decided to show his superiority by refusing to wear a dinner jacket in the presence of the Queen, some people muttered to themselves that this was the beginning of the end; they felt that revolution must be just round the corner. If they had looked over their shoulders they would have found that just the same sort of thing was happening in 1923. In March of that year Ramsay MacDonald, the first Labour Prime Minister, dined with the King and Queen at Buckingham Palace. There was an immediate crisis in the Labour Party . . . which was really very naïve of the Labour Party; they ought to have known what a dear old snob Ramsay was. The crisis died down, but not before twenty-five Scottish members had issued statements to the press that they did not intend to accept royal invitations, and that they would not besmirch themselves by attending 'plutocratic dinner parties'.

Everybody has done everything before; that is really the only lesson of history, and we forget it at our peril.

The twenties even had their own version of the Red Dean of Canterbury. This particular pestilent priest functioned in the charming village of Thaxted, in Essex. He was the Reverend Conrad Noel, and he followed the familiar pattern of all pestilent priests.

Services in Thaxted Church came to resemble a mixture between the mass and the music-hall. In an atmosphere drenched with incense hung the red and emerald flags of Russia and Sinn Fein. The Union Jack had been relegated to the cellars as an emblem of 'Snatch, Grab and Brag'. A table in the porch was loaded with piles of seditious literature, which bore the name of the Thaxted Tracts, urging a 'catholic crusade to shatter the British Empire to bits'. As a bizarre touch of colour, the girls in the choir wore veils of green and scarlet and white. From the pulpit the vicar thundered that the object of the Catholic Crusade was the Workers' International.

Such goings-on did not pass unnoticed. On May 21st, 1921, a meeting of five hundred parishioners condemned the vicar's action as 'outrageous and an insult to sensible and law-abiding citizens.' Meanwhile the Bishop of Chelmsford announced to the world that 'the deplorable affairs at Thaxted were engaging his most earnest attention'.

What happened? Needless to say—nothing. There are no laws of Church or State in our country for dealing with Conrad Noels or Red Deans. Noel, of course, was small fry, and was soon forgotten. But it will take a long time for England, or for the world, to forget the spectacle of the Dean of Canterbury, clinging like a senile limpet to the Rock of Ages.

Plus ça change. All history repeats itself, but British history repeats itself more often than any other. Here is a speech about Cyprus, delivered in the House of Lords in the year 1957, at the height of the Eoka terrorism.

I protest against the doctrine that you should give further and give more, not because Cyprus needs it, not because it is fair to the United Kingdom, but because crime has been more successful. Give it because it is right, give it because it is just, give it because it is good for Cyprus and the United Kingdom, give it because it brings peace and goodwill. But do not give it because you are bullied by the assassins of Colonel Grivas.

The reader must forgive me for the deception; the date of that speech was not 1957, it was December 1921. The speaker was Lord Carson, the subject was the Irish Treaty, and the 'assassins' were not led by Colonel Grivas but by Michael Collins.

And this reminds us that our silly season had sombre echoes. Throughout the decade, side by side with the latest news of bobbing and shingling, Valentino and the Charleston, were daily reports of bloodshed, terror and outrage from the Emerland Isle. Just as today Marilyn Monroe shares the headlines with death in Nicosia, so in the twenties Charlie Chaplin shared the headlines with death in Dublin. However, the Irish tragedy was bloodier and more tenacious, with roots deeply entwined in the soil of ancient hatreds, and since there were times when it overshadowed all our lives, we must give it, even in these careless pages, our brief attention.

CHAPTER TWELVE

GREEN AND WHITE

THERE are times when I am immune to the charm of the Irish. The sentimental legend has obscured the historical record. The legend is of a nation of near-geniuses, tender, sensitive, with a flickering, moonlit poetry. The legend portrays them as being for ever ground under the heel of a brutal oppressor, England. Ireland has never done anything wrong, and England has never done anything right. This legend has been fostered so artfully that even to this day there are a great many foolish people, particularly in the United States, who swallow it whole.

Women, elephants, and the Irish never forget an injury. On the only occasion when I visited the Emerald Isle I felt that the whole lovely landscape was clouded with ancient hatreds. When I went to a party I should not have been surprised if the door had opened to reveal a housemaid announcing Mr Oliver Cromwell. The faculty of memory, when developed to such extremes, becomes a form of neurosis. Fortunately for the Irish, the English memory is comparatively short. Otherwise the British people might still be feeling faintly embittered by the recollection that in the last war—thanks to the Irish— thousands of British sailors and merchantmen were drowned, blown up or burned to death because of the Irish refusal to grant us the facilities of their ports. The Irish decision was based, presumably, on the theory that Hitler was less of an immediate menace than Oliver Cromwell. Thanks to the British Navy this proved, indeed, to be the case. However, it might not do the Irish any harm, when assessing the comparative British and Irish casualties during the time of 'the troubles', to remember those drowning sailors.

During the whole of the twenties the Irish were making as much of a tragic nuisance of themselves as it is possible for any people to make in so comparatively restricted a space. In this they received the whole-hearted co-operation of a large section of the American people. Whenever a bomb went off in Belfast a procession began to walk down Fifth Avenue. These parades are always one of the most remarkable features of the political scene in the United States, and in the case of Ireland the Americans excelled themselves. Legions of middle-aged women who claimed Irish blood—usually on very slender grounds—bought miles of bright green ribbon which they stretched across their well-nourished bosoms and proceeded to march all the way from Washington Square to Central Park, shouting insulting slogans at their late allies. (Similar tactics were later adopted during the Palestine embroglio.) As a means of embittering international relationships such demonstrations could hardly have been improved upon, and one wonders what would happen if the long-suffering British had ever attempted to copy them. The height of the Irish troubles happened to coincide with the rise of the Ku-Klux-Klan, with its programme of medieval sadism. Quite a few of us would not have minded walking once or twice round Trafalgar Square to protest against *that*. But, in Britain, such things are not done.

The Irish troubles—with or without American fomentation —were certainly real enough. Roughly the situation was as follows. An 'Irish Republic' was actually in existence, and at the first meeting of its 'Parliament', in January 1919, delegates were elected to represent Ireland at the Conference of Versailles. Among these delegates were Eamon de Valera, Michael Collins and Arthur Griffith, who represented the brains and organizing ability of the Irish Republican Party . . . Sinn Fein. (Many of the short-minded British have probably forgotten that Sinn Fein is Erse for 'Our Selves'). These mens' hopes were centred on President Wilson, who was the current American Saviour of Humanity. Wilson was deluging Europe with moral platitudes, pious generalizations, and international principles . . . all of which were taken, *au pied de la lettre*, by the bleeding peoples of Europe, and all of which were subsequently and violently repudiated by the American people. However, de Valera, Collins and Griffith were not to know about that. They trusted Wilson. Surely Wilson would see, in the case of little old Ireland, an ideal subject for at least ten thousand words of moralization? For a conflicting number of reasons . . . the records are not very clear . . . the 'Irish Republic' was not recognized at Versailles. In spite of this, de Valera was elected the first President.

Partition was now inevitable, and it came in 1920 with Lloyd George's Government of Ireland Bill. This proved totally abortive . . . largely because it was a wholly practical measure, which recognized the facts of the situation. As such it was naturally unacceptable to the Sinn Feiners. The speech of King George V, when he opened the Parliament of Northern Ireland in June 1921, has an ironic ring, in view of subsequent developments. In it he made a moving appeal to all Irishmen . . . 'to pause, to stretch out the hand of forbearance and conciliation, to forgive and forget, and to join in making for the land they love a new era of peace, contentment and goodwill.'

The immediate result of these gentle words was an intensification of civil war. The barricades went up in Dublin and in Cork, in Belfast and in Londonderry; the mobs stormed through the wine shops; the Union Jacks and the flags of Sinn Fein clashed in an insane medley of red and blue and white and green . . . and Mr Sean O'Casey and a number of other dramatists filled their notebooks with a great deal of material which was later to be used, with considerable profit to themselves, on Broadway. In the great majority of these plays there were no half-shades; it was always a drama of white versus black, with Ireland in the white robe of innocence and England in the black garb of the villain. Perhaps it would be more accurate to describe it as a drama of green versus 'black-and-tan', for this was the name given to the members of the loyalist Royal Irish Constabulary, who were fitted with black hats, khaki uniforms, and police armbands. It is almost impossible for the young student of today to realize the odium with which the republicans, by skilful propaganda, invested the expression 'Black-and-Tan'. By comparison the word 'Hun' was almost an endearment. And yet . . . who were the Black-and-Tans? That there were scoundrels in their ranks goes without saying; but by and large they were brave, tough young men who had no intention of paying allegiance either to the Pope or to the self-elected President. If it is a crime to be Protestant, if it is a crime to be loyal, if it is a crime to be conservative, then the Black-and-Tans were undoubtedly criminals, and deserved to be shot in the back, as they so often were. And their crime was enhanced by the fact that they, and the people of Ulster whom they were protecting, were in a minority. For many years the intellectual has claimed, with considerable justification, that the 'minority is always right'. The Irish have given this phrase a new twist. To them, it would seem that the minority is always right, so long as it is left.

As this is now—for the British at least—ancient history, there seems no point in recapitulating the long and squalid story of back-street fighting, conferences and counter-conferences, which marked the struggle for Irish independence. I need not remind the reader that I am no historian, and even if I were, I should not choose so tangled and unrewarding a theme . . . particularly as that theme seems to be still unresolved. True, after the death in August 1922 of Michael Collins, the leader of the Free State Army, order was gradually restored, and by the end of the year all British troops had left, and the Irish Free State had been established by royal proclamation.

But murder and looting continued, and it seems likely to continue into the unforeseeable future. To this day, in Ireland, the ghost of Cromwell holds the stage.

All things considered, the impact of the Irish tragedy on the social life of Britain had been slight, but there were isolated instances of gangsterism that even the most phlegmatic John Bull could not ignore, such as the murder of a very gallant soldier, Field-Marshal Sir Henry Wilson, the former CIGS. One afternoon he was walking up the steps of his house in Eaton Place—he had just returned from unveiling a war memorial—when two Republican gunmen shot him in the back. They also shot a number of other people in their gay, irresponsible Irish way. This outrage, for a few weeks, aroused considerable indignation among the British, presumably, one suspects, because it occured in Eaton Place, which is a highly respectable district, where nobody expects to be shot in the back.

My own reaction to the Irish tragedy, as you may have observed, was a mixture of despair, exasperation, and sheer boredom, which led in its turn to an admittedly deplorable flippancy. Perhaps this was due to some of the personalities through whose eyes I saw it.

One of those personalities was the legendary Lady Lavery. Although she was a devoted friend of Michael Collins—the stormiest petrel of them all—and though, at her luncheon parties, she was sometimes apt to give vent to opinions that could have landed her in gaol, I could never take her seriously, because of her face.

Hazel Lavery had one of the loveliest faces of the century, but as she grew older it became increasingly difficult to see it. Not because she was elusive, nor because one's eyesight was fading, but because she applied her make-up so thickly that the face itself was almost totally invisible under thick layers of various shades of paint.

This paint was applied with a superb contempt for nature. There would be mauve triangles on the cheekbones, and vermilion streaks sloping upwards from the chin, and startling patches of beige. The effect was of an animated Picasso, and Lord Berners spread an unkind rumour that the First Lord of the Admiralty, after lunching with Hazel, had entirely revised his plans for camouflaging the Mediterranean Fleet.

Nevertheless she remained a very beautiful woman, far more beautiful than she appeared in the paintings of her husband, Sir John Lavery, which appeared in every Royal Academy with monotonous regularity over the years. I wonder how many a young Irishman today, when he licks a stamp to put on a letter to his girl friend, realizes that Hazel was the model for the colleen on the other side?

She was a very witty woman too. Often the *mots* which convulsed one generation are incomprehensible to the next. (*Vide* the average volume of royal memoirs . . . '*How* we laughed when the grand duchess tripped up and fell flat in the herbaceous border, and when His Majesty instantly observed "There's no place like loam!" The Emperor was *convulsed*!') And yet I think the humour that flickered around Hazel has not quite lost its sparkle. There is still, for instance, a ghostly chuckle in the pun about her own name. The story goes that on the day that John Lavery was knighted she was bidden to a reception at Londonderry House. As she ascended the celebrated staircase she was feeling nervous, because this was the first time that she was using her title in public. 'Lady Lavery,' she murmured to the footman who was announcing the names. To which he replied, with some embarrassment, 'At the bottom of the staircase, m'lady, and through the baize door on the left.' It was a sign of Hazel's good humour that for the rest of her life she cheerfully answered to the title of Lady Lavatory.

An elegant bawdiness characterized some of her stories. One of these greatly shocked Ramsay MacDonald, who was a constant visitor at her house. I shall always remember the occasion; lunching with Prime Ministers is not, to me, an everyday experience. To show her Labour sympathies, Hazel had put on a red dress and decorated the luncheon table with masses of red carnations. No doubt for the same reason her maquillage was basically composed of reds . . . crimsons and scarlets and vermilions. She looked very flushed.

So did the Prime Minister when he heard her story. It concerned a certain hermaphrodite who, in those days, was leading what might be called a dual existence in Mayfair. He was not merely an effeminate young man, but—so we were confidently assured—the real thing, such as one sees, or endeavours to see, in obscure corners of Italian museums. For Hazel he had great charm; more, she admired his courage; in spite of his disabilities—if such they must be called—he had gone to the wars.

She told all this to the Prime Minister, who looked increasingly bothered. Hermaphrodites, evidently, were not encouraged in the Labour Party. If such creatures really existed they would almost certainly be members of a Conservative club. He kept on trying to change the subject. But no . . . Hazel would not be put off. She went on and on.

'And then,' she concluded triumphantly, 'he went to the war. And do you know, my dear PM, what he went *as*?'

'No,' grunted the PM.

'He went partly as a corporal and partly as a *vivandière*!'

Another hostess at whose parties one often met distinguished Irishmen was Lady Colefax. Shaw would sometimes lunch there. I shall always remember his shudder of disgust when one of the old-fashioned, aproned parlourmaids offered him a lamb cutlet instead of the risotto which had been prepared for him. It was quite a nice lamb cutlet, with a slice of anchovy on the top, and a pretty little paper frill on the bone, but Shaw shrank from it as though it had been toadstools stewed in arsenic. As he had exquisite manners and would not have wished to embarrass his hostess, this betrayal of his feelings was obviously spontaneous and unassumed. Sometimes the poet Yeats would be there, but he was absent-minded and inclined to forget, so that there would often be an empty chair. This annoyed Lady Colefax, but was not regarded by the other guests as an un-mixed tragedy; there was not much elbow-room at her table. George Moore was another guest, which was a Colefax triumph, because Lady Cunard liked to regard Moore as her exclusive social property.

Sybil Colefax was the greatest lion-hunter of them all. She was, of course, a snob, but she was a snob for brains. True, she was not averse to having royals at her parties, but then, I suppose very few women are. To say that she was exalted if somebody like the Duke of Windsor was coming to supper would be going too far, but she was inclined to be restless, and to twitch at her dress, and speak rather sharply to the parlour-maids. So were her guests. But they would have been very disappointed if he had *not* come to supper. After all, a certain amount of good healthy curtseying is as beneficial to a woman's morale as to her muscles. However, Sybil's address book was not compiled from Burke nor the Almanach de Gotha; she was more drawn to *Who's Who* and *The Artists' and Writers' Year Book*. She was quite genuinely excited by talent in every shape or form, whether the talent was literary or political or musical or artistic. Should the talent have been recognized by the public, so much the better. No woman really minds having to invoke the assistance of the police in order to clear the crowds from her front door when she is having a star to luncheon. But stardom was not an essential passport to her friendship, and she never dispensed her favours with any regard to whether her friends were on the up and up or the down and down. Once a friend of Sybil's, you were always a friend. I have dined with Sybil when I was on the crest of the wave, with a couple of best-sellers and a play running to capacity, and I have dined with her when I was a complete flop, with nothing but an overdraft and an article in *The New Yorker*. On the latter occasion, she put me on her right.

After this little tribute, the ghost of Sybil will perhaps forgive me if I paint a portrait of her which suggests that she was, like all of us—thank God—a fallible, and occasionally a gently laughable human being.

Here goes. Lady Colefax. Dark, sharp featured, beady-eyed, with a voice that seemed to echo through a silver sieve. A questing, restless brain. A formidable knowledge of modern literature—though one sometimes detected, in her incisive comments on the latest fashionable novel, the echoes of the current reviews in the *Times Literary Supplement*. No woman, one felt, could possibly have read quite so many books in the intervals between giving six luncheon parties a week.

And of course, a perpetual cascade of Christian names. The Christian names of the great, the near-great, and those who might some day be great—one hoped in the not too distant future. The Christian names dropped from her thin, pinkish lips like the rattle of ornaments on an overloaded bangle. 'Darling Virginia,'[1]—pointing to a copy of *The Waves*, prominently displayed on the table in the hall (one had nearly put one's hat on top of it, which would have been unforgivable)—'insisted that I should read this before going to bed. But Arthur[2] came to supper and began to play that enchanting piece of nonsense that Willie[3] has written for Osbert's[4] *Façade*. So what is one to do?'

What she had in fact done, one suspected, was to read the *Times Literary Supplement*. What she might have done, if she had not been so harrassed by the social furies, was to read *The Waves* itself. In which case, if she had been honest, she would probably have put that pretentious work in its proper place.

I first met Sybil Colefax in Venice in 1920. She was then only Mrs Colefax, but she was already well on the way up the social ladder. I remember her standing at the window of some palazzo or other—(I don't remember which one but I vaguely

---

[1] Virginia Woolf.
[2] Arthur Rubinstein.
[3] Sir William Walton.
[4] Sir Osbert Sitwell.

recall that our hostess had been the mistress of the Kaiser)—
and I was much impressed by the way in which her beady eye
swept the Grand Canal, seeking whom she might devour.
'Surely,' she murmured, leaning over the balcony, 'surely
that is dear Jane[1] in the white gondola below?' It was not, in
fact, dear Jane; it was a drunken woman from Minnesota who
was to give us all a lot of trouble; but Sybil had made her
point, she had created the atmosphere.

Dear Sybil, standing at the palazzo window, raven-haired,
relentless—what a long time ago it all is! She had just come
from Rome, where she had met—once—that lively and rococo
figure, Lord Berners. ('Dear Gerald Berners—so many talents!
Serge[2] tells me that he is going to commission him to write a
ballet.') Like all of us, Gerald eventually came to dote on
Sybil, but he could not resist the temptation to tell malicious
stories about her. For instance, after the Roman meeting he
came back to London complaining bitterly of insomnia. 'I had
a room next to Sybil Colefax,' he said, 'and she never stopped
climbing all night.'

It was Gerald too, who played on Sybil one of the wittiest
and unkindest practical jokes of all time. During the war, not
long after Winston Churchill had come to power, a note was
delivered to Sybil's house by special messenger. When she read
it, her beady eyes sparkled as never before.

Dear Sybil,

I wonder if by any chance you are free to dine tomorrow
night? It is only a tiny party for Winston and GBS. I think it
important that they should get together at this moment. There
will be nobody else except Toscanini and myself. Do please try,
and forgive this terribly short notice.

Yours ever,

———————

Eight o'clock here and—of course—any old clothes.

[1] Princess Faustino.
[2] Diaghileff.

There was only one thing wrong about this heaven-sent epistle, which was written in longhand; the address and the signature were totally illegible. The address looked faintly like Berkeley Square, but it might equally have been Belgrave Square, and the number might have been anything from 11 to 101. As for the signature, she could not even tell whether it was male or female. A period of agonized activity ensued. Even Sybil had not the nerve to telephone to Downing Street to ask where the Prime Minister was dining on the following night. But she knew Shaw . . . ('dear GBS—what arguments we used to have about Saint Joan!'). So she rang him up, without effect; the master was in one of his habitual periods of retreat. And she rang up every hotel in London, in search of Toscanini, again with no effect, which was not surprising, for the maestro was in America. Maybe, if there had not been a series of air-raids at this time, which played havoc with many of the telephone exchanges, she would have discovered that she was the victim of Lord Berners' peculiar sense of humour. In which case she would have rung him up quite sharply ('Dear Gerald . . . such an *Edwardian*!'). As it was she stayed at home, grimly telephoning to the last minute, with the glittering figures of Winston, GBS and Toscanini slowly fading over the social horizon. There is something almost heroic in the thought of her small, thin, determined figure, sitting in her drawing-room in a hail of bombs, reaching out so desperately for the next rung of the social ladder that, for her, reached up to heaven.

This might perhaps be the place to pause, and bring Lord Berners, the author of this mischievous epistle, to the centre of the stage.

Gerald Berners deserves a niche in the gallery of amiable English eccentrics. He was a great figure in 'artistic London' in the twenties, and indeed until the outbreak of the war, which affected him more profoundly than might have been expected.

'Miss G. B. Stern, the well-known authoress, relaxing after a good day's work'

Elinor Glyn. She had a streak of exquisite felinity. She had the eyes of a cat, the purr of a cat and at times the claws as well

The Irish Free State Army at prayer

Crowd of women with banners at the Dublin Executions

Although he was rich and talented, he had always had a charming diffidence, possibly because he had never expected to succeed to the title—a respectable one, created in the year 1455. He told me that the only reason he became Lord Berners was because three of his uncles all fell off a bridge at the same time, on their way to a funeral, which seems a very strange thing to do. As Lady Brackenbury might have observed, to lose one uncle on a bridge would be a misfortune, to lose three would savour of carelessness. However, that was Gerald's story, and he ought to have known.

He was remarkably ugly—short, swarthy, bald, dumpy and simian. There is a legend that nobody who had ever seen Gerald in his bath was ever quite the same again. He did a little of everything. He wrote music well enough to compose a ballet on a theme by Gertrude Stein. (*There* was a glorious, rampageous fake for you, if ever there was one!) The ballet was produced by Diaghileff with mild success. He wrote books well enough to produce several delicate and nostalgic volumes of an autobiographical nature. He painted agreeably, in the manner of the early Corot. Usually he chose as subjects the stately homes of England, sometimes he chose humbler edifices.

Thereby hangs a tale. Once Gerald came up to stay with me at my cottage . . . the *Down the Garden Path* one. On Sunday morning he said he would like to paint the cottage, so out he went with his easel, and sat in a field and began to paint. He painted on and off all day, with a brief interlude for luncheon, and after tea, when the light was fading, he came in with a delightful picture. More of a Daubigny than a Corot, but very pleasing for all that.

Then he sat down on the sofa, opened the Sunday newspaper, and almost immediately burst into tears.

'Whatever is the matter, Gerald?' He really was producing an extraordinary amount of quite wet tears.

'It is too terrible. What is to happen to us all?'

'But why? What *is* it?' I hurried over to see what he was reading. The paper was open at the financial page, and there

L

was a rather gloomy leading article—the usual sort of thing. The pound was weakening, exports were falling, costs were rising, labour was striking, taxes were crippling . . . in fact, the mixture as before.

'Where is it all to *end*?' sobbed Gerald.

I suggested that it would end as it always did, in nothing much.

To which Gerald retorted that *I* was all right. *I* had a profession. *I* could always keep myself. But what had *he* got?

I might have reminded him that he had, apart from many other possessions, £100,000 in gilt-edged securities, a sum which had hitherto evaded me. But he was beyond comforting, and very shortly afterwards he went to bed.

This was the strangest example of an economic neurosis that I have ever encountered, and it was made all the stranger because Gerald was in private life, generous, open-handed, and indeed something of a spendthrift.

Some of his extravagances might perhaps be regarded today as conflicting with the principles of the Welfare State. Thus, he had a tiny piano built into his Rolls-Royce. In this vehicle he used to travel abroad, usually on his way to Rome, where he had an exquisite house in the shadow of the Forum. Most people, travelling in Rolls-Royces to exquisite houses in the shadow of the Forum, idly strumming snatches of Scarlatti as the chauffeur coped with the traffic, would feel that life was flowing by smoothly enough; they might even feel that the unforgiving minute was being fully filled.

But this was not enough for Gerald. In the back of the motor-car there was a strange object; a white, hideous mask, the mask of an idiot, fashioned by Oliver Messel. I once tried it on, in Oliver's studio, and the memory of it still gives me nightmares, seeing myself walking to the long pier-glass, with the cretinoid head and the swollen eyes.

This mask was part of his lordship's travelling equipment. Sometimes, when the light was fading, and the Rolls-Royce was purring through a tiny Italian village, he would put it on, and lean his head out of the window, to the terror of the local inhabitants—a terror that was enhanced by the fact that as the car vanished into the dusk there came, from inside it, the echo of ghostly music.

This was all, I think, very satisfactory. It isn't typical of the twenties; indeed it savours of the eighteenth and early nineteenth centuries. William Beckford might have conducted himself in such a fashion. He had much the same approach to life. (One of my favourite passages in literature comes from a letter which Beckford wrote to a friend at the height of the Napoleonic wars. He was planning a visit to Portugal, and discussing the composition of his private orchestra, which was accompanying him. This orchestra, he decided with patriotic resignation, must be greatly reduced. He would content himself with a mere matter of four fiddles, some woodwind and a harp. The troupe of performing dwarfs, too, would have to be cut down to the barest essentials. 'These are no times,' wrote the author of *Fonthill*, 'for travelling in state.')

Gerald, like Beckford, built a Folly . . . a tower which still stands, on a slight elevation, near his lovely eighteenth-century house at Faringdon. This Folly, I thought, was worthy of its name; it was a silly waste of money. His other follies were more fun. Among these was his *Berners' Book of Beauty*. This was a large album filled with photographs of all the reigning beauties of the day. Some of them he had cut out from magazines, but most of them had been given to him by the ladies themselves, who had been greatly touched because he had pleaded so earnestly for their likeness. They might not have been so pleased if they had known that as soon as Gerald received them he proceeded to paint moustaches on to their lips, to black-out most of their teeth, and add squints, warts and double chins.

There is no Gerald Berners in the life of London today. You may not think that a great loss; I do. Apart from his generosity, his occasional flashes of genius, and his very genuine passion for the arts, he was a sort of poltergeist, playing amiable tricks on the pompous; and his ghost will always walk with laughter.

All of this has taken us a long way from Lady Colefax. As we have seen, many people were malicious about her. When Mary Borden,[1] for example, wrote a short story called *To Meet Jesus Christ*, everybody said it was about Sybil. Mary, not unnaturally, said it wasn't. But it might have been. It was a sparkling, sinister little piece about a hostess whose ambition finally drove her mad, causing her to arrange a dinner party at which the seat of honour on her right was reserved for . . . Him. Sybil never referred to it herself. But she referred to Mary quite often, and when she did the silver-sieve voice was slightly grated ('Dear Mary . . . *so* talented.')

Osbert Sitwell was another who chose Sybil as a target. All of us are devoted to Osbert, and some of us think that his genius as a satirist has never received adequate recognition. But perhaps, on this occasion, he went rather far. It was during all that boring business about the Abdication . . . at least, to me it seemed very boring, perhaps because I had never met Mrs Simpson, and because my only encounter with the Prince of Wales was to tread on his toe at a dance, when he said a word much stronger than 'damn'. Anyway, Osbert wrote a poem of searing bitterness, called *Rat Week*, in which he held up to contempt—quite rightly—all those false friends of Edward VIII who deserted him as soon as he renounced the throne. Among these he included Sybil. He painted her, I remember, as 'Sybil Colefax in her iron cage of curls.' This was unjust . . . not the curls, but the ratting. The poem was for private circulation. Osbert was expressing a personal indignation rather than administering a public rebuke. But he was misinformed.

Here we are, with wars and abdications, and it is time that

[1] Lady Spears.

we returned to the twenties. It is time too, that we showed Sybil Colefax in a kindlier light. A woman who is neither nobly born, nor very rich, nor very beautiful, does not create a brilliant salon unless she has herself some brilliant qualities. She does not keep the friendship of men like Max Beerbohm, Bernard Berensen, Desmond McCarthy, Duff Cooper, Lord Birkenhead, Lord Balfour—the list is interminable—if she is a bore. Her husband, Sir Arthur, *was* rather a bore, in the opinion of most of us, but he wisely kept in the background. Sybil, as we have said, was a snob for brains, which is perhaps not so very deplorable. Moreover, she had a genius for spotting talent very young. In December 1924, on a dark, blustery night, a play called *The Vortex* was produced in the tiny Everyman Theatre at Hampstead. The author was Noel Coward. It is a long way to Hampstead, and in those days hardly anybody had heard of Noel. But Sybil had heard of him, and there she was on the first night in the front row of the stalls, with her beady eye fixed firmly and confidently on the young prodigy. And afterwards, of course, there was a visit to the dressing-room, and an invitation to supper, and another genius in the bag.

Sybil had an ideal setting for her parties—Argyll House, in the King's Road, Chelsea. This was—and still is—a charmingly proportioned eighteenth-century building of grey stone, with a miniature courtyard in the front and a large garden at the back, in which there grew one of the finest vines in London, producing real grapes which ripened well enough to provide jugs of rather wince-making juice at luncheon. The house adjoined two other houses of equal charm but less importance. In one of them lived Mrs Somerset Maugham and in the other the endearing but grotesque music hall artiste, Gwen Farrar. There were occasions when one would be bidden to luncheon at Syrie Maugham's on the same day that Sybil was entertaining, and there would be a great deal of curtain-drawing and window-peering to see if she had got hold of anybody particularly grand.

Once—it was during the summer—Syrie heard that Sybil had captured Charlie Chaplin. This news was embittering; Charlie had been received in England like a conquering hero; his leonine qualities were incomparable; wherever he went he was accompanied by vast crowds and troops of police.

'I can't believe it,' snapped Syrie, as we sipped our cocktails. 'I *won't* believe it. Beverley darling, be an angel and go out into the hall again and look through the window to see if there is any sign of a crowd round dear Sybil's door.'

I went. There was nobody but Lord Londonderry, getting out of a taxi and looking rather cross.

'There, you see! She *can't* have got hold of Charlie Chaplin. The whole of the King's Road would be in an uproar.'

'Perhaps she has managed to keep it quiet?'

'Beverley darling, you are a *child*. Can you imagine dear Sybil keeping a thing like that quiet?'

Luncheon was strained. Afterwards we went into the garden. From the other side of the wall came the sound of laughter. Syrie feared the worst. Perhaps Sybil had got Charlie after all. She could bear the suspense no longer.

'Beverley darling, be an angel and climb up and look over the wall.'

'I *can't* go climbing up walls to spy on Sybil.'

'Yes you can. I *must* know. You can stand on this chair. No ... perhaps not ... it's just been pickled and it might break. You can stand on the wheelbarrow.'

So I stood on the wheelbarrow and took a quick peep. There was Lord Londonderry, but we knew about him already. There was a very pretty girl called Paula Gellibrand, who afterwards became the Marquise de Casa Maury. There were several people I didn't know. There was no Charlie Chaplin. But there was somebody else, who to me was more important.

I went back and reported to Syrie, who was duly assuaged. Shortly afterwards I excused myself, because I wanted to waylay the 'somebody else' . . . whose name was Max Beerbohm. I hardly knew him, but that did not matter. And waylay him I did, quite shamelessly, by loitering at the corner of Oakley Street and catching him as he came out.

We walked down the King's Road together. Max was in an expansive mood; Sybil had given them a delicious risotto and the chianti had been admirable. There had been a rather curious incident after luncheon. Here he pursed his lips and turned to me with a beady look. It seemed that a face had suddenly appeared over the wall of the house next door. The face of a young man. He had only been afforded a brief glimpse of the face, but it had seemed vaguely familiar. However, he could not be sure, possibly because the features had been violently contorted by some emotional disturbance. (That, I thought, must have been when the wheelbarrow began to wobble.)

We walked through Sloane Square and through Eaton Square; we negotiated the chaos of Hyde Park Corner and at length we sat down, somewhat fatigued, on a bench in the Green Park. All the time Max was talking, and I would give a great deal to recall his conversation. It was flowing but stylized, colloquial and yet conventional, by which I mean that the laws of language were underlined. Thus, if he were saying that one thing differed from another, he would slightly accentuate the word 'from' . . . as though to remind an invisible, unlettered audience that some of them, who should know better, were saying 'differed to'.

Only one fragment of this conversation returns to me in any detail. I had asked him where, in his opinion, was the ideal place to work. 'But can there be any two opinions about that?' he said. 'Surely . . . the Charing Cross Hotel!' This was so startling a reply that I thought he must be pulling my leg. Apparently he was not. In the Charing Cross Hotel, it seemed, a writer could attain isolation and anonymity, and achieve his best. 'But the noise?' I suggested . . . and I nearly added 'And the people!' To which Max retorted that the noise of the station was also 'anonymous' and far from being a distraction,

it was an anodyne. I do not know enough about Max Beerbohm to state whether he ever put his theory into practice.
Perhaps he was pulling my leg, after all. If so, it was an experience I would willingly suffer again.

I do not care to cut this portrait in half merely to fit the
framework of a decade; for though Sybil's most glittering days
were in the twenties and the thirties, her true quality was not
revealed till later, in the days of adversity. One of the tests
of a woman's character—particularly of an older woman—is
her ability to accept assistance with grace and without embarrassing the donor. When Arthur Colefax died there was very
little money, and Argyll House had to go. Its sale was almost
a personal loss to many of us and as we knew that she needed
every penny she could get we clubbed together to buy various
things for her which otherwise she would have been obliged
to sell, such as the lovely piano on which Rubenstein had
played, and Rachmaninoff, and heaven knows who else.

Then there was the question . . . how was she going to be
able to afford to entertain? She had moved to a tiny house in
Westminster, where by astonishing ingenuity she managed to
carve out a sizeable dining-room on the ground floor. In due
course the luncheons and the dinners began again. But we all
felt slightly uneasy, accepting the hospitality of a woman
whom we knew to be hard pressed. Hence arose the institution
of 'The Ordinary', which must surely have been a unique
phenomenon in the life of social London. An 'Ordinary' was
a party to which one was bidden, in the usual manner, but for
which one was afterwards sent a bill. I do not know if it was
Sybil's own idea, but it was a great success. 'Ordinaries' were
usually given at the Dorchester Hotel; sometimes there would
be as many as thirty people, of considerable distinction, and if
Sybil had paid the bill herself it would have been at least a
hundred pounds. But we paid—all of us—even, and perhaps
especially, the very grand ones. In the hands of a woman who

was less sure of herself, an 'ordinary' might have been a tiresome affair; as it was, we all felt that it was quite natural. Indeed, there were certain definite advantages over the normal party; if one is paying for one's share, one can choose one's own wine.

Sybil, meanwhile, had to take a job; inevitably, with her huge circle of acquaintances, she turned to interior decoration. She had not the flair of Lady Mendl, nor the genius of Mrs Somerset Maugham, but she had a quiet, cultivated taste, and she had the sense to choose as partner a brilliant young man called John Fowler. The energy which she put into this new enterprise was astonishing. By now she was very nearly an old woman, and very certainly a sick one; she had always stooped, but in the later days she was bent almost double. And yet she would be up at six in the morning, scribbling invitations on postcards for an 'ordinary' or—when funds were more plentiful, for a dinner at her own house—and after that, when most people were still in bed, she would set off in all weathers to some sale in the country, return to her shop, go out to luncheon, write more postcards, attend a debate in the House, bring back a cabinet minister to tea . . . it never stopped. And always she had read the latest book, seen the latest play, discussed the latest opera, delighted in the latest ballet . . . and in all probability asked the latest ballerina to an 'ordinary' and sent her the bill.

The last time I saw Sybil was at my own house, Merry Hall, after the war. She had heard about my lilies, and she wrote to say that she must come down to see them. But she was in hospital . . . so tiresome, a temporary setback . . . would I come up to see her and discuss ways and means? So up I went, to some gloomy house of sickness near Paddington Station. 'She ought not to see any visitors,' said the matron, with a sigh of resignation, 'but she is expecting you, so I suppose there is nothing to be done about it.' As I entered the room Lady Diana Cooper was just leaving, and I gathered that Max Beerbohm was also on his way up, and Desmond McCarthy had just left some flowers, and Fred Behrman was sitting by the side of the bed talking about the first night of his new play which was opening in a few days' time. Sybil—who was obviously very near to death—was saying to him: 'You will be sure, won't you, that my seat is on the gangway.'

But she did not leave us for a little while, and before she died she came down to see the lilies. She was so bent that her head seemed almost as low as her waist; she could only walk one step at a time; and she was as thin as a shrivelled leaf. But her spirit was indomitable; she rattled on and on; and she knew a great deal about lilies. She knew, indeed, so much that I am quite certain—bless her heart—that she had read them up before she came.

CHAPTER THIRTEEN

STRIFE

THE decade marched on. The House of Commons, in one of the grandest dinners it had ever organized, paid tribute to Britain's leading novelist. The occasion was the publication of a novel called *The Master of Man*. It had a sub-title, which honourable members pronounced with pursued lips: *The Story of a Sin*. The name of the great man, whom the King had honoured? Sir Hall Caine. Now—as we have observed before —out of print.

The decade marched on. The Poet Laureate, Alfred Austin, died. Austin, however, is assured of immortality as the worst poet who ever lived. And yet . . . can we be so certain? Is there not a danger that one day we may forget these master-pieces of bathos, which he produced with such a resounding thud of doggerel on all ceremonial occasions? Let me remind the younger generation of one of them. The subject of his inspiration was the illness of King Edward VII. This, obviously, was a misfortune which demanded the Poet Laureate's most earnest attention. It got it. Screwing himself up to a frenzy of righteous emotion—and remembering, at the same time, that he was a man of the world, living in an 'age of science'—he penned these deathless lines:

> Across the wires the electric message came
> 'He is not better' . . . 'He is much the same'!

The decade marched on. The King's wine merchant sold a

great deal of excellent claret at 3s. 6d. a bottle. Lady Astor entered the House of Commons. The Prince of Wales shimmied round the world in the *Renown*, smiling and smiling, to blacks and whites and near-whites and off-whites. The greatest genius of modern journalism, Lord Northcliffe, died in his mansion in Carlton House Terrace. Compared with Northcliffe a man like William Randolph Hearst was a pygmy, for all his wealth and influence. Northcliffe, in more ways than one, was Napoleonic; indeed, in some ways he was more successful even than Napoleon, for his empire, thirty years after his death, is still largely intact.

The decade marched on. At about the same time as Lady Diana Cooper was astonishing the aristocracy by appearing as the nun in Reinhardt's production of *The Miracle*—('How does she manage to stand so still, for all that time, in that niche?')—70,000 people were killed in an earthquake in Japan. But there was still hope for mankind; Dr Serge Voronoff had just appeared on the horizon, with his promise of eternal youth—for those who could afford it—by the injection of monkey glands. A gleam of hope, indeed of reviving lust, was observed in the heavy-lidded eyes of many old gentlemen sitting in the bow-windows of their Piccadilly clubs. The gleam faded when they read that Dr Voronoff himself had been so inconsiderate as to die at a comparatively early age. The Faust motif is recurrent in every era.

The decade marched on. The first Blue Train puffed its way out of Victoria Station, and Londoners thrilled to the slogan: 'Sleep your way from the city's fogs to the Riviera sunshine.' Tutankhamen's tomb was prized open, and the priceless bric-a-brac of death was displayed to the wondering eyes of the twentieth century. And a young man called Beverley Nichols published an impudent volume of memoirs called 25—because, as he shrewdly observed, twenty-five seemed to him the latest age at which anybody should publish an autobiography.

Quite possibly he was right.

.   .   .   .   .

And then, of course, there was the wireless.

In these days, when a television set is considered as essential as a water-closet—and is often apparently designed to meet the same requirements—it is difficult to remember how recent is the development of sound broadcasting itself. A picture in a scientific magazine of the twenties shows a British family grouped round one of the early receiving sets, listening with awe, indeed with apprehension, to 'music transmitted by wireless from Holland'. There, on the parlour table, is something like a miniature atomic station, attached to a gigantic trumpet. Wires curl in all directions. (The caption tells us that 'a copper wire is suspended at one end of the garden, with the other end of the wire coming through the window. This is attached to the receiving set. Another wire from the receiver is fixed to a water pipe. That is all that is required for listening to transmissions hundreds of miles away'!) Over this formidable apparatus bends a young man encumbered with earphones. ('The head-telephone'—it is explained—'need only be worn for tuning-in. Afterwards, it may be discarded'.)

Frankly, I do not remember these contraptions. They certainly never encumbered my parents' house; they would have been too expensive; apart from that, we had an old but beloved piano by Bechstein, which seemed able to say quite a lot to us, if properly asked. And yet . . . here it all was, in the twenties. All the wires beginning to curl, all the trumpets beginning to spout, all the terrible noise and din which was to deafen the world and distract it, and maybe . . . finally doom it to destruction. Or is that being too melodramatic? Pause for thought. Yes, I believe it is. For the story really ends, not with a bang but a whimper—the hideous whimper of podgy transatlantic pianists murdering the ghost of Chopin.

However, all this was in the future. Today's popular entertainers were not even an awful stirring in the womb of Time. As for the thought of Lord Haw-Haw's voice, poisoning the night sky, or the screams of Nasser, drilling his phantom armies, let alone the logical culmination of it all in Mr Orwell's *1984*

. . . these would have been conceptions too fantastic even for the consideration of Mr H. G. Wells. 'The wireless'—it had not yet been Americanized into 'radio'—still spoke in dulcet accents; we listened to it with wide, innocent eyes, feeling— poor dupes—how much luckier we were than our fathers.

And always there was this sense of standing on the threshold of a new world. In March 1923, all England thrilled to the news that a 'wireless apparatus' had been installed in the dining-car of the London to Liverpool express, and that London had been received 'up to fifty miles out'. Later on, we were informed, Birmingham broadcasting station was tuned in to the train, though with 'not quite such favourable results'. In the same month, at the *Daily Mail* Ideal Home Exhibition, by far the most popular item of entertainment was a wireless concert. A vast audience sat enthralled before two giant golden trumpets, marvelling at the news they had read in their morning newspapers . . . 'The music of one band is being distributed to no less than six audiences at once!' A few months later the first radio advertisements began to be printed . . . 'Don't bother to entertain your friends; the British Broadcasting does that for you.' At the same time the first portable radios appeared in the shops. Unless my memory is at fault, they were the size of small cabin trunks.

I cannot claim any special prescience, and it would certainly be an exaggeration to suggest that in those preliminary trumpetings I heard the voice of doom. But I do remember, very clearly, reading a sentence in a contemporary essay by G. K. Chesterton, which struck me as very much to the point: 'How strange it is that mankind should have invented a machine for speaking to the whole world at precisely the moment when no man has anything whatever to say.' The occasion of this essay was the General Election of 1924, when, for the first time in history, the leaders of the three parties, Baldwin, Asquith and MacDonald, made use of broadcasting. The first two were quite successful, MacDonald was a flop. Even his supporters were bound to admit this. One London paper commented: 'Mr

MacDonald has yet to learn the technique of this marvellous invention; he must curb his tendency to stride about the platform, raising and lowering his voice. As a result of these habits, large portions of his address were totally inaudible.'

The wireless played only a small part in the General Strike of 1926. Even in these airy pages an event of such historical importance cannot be entirely ignored. However, since most accounts of it are—to me at least—completely unreadable, I propose to introduce it in the form of a short story. The story happens to be true.

'We seem to be stuck in this tunnel, old boy.'

'What's the matter?'

'All the water seems to have come out of the old engine.'

'Can't we put some more in?'

'To tell the truth, old boy, I'm not quite sure how one puts the water in engines. Even when one's got the water to put in, which at the moment, one hasn't.'

'I suppose I'd better go and see if I can get another engine.'

'I say, old boy, that'd be jolly decent of you. There must be a spare one knocking around somewhere in Liverpool Street.'

'I'll go right away.'

'Good man. And by the way I think it'd be a good idea to put on the fog signals as you go down the line. We don't want a great walloping express crashing in our rear.'

'Where are the fog signals?'

'Don't you remember? They're those things by the side of the rails that look like sort of perverted poached eggs. They go off with a bang. Can't miss 'em.'

The young man wanders off into the Cimmerian darkness of the tunnel, in the direction of Liverpool Street, which is about two miles away. On the arm of his sport's jacket he wears a band marked 'Guard. No 4156'. As he walks, he reflects that this is a much pleasanter way of spending an evening than writing an essay on the Elizabethan ecclesiastical settlement for his tutor at Balliol. He rather hopes that the general strike will go on for quite a while. And then—he is not quite so sure. For as he emerges from the tunnel he is greeted by a hail of stones from a group of toughs on the bank above, and shouts of, 'Go back home you bloody blackleg . . . go back home !' The young man decides it might be politic to break into a sharp trot.

Incredible as it may sound, the young man got his engine at Liverpool Street. There was another youth standing on the footplate; he did not seem at all surprised to be asked to come to the rescue. When questioned about the water problem he said it was quite simple; you put it in through one of those leather things. Always been fond of engines, he had. So off they went, dodging the stones of the strikers, and greatly enjoying the bangs made by the fog signals, and when they got to the tunnel, slowing down and stopping in the most professional manner. True, the next quarter of an hour was not quite so professional. 'The best thing to do,' said the first engine driver amiably, 'is for me to go back to my engine, and I'll give two hoots and you'll give two hoots, and then we'll push like hell.' That seemed a very good idea to the second engine driver too. So they hooted and they pushed like hell, and by a miracle, the train started. When they reached their destination, which was Stratford, they were only two hours late, and the passengers made a silver collection in a bucket, which was very acceptable to the young volunteers.

At the end of the general strike a grateful government gave Guard 4156 the sum of £4 5s. 6d. with which he rushed off to buy a Briggs umbrella, an object that he had always coveted.

And then he went back to finish his essay on the Elizabethan Settlement.

As I observed above, I have introduced the General Strike of 1926 in this manner because every other account I have ever read of it has bored me to death. Moreover, most of the strike's historians seem to me to have missed the point. They have spotlit the wrong things and the wrong people. Out of all the mob that swept across the stage, which seemed to be lit with the blood-red glow of revolution, there was one figure which the limes should have picked out . . . one figure who should have stepped towards the floats, while the stage-manager brought the extras to a halt . . . the tall, spare, thin-lipped figure of Sir John Simon. (The adjective is not taken from stock; he really had extremely thin lips.)

Here was a country in the full flood of revolution . . . so we were told. And it is true that the stones which were hurled at our young friend Guard 4156 were not thrown for fun; the mood of the great majority of the workers was ugly. The glossy magazines, when it was all over, were full of dainty pictures of débutantes carrying boxes of tomatoes at Covent Garden, but they might have been just as full of pictures of volunteers lying in the gutter with bloody heads.

And then, five days after the General Strike was declared, when paralysis was creeping over the country, when public transport was at a standstill, when Whitehall was packed with troops, when the Press was stifled, and when the Royal Family were, for all practical purposes, unable to venture abroad, up pops Sir John Simon, to declare the general strike is *illegal*, on the grounds that it was not covered by an act of twenty years previously which rendered trade union funds immune from claims for damages caused by industrial disputes. As a result, he claimed, every trade union leader was 'liable in damages to the uttermost farthing of his personal possessions'.

That was really the beginning of the end of the strike. This must be the most astonishing example that history can offer of the docility of the British people. It is as though the Court Chamberlain of Louis Seize were to stroll out into the courtyard at Versailles and dispatch a mob of *sansculottes* with a whiff of snuff from a jewelled *vinaigrette*. For, if this was indeed

M

Lady (sweetly). "Do you go to Park Lane?"
Volunteer Conductor (gallantly). "Well, we don't, but I've no doubt we could"

revolution, it was finished with the gentle tap of a legal finger on a piece of faded parchment.

In view of this national docility, the behaviour of the Tory government was regrettable, to say the least of it. If there had been cooler heads and warmer hearts the strike need never have occurred at all. The actual spark which lit the blaze was fired in the printing department of the *Daily Mail*. Here are the facts, from the leading article of this newspaper, dated May 4th, 1926:

> On Sunday night the leading article which appeared in the editions of the *Daily Mail* published in Manchester and Paris was written and set up. When it was in type a number of Trade Unionists in our London office demanded the right to exercise a censorship over the contents of the paper. Certain passages of the leader article, they said, must be omitted before they would print it. The editor refused. The Trade Unionists in question ceased work when they found they were not to be allowed to dictate its policy, and our London edition was not published on Monday morning.

This isolated act of intransigence on the part of a few hot-heads was treated by the Cabinet as an act of war. They assumed, without even asking any of the responsible leaders of the TUC, that this was an act that would receive their blessing. They also assumed that the general strike had actually begun.

The truest account—and the most damning criticism—of this first stage of the strike was published a fortnight later in the *New Statesman*.

> The action of the workers who refused to publish the *Daily Mail* leading article had, in spite of the government's contention, nothing whatever to do with the General Strike. It was an act of mutiny which the Trade Union leaders would instantly have condemned and repudiated, since they were still hoping that there would be no strike at all. They were offered no opportunity, however, either of repudiation or of explanation. They had

heard nothing of the events in the *Daily Mail* office, and when
they returned to the conference room with the agreed formula
they found it dark and locked. The Cabinet had declared war
and gone to bed.

For those whose admiration of some phases of Sir Winston
Churchill's career amounts to hero-worship—and I am among
them—a study of his activities in the General Strike is sadden-
ing. He had the whole-hearted co-operation of most of his
colleagues, but Sir Winston must bear a special responsibility
because of his direction of *The British Gazette*.

The British Gazette may have been British in name but it
was hardly British in principle, and it seldom deserved the
title of 'Gazette'. Its ostensible purpose was to fill the vacuum
created by the absence of newspapers. In fact, this vacuum was
by no means complete... *The Times*, for example, struggled on
with limited resources, and the *Daily Mail*, by a series of brilliant
improvisations, stepped up its continental organization and
managed to supply a large number of readers by air. However,
since the government commandeered the supply of newsprint,
the nation's main source of information was *The British
Gazette*, and a very unreliable source it proved to be. Obviously Sir Winston, coping with a thousand practical problems,
cannot be held responsible for everything that went into the
Gazette but surely he cannot have been ignorant of one vital
item that did *not* go into it—the appeal of the Archbishop of
Canterbury. At so grave a moment one would have thought
that even the King would have hesitated before informing the
spiritual leader of the nation that his advice was not required,
but this is precisely what the government did, and if Sir
Winston made any protest on this occasion history has not recorded it. The Archbishop, denied the courtesy of *The British
Gazette*, had perforce to be content with publication in *The
Times*. This fantastic situation brought Mr Lloyd George to
his feet in the House of Commons. Why, he demanded, had

the Archbishop been gagged? A government spokesman replied that it was impossible to find space for *everything* in *The British Gazette*! Considering that its pages were largely filled with trivialities, this was a piece of insolence.

When one turns the yellowing pages of *The Times* to find the nature of the Archbishop's appeal, one is at a loss to discover any reason why anybody should have been reluctant to publish it. There have been times in the past thirty years when the heads of the Established Church have delivered themselves of statements which have violently conflicted with public opinion. But on this occasion the Archbishop was animated by simple Christianity and plain common sense—two principles which are not always incompatible. He asked for three things. First—a cancellation of the General Strike. (Hardly a revolutionary demand.) Second—a renewal by the government of its offer of assistance to the coal industry 'for a short period'. (When one thinks of the tens of millions which we are apparently able to afford to the nationalized industry in these days, such a request seems not only modest but timid.) Lastly he asked the mine-owners to withdraw their new wage scale and think again. Any Christian, and any man of common sense, would have been behind him.

But there was precious little Christianity, and precious little common sense. As one grows older one is supposed to grow more conservative; and when I began to study the files of the contemporary newspaper which recorded the whole bitter story, I suspected that I should no longer feel the indignation that I had felt thirty years ago. To my surprise, and indeed to my relief, I felt it more strongly than ever.

Listen to this dessicated, inhuman comment from the Earl of Balfour:

No revolution in Britain, however triumphant, is going to diminish foreign competition in neutral markets.
No revolution is going to augment the demand for coal at home.

No revolution is going to compel a mine owner indefinitely to carry on his industry at a loss.
Revolutionary methods would be completely powerless except for evil.

All, of course, true. And all, of course, bloodless and blind. Those words were written by an elderly, fatigued aristocrat, at a desk heavily gilt with ormulu, with a lapiz lazuli cigarette box at his side. They were written, as it were, in rich purple ink, assisted by a glass of Tio Pepe. This all sounds like Ouida ... but Balfour, in spite of his first-class Balliol brain, was not so very unlike Ouida's idea of a great Tory statesman. When I met him, I thought that he showed too much cuff, and that his handkerchief had been dipped too heavily in eau de cologne.

Balfour was typical of the average House of Lords mentality. At the basis of the general strike there was the stark fact of hunger, the whole revolutionary impulse stemmed from an ache in the belly. Most of the nice, kindly upper class people of that period seemed quite unable to imagine that ache, to transfer it, as they should have done, to their own bodies, and to re-plan their thinking accordingly. Unless you can imagine pain and really suffer it on your own body you are not likely to cut much ice as a reformer. The Duke of Windsor could do precisely this; when, years later, he went down to the distressed areas, he said four simple words, so trite that they might lend themselves to parody. But he said them with a throb in his throat. 'Something must be done.' Those four words, coming from such a source, were remembered long after the learned arguments of the economists were forgotten.

I had perhaps more reason than most young men of the period for detesting *The British Gazette* and for backing the suppressed Archbishop. One of the great coal-owners of the period was the Marquess of Londonderry. I had walked up the staircase of Londonderry House in a tail coat—rather frightened because all the women were dripping with diamonds. I had also crawled in the caves of the Londonderry mines, even more frightened, because the low roof was dripping with water. I remember turning my coal-blackened face to the man behind me and gasping, 'Why is this water coming through?' 'That's O.K. mate,' he said. 'We're under the sea.' I licked my lips and they tasted very salt. This, I trust, will not be regarded either as communist propaganda or as a sneer at the late Marquess of Londonderry. He was a far-sighted, enlightened employer, with flashes of inspiration; his men adored him; and if his recommendations had been heeded the state of the coal industry today would have been very different. But he was a victim of circumstances and he was caught up, like all the rest of us, in an impossible situation.

The General Strike, as we know, fizzled out; the miners went back to work in even worse conditions than they had known before; and the country reverted to 'business as usual'. But it was not quite 'business as usual'. The strike had left a legacy of bitterness which lingers to this day.

The last words of the final issue of *The British Gazette* ran as follows: '*The British Gazette* may have had a short life but it has fulfilled the purpose of living. It becomes a memory but it remains a monument.'

It does indeed . . . a monument that should be hung in crêpe.

CHAPTER FOURTEEN

SET TO MUSIC

It is time that we had some music; nothing so vividly recalls the past as an old tune. One of my earliest recollections, as a schoolboy, was the lilting march of *Tipperary*, sung by a platoon of Grenadiers swinging down Piccadilly in the rain. I remember thinking what a good tune it was, and how well it would orchestrate, with the dark sweep of cellos for the men's voices and the tap of muted drums for the thud of their boots.

And that leads to another memory . . . to a cocktail party in Mrs Asquith's pretty, sunlit drawing-room in Bedford Square. Dame Ethel Smyth had called. She was of course a brilliant woman, and it was a mystery how so vivid, masculine and questing a brain could compose such singularly boring music. Her chief opera *The Wreckers*, which created such a sensation in its time, sounds today as if it had been composed by an elderly female academician after a powerful soporific. However, Dame Ethel, as a conversationalist, was far from elderly and not noticeably feminine. On this occasion she was making an impassioned defence of *Tipperary*, which Mrs Asquith had condemned. 'Damn it, Margot, sometimes I think you must be tone-deaf. It's a damned good tune. It's clear-cut; it's got a fine shape; it says what it means and then it stops. That's something *you* might learn to do with advantage.'

Dame Ethel, whose threadbare little tunes have now tinkled over the hills and far away, made a tremendous impact on many people who, one would have thought, might have

known better, such as Virginia Woolf. In *A Writer's Diary* she
draws a picture of Dame Ethel rehearsing in a vast cold room
in Portland Place, and a very vivid picture it is; she leaves
nothing out . . . the battered felt hat, the short skirt, the jersey,
the stridings up and down, the baritone bellowings suddenly
emerging from the flat chest . . . even the drop on the tip of her
nose. Miss Woolf was evidently enthralled. And though she
confesses that the music was perhaps 'too literary . . . too
didactic' for her taste, she pauses to ask the question: 'What if
she *should* be a great composer?' Time has answered that
question, with some finality.

However, Dame Ethel was certainly right about *Tipperary*,
and she more than held her own in the amiable duel with Mrs
Asquith, which I will not attempt to reproduce. It struck me at
the time as very witty. This was more than could be said for
another exchange which had taken place, that very morning,
between Mrs Asquith and Melba. They had met in Mr
Reville's dress shop. (Melba was still flushed with triumph
when she narrated this story at luncheon.) Mrs Asquith came up
to Melba and said: 'Melba, you're too fat.' Without an
instant's hesitation the diva retorted, in her ringing treble:
'And *you're* too skinny!' She was so pleased with this riposte
that she repeated it about six times with the lobster thermidor,
and each time the word 'skinny' rose higher and higher, till it
sounded like some exquisite bell being struck by a rather dis-
gruntled cherub.

But we were waiting for the music to begin . . . the music of
the twenties. I wish that instead of writing this passage on a
silent piece of paper I could sit down and play it on a piano.
However, even the titles must carry, for the middle-aged, an
echo of happiness, beginning with Kern's *Look for the Silver
Lining*, a tune to which we were all dancing at the beginning
of the decade. This was a melody that wound its way up and
down the stave as prettily as a silver thread. Then we hear, far
off in 1922, the voice of Gracie Fields singing *Sally*—and what a
voice—sexless, serene, soaring to incredible heights! And what

a tragedy that Gracie, instead of treating it as the priceless and delicate thing that it was, proceeded to use it with such prodigal generosity that its magic faded before its time.

Towards the middle of the twenties the melodies come flooding thicker and faster; in the space of less than three years we had such shows as *Rose Marie, No No Nanette, The Student Prince, Lady Be Good* and *The Desert Song*. And though many of these productions, no doubt, would raise a smile on the face of a modern audience, their music is as fresh and sparkling as on the day it was written. The average errand boy can still whistle 'Spread a Little Happiness' by Vivian Ellis . . . or indeed, a dozen other melodies which this distinguished composer created during the decade. Vivian has never been a good publicity agent for himself. If he had stood up boldly and proclaimed himself a second Puccini . . . if you study one of his scores, the claim is not so exaggerated . . . people might have taken more notice, and Drury Lane might not have become a shop-window for Broadway.

The modern young man is very much in error if he thinks that the melodies of the twenties, in content and construction, were simpler and less sophisticated than the melodies of the present day. The reverse is the case. How many of the guests at a modern party could sit down and rattle off a number like *Kitten on the Keys*? This was published in 1923 and was the first 'novelty piano solo', in pure ragtime, to sweep the country. Although it demands a fairly high standard of technique, it was in every amateur pianist's repertoire. So were the early Gershwin numbers such as *Fascinating Rhythm*. If you were to place the music of this in front of the average Rock-'n-Roller, the result, if any, would be a shambles.

Round about 1927 a note of melancholy began to creep into popular music . . . a note which has never quite left it. This was the year which saw the publication of *The Birth of the Blues*, and the year in which Gershwin wrote one of his finest tunes, *The Man I Love*, which has a quality not inferior to the organ music of Cesar Franck. Was there anything in the condition of world

affairs to account for this note of sadness and disillusionment?
Were the first faint rumblings of the great depression making
themselves heard in the composers' brains? We cannot answer
that question; we can only note the fact that gradually music
began to creep from the major to the minor. In 1925 we had
sung *I want to be happy* and had left it at that; in 1927 we were
singing *Sometimes I'm Happy* only to observe in the next line of
the same song 'sometimes I'm blue'. This was the year of the
St Louis Blues, of the *Yale Blues*, of *So Blue* and many other
blues beside, and even a straightforward love song like Rogers
and Hart's *My Heart Stood Still*, or the exceptionally nostalgic—
for me, at least—*Bye Bye Blackbird* had this subtle note of sadness;
they were melodies that were orchestrated, as it were, with sighs.

Even *Ol' Man River*, which swept across two continents a
year later, could hardly be called a musical jollification. Those
to whom this song is part of the pattern of their youth may be
interested to know that it was composed at the last minute,
almost as the result of an accident. On the day before *Show
Boat* opened, Hammerstein came to the composer, Jerome
Kern, and said, 'We've got a fine singer in that man, I want
you to write him a song.' Kern replied, not unnaturally, that
he could hardly be expected to turn out a song at such short
notice. 'Never mind about that,' retorted Hammerstein, 'go
ahead and do it.' Somewhere in the orchestra pit, during this
conversation, a banjo-player had been strumming a conventional bass arrangement—the sort of tumty-tum that
accompanies a hundred Southern folk-songs. Kern listened
to it, and pricked up his ears. Supposing one took those two
bars and slowed them down, and then—still keeping to the
same key—made them climb up the scale? Which was precisely what he did, in the next twenty minutes. The result was
Ol' Man River. It is a pleasant way of earning one's living.

Now that we are on the subject of tunes and their inception,
here is a story about *Sonny Boy*. This number, as sung by Al
Jolson, became one of the most efficient tear-jerkers of all
time. Jolson did it with terrifying sincerity, going down on

his knees, almost choking with emotion. The results on the audience, particularly on the middle-aged females, was not dissimilar to those obtained by a religious revivalist. One wonders what they would have felt if they had realized that the song was originally written as a joke. De Litta Brown and Henderson in search of a comedy number, decided to write a vicious parody on all the mummy-sonny songs that had ever been known; they scoured the records for every old cliche and every worn-out metaphor and fitted them to a tune that was pure treacle. Nobody was more astonished than themselves when Jolson decided to sing the number straight . . . and got away with it.

Glancing through the pages above, I seem to detect a suggestion of middle-aged intolerance, as though I were reluctant to allow any merit at all to the popular music of today. This was far from my intention, but I *am* intolerant when I see illiterate and tuneless scullerymaids and pantry-boys making vast fortunes by poisoning the night air with their catterwauling. When I protest to the intelligent young man of today about these creatures, when I point out to him that the timbre of their voices is odious, that the tunes of their songs are spineless and derivative, and that the content of their lyrics are insulting to the intelligence of a backward aboriginal—to put it very mildly indeed—I am usually fobbed off with some answer which, when analysed, proves that the real attraction of these popular horrors has nothing to do with music but a great deal to do with sex appeal. If this is indeed the case, why do the aforesaid scullerymaids and pantry-boys confuse the issue by singing at all? Why do they not merely stand in front of the cameras and undress? However, perhaps this would prove disappointing; it usually does; dress is the first and last refuge of the physically repulsive.

Let us forget these monsters. Let us dispel them with such evocative titles as *All Alone, Heaven, What'll I do, Blue Skies,*

The Song is Ended—all by Irving Berlin. For pure melodic line Irving Berlin can seldom have been equalled. He was— although he is still very much alive I put him in the past tense because I am speaking of his early work—something of a mystery. He would have been the last to call himself a 'musician'. His own piano playing was so rudimentary that he could only play in one key, for which reason he was obliged to use a specially constructed instrument which transposed mechanically. His lyrics were almost unbelievable naïve; a man who could write a song called *You forgot to Remember* can hardly be accused of understanding the subtleties of the Queen's English. And yet, he wrote melodies which were as fresh and inevitable as a spray of apple blossom, and though the words which he invented for them should have been hot-making—('hot-making' is a very 'dating' adjective, implying embarrassment) —somehow or other they weren't.

Yes Sir, That's My Baby; I'm Sitting on Top of the World; Let's Do It; You're the Cream in My Coffee; There's a Rainbow Round My Shoulder—but really, I can't go on. As I suggested above, this is a chapter that should have been played at a piano rather than written on a page. As I played, all sorts of old friends would hover round, and they would have for me a special charm, in spite of their crowsfeet, their double chins, their receding hair and their advancing waist-lines. Did I say 'in spite of'? I should have said 'because of'. That is something that young people should remember. As one grows older one's friends grow more endearing in almost precise ratio with their physical decay. One feels more and more deeply attached to people who are ageing—or so one flatters oneself—rather more rapidly than oneself.

Needless to say, the popular music of the twenties, particularly when it began to experiment with broken rhythms, evoked the strong disapproval of our elders and betters. 'Oh, for an hour of Sullivan!' the dowagers would sigh, after a couple of hours of Gershwin. Sullivan never gave one that odd twitching in the spine—so disturbing for young people; Sullivan never gave one pins and needles in one's toes; there was really something not quite *nice* about this new music. And they would trundle home in their barouches, shaking their heads and humming *Poor Lonely One* to themselves. In which, of course, they showed their very good taste, for this lovely, lilting waltz has a cleaner, sweeter melodic line than even Weber's *L'Invitation a la Valse*.

This disapproval of the music of the period was extended to some of its performers, in particular to a young lady with straight black hair, horn-rimmed glasses, and square shoulders, who was called Gwen Farrar. Really, said the dowagers, there was no excuse for Gwen; after all she was a *lady*; she was quite rich, she had a delicious panelled house in Chelsea, and she played the cello more than passably. The trouble was that she also insisted on singing, which was the gravest mistake, since her voice was only a semitone higher than dear Mr Chaliapin's. Moreover, she insisted on singing in public, on the music-hall stage, with that young Norah Blaney at the piano. True, they drew the town, but somehow when one remembered Gwen's dear father, who was a near millionaire, it all seemed a great pity.

It did not seem a pity to me. Gwen, alas, has departed this life. The last time I heard from her was at midnight, when the telephone suddenly rang. I answered it and was greeted by the sound of a cello, playing *Softly Awake My Heart*. I said 'Stop it, Gwen darling'—for it could be nobody else—'and go to bed.' To which she replied, 'I've got a temperature of a hundred and four.' So I said I was very sorry but she must go to bed and stop playing *Softly Awake My Heart*, which was not one of Saint-Saens' best, anyway. But she went on and on. And she *had* got a temperature of a hundred and four, and very soon afterwards she died. But Norah Blaney is still with us, as pretty as a picture and as clever as a bundle of monkeys. Only a few days ago she sat down at a piano and played—after a

lapse of nearly thirty years—a little number that I wrote for
the two of them when they were starring at the Palace Theatre.
Though I say it myself, it had a pretty tune. The words, which
were the result of an unhappy love affair, were not so hot. I
called it *Another One Gone* . . .

> Another one gone
> And left me alone for week-ends,
> Another one gone away. .
> They always pass on,
> Love's passionate hide-and-seek ends
> So emptily every day . . .

One took things very seriously in those days.

The mention of Gwen has started a train of thought. Are we,
in these days, more drilled and dragooned and bludgeoned and
generally b——d about? When one thinks of Gwen one is
inclined to say yes. One night, coming out of the Savoy Grill,
Nora found a policeman standing by her motor-car, which
she had parked without lights. The policeman began to
reprimand her, but unfortunately his mouth was full of
Mackintosh's Toffee de Luxe, with which he was relieving the
monotony of the night-watch. This was too much for Gwen.
'Don't speak to me with your mouth full of Mackintosh's
Toffee de Luxe!' barked Gwen in her *basso profundo*. She then
gave him a brisk blow in the navel, and was promptly carted
off to Bow Street. How many darlings of ITA would behave
with such natural, girlish charm today? And how many—
having engaged the services of Sir Henry Curtis-Bennett on the
following morning—would stride from the wings, on the
same night, dressed as a convict, and bring down the house?

Yes. Nowadays we *are* more drilled, dragooned, bludgeoned,
and generally b——d about.

Such goings-on, in social-dramatic circles, gave rise to the
gravest misgivings. As for the Charleston . . . !

Since the word 'Charleston', which should be as inoffensive
—and as explicit—as the word 'minuet', has degenerated into a

sort of verbal guffaw with which to ridicule the twenties, let us talk some sense about it; very few people do. Even at the height of its popularity it was regarded by many as a sort of black magic. YOU ARE EARNESTLY REQUESTED NOT TO DANCE THE CHARLESTON was a notice prominently displayed at the Hammersmith Palais de Danse, which could hardly be described as an exclusive establishment. Similar injunctions were placed on the supper tables at the Piccadilly Hotel. 'Freakish'— 'degenerate'—'negroid'—were among the many adjectives used to describe it. And in one newspaper the inevitable 'Harley Street Specialist' was dragged in to warn the public that the Charleston would lead to 'a permanent distortion of the ankles'.

What was all this fuss about? Nowdays, it is difficult to answer that question. Compared with rock 'n' roll the Charleston was a gavotte. Moreover it was a dance that allowed no liberties; it was rigidly defined, with one basic step and a few established variations. This basic step demanded an exceptionally supple movement of the knees and perfect co-operation between the partners. As danced in *The Boy Friend* the Charleston is admittedly ridiculous; as danced in the twenties it was—sometimes—as graceful and dynamic as in the country of its origin.

Proof of the difficulty of this dance was once afforded by— of all people—Noel Coward, during one of his revues in New York. I have written so many nice things about Noel over the past thirty years that he will forgive me if I remind him that on this occasion he was very bad indeed. He came on at one end of the stage and Charlestoned with agonizing intensity over to the other; the effect was *macabre*, as of a patient afflicted simultaneously by rheumatoid arthritis and St Vitus' Dance. When he reached the far end of the stage, not only Noel but the entire audience breathed a sigh of relief. I was so moved by this almost unique spectacle that in a mood of masochism—for I was and am devoted to Noel—I went again on the following night. The Charleston was out.

The Times

No. 44263   London Wednesday, May 5, 1926.   Price 2d

WEATHER FORECAST. Wind N.E.; fair to dull; risk of rain.

THE GENERAL STRIKE.

A wide response was made yesterday throughout the country to the call of those Unions which had been ordered by the T.U.C. to bring out their members Railway workers stopped generally, though at Hull railway clerks are reported to have resumed duty, confining themselves to their ordinary work, and protested against the strike. Commercial road transport was only partially suspended. In London the tramways and L.G.O.C. services were stopped. The printing industry is practically at a standstill, but lithographers have not been withdrawn, and compositors in London have not received instructions to strike. Large numbers of building operatives, other than those working on housing, came out. The situation in the engineering N. Derbyshire and Monmouthshire.

Evening papers appeared at Bristol, Southampton, several Lancashire towns and Edinburgh, and typescript issues at Manchester, Birmingham and Aberdeen.

The Atlantic Fleet did not sail on its summer cruise at Portsmouth yesterday. The men went on shore duty.

Road and Rail Transport - There was no railway passenger transport in London yesterday except a few suburban trains. Every available form of transport was used. A few independent omnibuses were running, but by the evening the railway companies, except the District and Tubes, had an improvised service.

Among the railway services to-day will be 6.30 a.m. Manchester to Marylebone; 6.30 a.m. Marylebone to Manchester; 10. 10 a.m. Marylebone to Newcastle; 9 a.m.

The proverbial British talent for grinning and bearing it

Mrs Somerset Maugham. White from tip to toe. All her flowers were white, all her furniture was pickled and she bitterly resented the absence of a white cocktail.

Perhaps the uproar that greeted the Charleston was only to be expected. History never repeats itself so monotonously as in the saga of the dance. After every time of ferment there is a dancing mania and always the moralists rise up to condemn it. When Lord Byron denounced the waltz, which swept Europe in the twenties of another century, he was animated by personal spite but he was speaking for the vast majority of the people. And when Noel—it seems impossible to keep him out of these pages—wrote *Dance Little Lady*, he suddenly found himself, to his considerable astonishment, congratulated by a number of earnest clergymen who concluded that he had composed a tract for the times. Well, in a sense he had done so. All popular songs of genius are, in a sense, tracts for the times. This song had genius; here is a word about it.

Dance Little Lady was a classic example of the perfect mixture of four ingredients, the composer, the producer, the designer, and the date. The melodic line is perhaps its least important element. (Indeed, the first four bars, as Noel once admitted to me, are an unconscious echo of a sentimental song by Liza Lehmann.) But the lyric is brilliant. It hisses and sizzles with irony . . . 'so obsessed with second best, no rest you'll ever find.' Then came Cochran, who had the inspiration to engage Oliver Messel to design the masks for the chorus. There was nothing pretty about those masks; they were vacant, chalk-white, with the stamp of idiocy. Nobody who attended the first night of the revue at the London Pavilion is likely to forget the almost frightening impact of that line of pale-faced automata dancing till they dropped. As for the date . . . that speaks for itself. The song summed up an era, musically and pictorially. If there has been such a song to sum up the era of the fifties, I have yet to hear it.

N

CHAPTER FIFTEEN

CURTAIN UP

THE twenties, as we have seen, were drenched in melody; moreover, many of us were still able to play those melodies ourselves, and to sing them, standing up by the piano, pulling in our tummies, and properly enunciating the words. We did not merely lie back in a chair and turn a knob.

True, we had come a long way from the days of my boyhood, when my mother used to end her invitation with a tactful postscript, 'I do hope that you will bring your music.' This request was seldom ignored, and as the guests alighted from their high, trundling motor-cars there was a rustle of paper underneath their cloaks, indicating that they had come armed with their songs, with which to delight us after dinner, if sufficiently pressed. If they had been insufficiently pressed, they would have been much offended.

'Please bring your music,' was, I suppose, an echo of the Victorian era, for we were an old-fashioned household. I remember my mother telling me that once, when she was a little girl, and when *her* mother was giving a dinner party, she had come downstairs, and tiptoed into the hall, and rummaged among the ladies and gentlemen's cloaks to see what music they had brought. To her dismay, they had all brought the same song—*Tit Willow!* In my childhood, it would have probably been that glorious piece of slosh *Because*. Do you remember? 'Because—pom—you came to me—pom—with thoughts of lo - - ve.' I used to take great pleasure in accompanying this song, as a small boy, adding my own variations, which consisted in a powerful display of double octaves in a minor key. This was much admired by the guests, but was not so popular with the vocalists.

But though we may not have 'brought our music' in the twenties, we certainly played it more competently. That nasty little mechanical trick, the boogey woogey bass, had not yet become popular; and since our ears had not yet been dulled by dissonance it was still thought generally desirable to play the right notes of a melody. It was even considered a good thing to keep to the rhythm. One of the few times when I feel very old—and very angry—is when I hear a modern crooner murdering rhythm. There he stands, in front of the microphone, with his pigmy voice and his drooling lips and his oversexed uvula, singing a blues number which is a rhythmic nightmare. Sudden breathless *accelerandos*—sudden inexplicable *rallentandos*—sudden gulps and pauses—the voice and the orchestra in a lunatic conflict. Such creatures should be stripped, dipped in cold water, incarcerated, and made to sit on hard planks, while a metronome ticked some sense into their peanut brains.

Perhaps it is significant that one of the last melodies that really caught the ear of the British people a little while ago— a melody that echoed down the streets and over the hills and through the country lanes—was the work of a man who was essentially a product of the twenties, Ivor Novello. I refer, of course, to *We'll Gather Lilacs*.

Once, at his country house, Redroofs, Ivor told me how he had written it. Alfred Lunt and Lynn Fontaine were staying with him. One morning, when he was sitting at the piano, Lynn walked across the lawn in a white dress and stood under a white lilac tree and lifted up her hands. Something in the grace of her gesture gave Ivor the tune. He wrote it at that moment, without glancing at the keyboard, looking out across the green lawn at Lynn in the white dress.

That was typical of Ivor's method. The main theme of

King's Rhapsody, his last great success, was composed while he was on the stage, playing the lead in *Perchance to Dream*. This was a waltz called *Some Day My Heart Will Awake*; he composed it, *sotto voce*, while sitting at the piano in the background, waiting for his cue. The cue came, but Ivor ignored it; he was feverishly scribbling the top line on a piece of manuscript. Again the cue came, but Ivor had not finished. Not till the third cue—by which time his fellow actors were becoming desperate—did he rise and get on with the show. He had given everybody an agonizing sixty seconds, but he had caught his melody. Writing a melody is like catching a butterfly; you never know when it is going to fly into your life.

Music poured out of Ivor; there was more music in his little finger than in the hands of the whole fraternity of contemporary English composers. To prove this you need only refer to the score of any of his works in the twenties—revues such as *A to Z* or musical comedies like *The Golden Moth*—and compare them with the 'scores', if they can be dignified by such a term, of some of the successes of the fifties. If Ivor had conceived anything so pedestrian as the monotonous jog-trots on the tonic and the dominant to which we have recently been treated, he would have thrown the manuscript into the wastepaper basket. But then, of course, Ivor couldn't have conceived such things, for he happened to be a fine musician. Nor, in the twenties, would audiences have listened to them.

If a competent pianist sits down to play the melodies of the twenties to a bunch of young people, he soon has them spellbound. Consider a number like *And Her Mother Came Too*. The title does not sound musically inspiring, but Ivor invented a melodic line for it that was as clean and as buoyant as an air by Schubert.

> We lunch at Maxim's
> And her mother comes too;
> How small a snack seems
> When her mother comes too!

Those words, and the tune which accompanied them, have a nostalgic echo for the middle-aged. They were sung by a slim, debonair Jack Buchanan, in a voice which had all the charm of a sophisticated corncake. At the end of the song he did a little dance which, if analysed, would have proved to be a few elementary taps and a couple of turns on the heel . . . and yet such was his star quality that you could have heard a pin drop in the gallery. And since melody is a quickener of the memory, the moment in which I heard it is still vivid in my mind. This occasion has some of the qualities of a period piece; perhaps we might pause to recall it.

I was very much 'in' on the birth of this song. I first heard about *And Her Mother Came Too* when I was lunching with one of the most vivid characters of the twenties, the young Earl of Lathom. Ned Lathom was a tragic figure. He ran through a vast fortune and died of consumption, in comparative poverty, before he was thirty. He adored the theatre, and himself wrote several plays which had considerable talent, such as *Wet Paint* and *The Way You Look At It*. (He had a flair for titles.) *The Way You Look At It* caused nose-wrinkling in Mayfair; it was about a young man who was kept by a middle-aged woman, and Ned wrote it in a way which showed clearly that he considered this a perfectly proper arrangement. Mayfair did not think that an eligible young earl should express such opinions, particularly if—as in Ned's case—his grandfather had been Lord Chamberlain under Queen Victoria.

Back to *And Her Mother Came Too* and to Ned's luncheon party at his house in Great Cumberland Place. As the footman flings open the door our nostrils are assailed by a powerful and sickly perfume, and we see another footman, in the background, scurrying away with a white-hot leaden spoon in his hand, from which fumes of scented smoke are drifting. This was another habit of Ned's which caused Mayfair nose-wrinkling, in more senses than one. The footmen of eligible young earls, people felt, should be better employed than dropping scent onto hot spoons just before luncheon. I rather enjoyed the habit, and one day I bought some of the scent myself. It was called Omy, and was really meant for putting in one's bath. However, I gave it up; it seemed pretentious for a tiny house in Pimlico; apart from that it alarmed the cats.

The door closes and we follow the footman upstairs. Just in front of us is Marie Tempest, who has paused to powder her small, adorable nose. She is looking cheerful, in spite of the fact that her return to the London stage, only a few days ago, was an unmitigated disaster. That was a first night I shall never forget. For years the legend of Marie Tempest had entranced us; she had been held up to us as an example of everything that was witty and elegant and civilized; no star in the whole world of comedy, we were assured, could compare with her. The young men of my generation had not been able to confirm this legend for themselves; during the whole of the First World War Marie had been touring the Empire, and when she returned to the London stage, ten long years had rolled by.

We flocked to the theatre in a mood, almost of exaltation. Now at last we would be able to see for ourselves this delicious creature of whom we had heard so much. Then the curtain went up, and it was all quite, quite dreadful. The play itself was of an ineptitude that baffles description, and the production would have been regarded as amateurish by an audience of aboriginals. Even a heaven-sent genius could not have produced comedy from such a hash and Marie, that night, was very far from being a heaven-sent genius. She wandered about the stage in a hideous frock, fluffing her lines, shaking with nerves. The worst moment came at the fall of the curtain which, inevitably, was accompanied by an uproar from the gallery. Instead of keeping the curtain down, returning to her dressing-room, having a good cry and calling it a day, Marie had the curtain raised again, and stepped forward to the footlights. Thereupon, to an audience who by now was frozen into silence, she proceeded to deliver an interminable speech of thanks which had been written for her by her husband, Graham Browne, on the assumption that she would have just enjoyed a triumph. This, she assured us in quavering tones, was the happiest moment of her life, and she thanked us from the bottom of her heart. Then—while the silence froze thicker and thicker—she launched into an extremely involved dissertation on prodigal daughters and fatted calves, ending up with a peroration about the Empire which would have brought a hot flush to the cheeks of Miss Whilelmina Stitch.

To this day I have nightmares about that premier, not only because of its intrinsic horror but also because it was almost the first occasion on which I sat in the stalls as a dramatic critic. Why I was made a dramatic critic I cannot imagine; judging from the results—which I have recently re-read for the first time in thirty years—it must have been because the proper critic had been stricken with some very painful disease. My standards were crude, my knowledge of the theatre was nil, my approach to the art of acting was ludicrously limited, and my style, if such it may be called, was vulgar and derivative. The one thing which might be said in my favour was that I was never deliberately unkind; I always tried to make the best of a bad job. And I was accurate. Only once did I fall into serious error. This was after the production of Karel Capek's *The Insect Play*, which I attended on a Saturday night while sickening for the flu. Hurrying back to the office I rashly paused to fortify myself with two large glasses of whisky, which, in my fevered condition, went straight to my head. As a result I got all the insects mixed up, and said that the ant had given a terrific performance when, in fact, all it had done was to come on for a brief moment, make a noise like a raspberry, and exit to have a Welsh rabbit at the Queens.

I must not let the memory of Marie Tempest fade out to the accompaniment of boos. Five days after that ill-fated premier she closed the show and like the 'indefatigable trouper' that she was—the cliché is inevitable—she proceeded to the suburbs and the provinces in one of her old successes—*The Marriage of*

Kitty. Thither I followed her, and learned that the legend about her was true. She was a diamond of an actress; all sparkle and polish and white light, with occasionally the flash of a deeper fire. She was also, when she felt like it, what she herself would have been the first to call a bitch. My favourite story about her, in this connection, concerns a chair. This was the chair in which she sat during an important dialogue in a play which had a long London run. Her partner in the dialogue was a young actress whom we will call Miss X, who sat facing her in another chair. At the beginning of the dialogue, the two chairs were always immediately opposite one another, but as the conversation proceeded Miss X discovered to her dismay that Miss Tempest always 'upstaged' her—in other words that she slowly pushed her chair to the rear, so that the wretched Miss X was obliged to turn away from the audience in order to address her, thereby losing all the effect of her best lines. After a few such experiences Miss X decided that she had had enough, so she arrived at the theatre very early with a hammer and nails, and proceeded to nail the chair to the boards. I would have given a great deal to see the expression on Marie Tempest's face as she began to push the chair back and found it would not budge. But she bore no resentment against Miss X, and probably admired her for her enterprise. It was the sort of thing she would have done herself.

Towards the end I often used to go out to see her when she lived in St John's Wood and sometimes I would play the piano for her. She would sit by my side, like a music mistress, beating time, and keeping up a perpetual stream of injunctions, which were not very helpful to the interpretation of Chopin. 'You are hunching your shoulders, my dear boy. That is better. Keep the wrists loose, and watch that little finger of the right hand. There, that was charming ... charming! But now you are hunching your shoulders again. When will you learn to *breathe*?' And she would stop me, and switch me round, and place my hands firmly on her small, hard, tummy, and tell me to study how she breathed. 'Do you see? Do you understand?

Do you *feel*? Life is simply a matter of correct breathing.' I said yes, I was sure it was; but I was not so sure. When one is twenty-five, and when one's hands are pressed against hard, elderly tummies after luncheon, and when one is at the same time being fixed with a stern, disciplinarian eye and told not to hunch one's shoulders, it is difficult to be sure of anything.

This luncheon party, as you may have observed, is taking a long time to get going. Where were we? At Cumberland Place, going to luncheon with young Lord Lathom, and Marie Tempest has just paused to powder her nose. And by her side is another ubiquitous figure of the twenties, Miss Olga Lynn, whom we all knew as 'Oggie.'

There are countless stories of Oggie, but the most vivid concerns the late Mr Douglas Fairbanks, when he was lunching at the Ivy Restaurant. Turning to his companion he inquired, 'Who is that remarkable looking woman over there?'

'That is the celebrated Olga Lynn.'

'Really! What does she look like when she's standing up?'

'She *is* standing up.'

Oggie, indeed, was almost as broad as she was long. She seemed to come up to one's knees. She had a face like a Jewish baby doll and the most exquisite speaking voice I had ever heard. Her personality was so intensely dominated by music—I once told her that I was sure her heart was made in the shape of a harp—that she gave even to the spoken word a melodic line; even if she said, 'No thank you I would rather have a soufflée,' you saw it as a phrase of music, with a *legato* mark above the melody.

Oggie was an opera singer *manqué*. She made her debut at Covent Garden, as Musetta in *La Boheme*, where she incurred the hatred of Melba. After that, she sang with Chaliapin at a number of Beecham's concerts. But her appearance was against her, and finally she settled down as a teacher and—in a highly individual way—a sort of social star.

How does one 'place' Oggie? The *Daily Worker* would probably have labelled her as a parasite, because she had a great many rich friends, and she organized parties and concerts for them in their houses. She arranged smart Christmas carol parties, which rolled round the streets of Mayfair and were occasionally moved on by the police. From time to time she would take a theatre for Charity tableaux; I myself appeared in one of these as Lord Byron, and had the alarming experience of walking down a long staircase in trousers that were far too tight, gazing adoringly into the eyes of a young woman who loathed the sight of me. This spectacle afforded great pleasure to one member of the audience, Mr Noel Coward, who had strong views on amateur performances.

Not everybody liked her. Melba, as we observed, detested her, and moved heaven and earth to get her out of Covent Garden. Oggie swore that this was because the Diva once heard Oggie imitating her behind that old tree which they always stick in the middle of the stage in the second act. She was entertaining a group of enraptured stage hands with a version of 'me chiamano Mimi', in an Australian accent. Melba's Italian, of course, was hot from Sydney, but the voice was such that she could have sung Mimi in the broadest Cockney and still have brought a lump to one's throat.

Another who loathed Oggie was Mrs Patrick Campbell. There is a story that Mrs Campbell was once attending a charity concert that Oggie had organized in Lady Howard de Walden's house in Belgrave Square. Stalking slowly up the staircase the great actress paused in front of a mirror. She had perceived a small, round, female object behind her, swathed in pink tulle—Oggie. Mrs Campbell glared at herself in the mirror, gave a dramatic switch to her false pearls, and boomed, 'I try to look like a lady, but all I look like is Olga Lynn.' After which, she resumed her course up the staircase, and sat down to listen to Mozart on a flimsy chair, which was too small for her behind. Mrs Campbell deplored her own behind, which was, indeed, substantial. Melba, on the other hand, delighted in hers. She would stand in front of a glass, and clap her hands, and declare, 'No bottie ! No bottie !'

But we were trying to assess the place, in art and society, of this figure who, I fear, is still vague to you. Olga Lynn. A very, loveable, sensitive, fallible, female footnote to a decade. Serious critics would probably dismiss her as a trifler, because her musical career was conducted at so high a social level. It was as though, on her writing desk, Burke's *Peerage* was next to the *Life of Beethoven*. I take a kinder view. True, when she started the Aeolus Concerts, they were attended by a great many duchesses, but Oggie did not play down to her duchesses. She gave them Bach and she got Horowitz to play it; she gave them the songs of Faure and Hugo Wolf and Ravel and she sang them herself, impeccably. No other singer I have ever heard, with the possible exception of Maggie Teyte, phrased so exquisitely, nor blended the words so magically with the music. When Oggie was over seventy that distinguished critic Desmond Shaw-Taylor tried to persuade her to make a record of some of her songs for the benefit of future generations. I remember the occasion well. It was just after luncheon in the tiny flat where she ended her days. And though the poor darling had recently had a second stroke and, even more recently, a second helping of chocolate soufflée, she suddenly set down her coffee cup, and sang the opening bars of that ravishing song Duparc's *Clair de Lune*. Was there ever a lyric that began with so enchanting an image? *'Dans ton coeur dort un clair de lune, un beau clair de lune d'été'*. As the old lady sang it, with her twisted mouth and her raddled doll's face she seemed suddenly to become beautiful, and the nightingales really did sing in Berkeley Square—or rather, in Chesham Place.

I can imagine nothing more calculated to make me close a volume of memoirs with a sharp snap than to be told that somebody or other, whom I never knew, was a great mimic. I must take that risk—and quickly, before you have time to close this particular volume. Here is a story. Oggie mimicked everybody—Syrie Maugham, Sybil Colefax, Gladys Cooper—

the lot. One of her favourite subjects was Lady Oxford. The scene was set at a wedding to which, so Oggie said, Lady Oxford had not been invited. However, Lady Oxford wanted to go, and went. She also went into the vestry to sign the book. As she was signing it she turned to Oggie with a scowl of disapproval, and hissed in a stage whisper: 'Hideous bride! *Too* hideous! I can't think why I came!'

But no. I have proved my own point. Flat as a pancake, that story. Too many undertones lost, too many echoes flown away over the hills. We had better return to luncheon.

CHAPTER SIXTEEN

AND HER MOTHER CAME TOO

WE shall never get to Ivor's song *And Her Mother Came Too* at this rate but I do not greatly care, because I am enjoying myself at this luncheon party of the twenties. Besides, here is Ned, fifth Earl of Lathom, advancing towards us in a state of febrile exhilaration, waving a letter from Somerset Maugham, and letters from Somerset Maugham are not to be lightly dismissed. Particularly this letter.

'Darlings!' he exclaims. 'Here is the most divine letter from Willie. It's about Syrie and her shop!'

Syrie was Mrs Somerset Maugham, and she had just startled everybody by opening a shop . . . though that is perhaps an inapposite word for her elegant establishment at the corner of Grosvenor Square. I remember it as a place that was filled with exquisite but faintly dubious objects of furniture that were liable, if examined too closely, to fall to pieces. However, they were seldom examined too closely; Syrie's brilliance and charm attracted most of the attention to herself. Besides, her clients, who were mostly American millionairesses, had usually lunched with Syrie beforehand, and luncheon with Syrie demoralized one for the rest of the day. Hence an astonishing collection of old bits and pieces of French provençal armoires, Biedermeyer sofas, nineteenth-century Italian chests, etc., etc.— all most delicately 'pickled' and tarted up—passed across the Atlantic, at fabulous prices, and slowly decomposed in the mansions of Long Island.

After which slightly acid paragraph I feel obliged to admit that Syrie had the most delicate and civilized touch in decoration of anybody I ever knew. Her sense of colour was impeccable. And even if she charged a Texas oil merchant a thousand dollars for a pickled Spanish harmonium—which on one occasion, in fact, she did—the result was enchanting.

Before it is too late, somebody should try to re-create a typical Syrie Maugham interior, to be preserved in some museum as a proof that the taste of the twenties was not entirely represented by knee-length frocks and bobbed fringes. On the walls would hang Ambrose MacEvoys delicate, elusive portrait of her daughter Liza (Lady John Hope) as a girl, and opposite it Glyn Philpot's painting of a negro boy—a study in chocolate and mauve and lime green. There would probably be a Boudin, too. Somewhere on a painted Italian table, there would be a vase with a few blossoms of magnolia. The curtains would be exquisite; they might be of faded olive green satin. The carpet would probably be Bessarabian, with a flamboyant design of full-blown roses. All round the room there would be charming, unexpected objects which Syrie had picked up in some junk shop—a tiny Venetian monkey in a cloak of cherry-coloured silk, a slab of lapiz, a lotus in white jade.

But alas, very few people today have either the taste or the flair or the knowledge—or the memory—for such a task. Indeed, the only candidate who occurs to me is Bob Lebus—a name that may not be familiar to the general public, but one that was, and is, very familiar among the friends of whom we are writing. One day I went down with Syrie to luncheon at a charming cottage which, at that time, he owned in the country. Bob's taste was always impeccable, but he was beginning to get bored with the cottage—English Tudor was never really his cup of tea. To relieve his boredom he had carried out a number of decorative schemes which were, to say the least of it, unconventional. Over the old barn, for example, he had caused to be hung a pink stag's head. 'But why pink, Bob?' I inquired. 'Because I'm not mad about stag's heads in any case, my dear

Beverley, so it might as well be pink.' To which faintly sur-
realist remark there was no reply.

Bob had the greatest respect for Syrie's taste—and she for
his. Throughout the twenties there was an affectionate and
mysterious feud between the two of them concerning a pair
of seventeenth-century Meissen camellia trees, which both of
them claimed to have bought but neither of them ever seemed,
actually, to possess. At unexpected moments Syrie would
suddenly hiss: 'I'm sure that darling Bob has spirited my
camellia trees away!' And Bob would return from Paris
saying: 'I'm almost certain that darling Syrie has sold my
camellia trees to Boudin.' It was all most amiable and endearing, and we longed for the feud, if such it can be called, to go
on for ever.

But we were talking of Bob's luncheon party. He was
feeling a little nervous at Syrie's arrival; in particular, he was
worried about a pair of large negroes standing on their heads
in the dining-room fireplace. They were very pretty negroes,
with nice striped trousers, and I, personally, could think of no
pleasanter accompaniment to the *sole colbert* which, as I had
ascertained from Bob's cook, we were shortly to enjoy.
However, the conventional decor of a Tudor cottage, deep in
the heart of Surrey, does not normally provide for a pair of
large negroes standing on their heads in the fireplace, and Bob
was restless. Syrie arrived. She was gay, she was elegant, she
was witty, she was the tops. She admired everything. Never
had she seen such divine mixed bunches of flowers. *Where*
had Bob discovered those adorable pieces of goldstone? *What*
taste! We went in to luncheon. It was a small room and Syrie
nearly knocked over one of the negroes but oddly enough she
appeared not to notice it. The iced soup was delicious. *What*
a cook! Her eyes fluttered round the room. *What* charming
rice paper pictures! (No mention of the negroes.) The *sole
colbert* was heavenly. And *what* a good idea, those stuffed birds
in the corner, superimposed on the wall and surrounded by
mirrors! (Negroes still off.) Finally, Bob could bear it no longer.

'Syrie, darling, you don't seem to have noticed my negroes.'
Pause. And then: 'Yes, Bob darling. I did notice your
negroes. But I thought it better . . . *much* better, darling . . . not
to mention it.' A ravishing smile to Bob's servant, and the
flash of a white hand over a wine glass. 'No more wine,
George, thank you. I shall be quite tiddly.' Somewhere, in the
distance, I seemed to hear the faint rustle of camellia trees.

I cannot recall this gay, provocative, sparkling woman
without bringing forward her American counterpart, the
fabulous Elsie de Woolf . . . who in later life was Lady Mendl.
Each by herself was stimulating; together they were almost too
much; they went to one's head. I discovered this one week-end
when I motored down with them to Cecil Beaton's house in
Wiltshire. Syrie and Elsie sat in the back and I perched on a
sliding seat opposite to them. By the time we arrived my knees
must have been black and blue; Elsie had a strange habit of
reinforcing her conversation with sharp slaps. 'Beverley my
dear, that tie of yours is the shickest[1] thing I ever saw'—(slap)
—'isn't it the shickest thing, Syrie darling?'—(slap). 'It's
given me an idea for my noo bathroom.' (Slap, slap, slap.)
We sped down the country roads to a babble of feminine
salesmanship. Elsie was creating a bathroon for the Prince of
Wales at Fort Belvedere, of incomparable 'shick'. Syrie was
doing a dining-room for Gertie Millar at Le Touquet. It would
be too divine. The conversation had a strongly financial
flavour; I learned a great deal about the value of velvets and
brocades—the proper price to pay for a set of Regency chairs
—where to go for a Bokhara rug in Paris and where not to go
for one's glass in Venice. There was a great deal of head-shaking
about people who did not pay their bills, and once, after Syrie
had poured out a tale of woe about the Marchioness of X, who
owed her seven hundred pounds, Elsie shouted, 'You should
soo her, darling, *soo* her.' so loudly that the chauffeur nearly

[1] Most chic.

Emerald and Hazel. They were not over-fond of one another

Sybil Colefax: 'a snob for brains'

Lord Berners . . . the last of the great eccentrics?

Lady Mendl. If you had asked her to stand on her head she
would have obliged

swerved into a ditch. The only time when they ceased to talk
about money was when Elsie changed the subject to health.
She was a demon for diet and breathing exercises and vitamins
and Yogi and Gaylord Hauser and the whole works. On this
occasion I was the target. 'That creme Vichysoisse you had at
luncheon, Beverley darling'—(she made it sound like some
fearful concoction of the Borgias)—'it was *poison* !' (Slap.) 'Did
I have it? No! Why? Because I do *not*'—(slap)—'build my
meal on a *lake* !'

Elsie used to do a great deal of standing on her head. Once,
in Paris, at an age when most other women would have been
giving poignant impersonations of Whistler's mother, she
went to a very grand party at the Comte de somebody or
other, and made her entry as a *gamin*, standing on her head.
There was a great deal of plucked eyebrow raising and Fau-
bourg St Germain pursing of lips. After all, she *was* Lady
Mendl, connected with the British Embassy, and though the
title was not exactly ancient nor Sir Charles Mendl's post
particularly elevated—(it was something to do with the press)
—it was felt that *ça ce ne faisait pas.* When Elsie was told about
this she observed, tersely, that the ladies in question would
have been damned glad if they could do it themselves.

So we sped down the country lanes, in a whirl, as it were,
of faded velvets and pickled chests-of-drawers, and at last we
came to where Cecil was waiting for us.

And now I am tempted to leave our two ladies, for Cecil,
as he comes to greet us, is evidently at the top of his form, not
only intellectually but sartorially; he wears shorts and pale
yellow stockings and a Tyrolean jacket with a gardenia in the
button-hole. And yet the effect is not bizarre; one feels that
if there were country squires in the pages of Firbank, they
would dress in precisely such a fashion.

Under their soft exterior the aesthetes of the twenties concealed an unexpected toughness. Cecil Beaton is perhaps the
most vivid surviving example of this fact. When he first
burst upon London from Cambridge—no, he did not 'burst',

o

he floated languidly from the wings—I did not care for him overmuch. He seemed to have mistaken his decade, to have retreated, quite deliberately, into the nineties. He might have walked straight out of some revised version of *Patience*, with his languid gait, his extravagant adjectives and his voice . . . above all, his voice. It was, and still is, one of the most astonishing sounds in the contemporary symphony. When he is serious it resembles the sounds made by an extremely fatigued corncrake, when he is amused it recalls an obscene laughing jackass.

Nor are those the only birds whose cries his voice evokes. In moments of depression he has a seagull wail and when excited he can chatter like a spiteful starling. Oddly enough, though the voice is totally unmusical, it is not displeasing, but it is definitely an acquired taste. However, at the beginning of the decade I had not acquired that taste. Nor did I share his passion for dressing up. The Bright Young Things of the twenties never missed an opportunity to dress up . . . any excuse was good enough for putting on a wig and painting one's face and roaring round the town. Cecil was always a ringleader in these expeditions, and I did not realize at the time that this passion for fancy-dress was the first indication of his longing to design, to create beauty in line and colour. He has, as yet, no real theatre in which to clothe his fancies, so he made a theatre of the drawing-room.

But even I was bound to admit that his photographs were extraordinary, and now, at a distance of thirty years, I suspect that his camera made a decisive impact on the decade. Today his experiments have become commonplaces all over the world . . . the multiple heads against a dark backcloth, the startling poses, the rich, rococo settings. But in the twenties their effect was explosive. 'My dear,' people would cry, opening *The Tatler* or *The Sketch*, '*look* what Cecil's done to Edith Sitwell this week. He's stretched her flat on the *floor*, my dear!' Even at the outset the intelligentsia realized that his little camera was no ordinary apparatus; they posed for him with alacrity; and we had the refreshing spectacle of Siegfried

Sassoon against a background of polka dots and Max Beerbohm under the dramatic stripes of an awning.

And then, of course, there were always Baba and Nancy, his
exquisitely pretty sisters. 'He's surrounded them with *balloons*,
my dear, and hung a lot of delicious *cellophane* round their
necks, and lit them from *behind*, and they look *too* ravishing,
my dear, and I can't wait to be done myself.' Cecil took thousands of pictures of Baba and Nancy, and some of the other
débutantes were inclined to resent all the publicity that they
got. Round about the middle of the decade there was a terrific
hullabaloo because some young man dragged the poor girls
to a dance to which they had not been invited and to which
they did not particularly want to go. The hostess was called
Lady Ellesmere, and she banished them from her ballroom
as indignantly as if they had been fallen angels endeavouring to
storm the gates of Paradise. The less successful débutantes were
delighted and so were the gossip writers, and for several days
the papers were filled with leading articles on the heinousness
of 'Gate-Crashing'—(very much a word of the period)—and
the necessity for protecting the sanctity of the English home,
particularly if it was the home of a countess.

All this was a very long time ago. Gradually I began to
realize that there was more to Cecil than one had suspected. I
was even photographed by him, in Paris. This was an interesting experience. He appeared to be extremely vague about
it, and not quite sure how the camera worked. His running
commentary was disconcerting. The corncrake voice would
suddenly bark 'Beverley my dear, you're making a face. I
do *wish* that people would not make faces.' Click of the camera.
'I shouldn't be surprised if that *ghastly* woman had forgotten
to put in a film.' Click of the camera. 'Stop that astringent
smile, for heaven's sake. No, you'd better put it on again,
you've gone all prunes and prismy. It's all too depressing.' Click
of the camera.

And then his drawings began to force themselves on our attention—curious, spidery little sketches of society beauties, glimpsed through razor-sharp eyes and traced with a very sharp pen. The likenesses were quite uncanny. Emerald Cunard, for instance, had a face that one would have thought impossible to catch on paper, for it was an entirely artificial product, varying from hour to hour in proportion to the amount of astringent lotion which was holding it together. But Cecil caught her, as it were, with a flick of the wrist, and perched her in her box at the opera so that she looked like a strange painted bird in a gilded cage.

Yes, there was more, much more, than one had expected. Perhaps his forte was caricature? But even as one asked the question he began to design for the stage and the ballet, and some new colours began to creep into the decade.

I have emphasized this early aspect of Cecil Beaton not only because it happens to coincide with the period of this book but because it is a healthy reminder of the folly of judging by appearances. (I have a story to tell about that in a moment.) It might also be a healthy reminder to the modern young man —whether 'angry' or indifferent—of what can be accomplished by sheer hard work. Today Cecil is one of the very few international designers to whom one can, on occasions, apply the word 'genius' without wondering whether one is going to regret having done so. Some of his stage sets, such as the Olivier production of *The School for Scandal*, are worthy of Rex Whistler at his best. But the stage absorbs only a small part of his prodigious energy. The portfolios of portraits swell ever thicker, and today the society beauties are in a minority, for he has taken as his study the broad face of humanity. And accompanying the portraits is a commentary of the most curious and compelling prose . . . a liqueur of a prose, heady with adjectives, spices with rare flavours. His prose is, I think, Cecil's last link with the nineties, recalling the distant echoes of Beardsley's *Sous La Colline*.

Now for my little story, with its moral about the folly of judging by appearances. Towards the end of the decade Cecil began his conquest of America, a continent in which he now needs no introduction. I was at that time in New York, trying to edit a magazine called the *American Sketch*. I had friends who might, I thought, be useful to Cecil, and one day, at a large luncheon party at Bessie Marbury's—a powerful hostess whom we shall meet again— I began to talk about this brilliant young Englishman who had just arrived.

'He hasn't found himself yet,' I said, 'but he will. He has a genius for caricature. He takes ravishing photographs. He has a superb sense of the theatre. He . . .'

I found myself talking in an echoing void. I stopped.

Bessie heaved her immense bulk in her chair. 'I've met him,' she snorted.

'Well?'

'He paints his face.'

'My dear Bessie, don't be idiotic.'

'I *know* he paints his face.'

'How can you know anything of the sort?'

'No young man could have such a complexion and such eyelashes if he didn't paint his face.' She sent a challenging glare round the table. She had given her verdict. And because she was the hostess, and because she was Bessie Marbury, and because she was a social heavyweight, mentally as well as physically, nobody ventured to contradict her.

I left the luncheon party in an ill humour. This piece of malicious gossip was a typical manifestation of the anti-British propaganda which periodically swept America throughout the twenties. Only a year before, a baboon-like politician called Mayor Thompson of Chicago had won an election on the sole issue of 'keeping King George out of Chicago'. The inhabitants of that enlightened city believed, in all seriousness, that the British King was planning to attack them. It was this fantastic episode which convinced me that American ignorance of world affairs—sheer crass ignorance—was one of the greatest dangers to the peace of the world. That conviction has not been weakened with the passing of the years.

So I felt indignant about Cecil not only as a fellow-artist but as a fellow Englishman, and I decided to tell him what had happened, without delay. I hurried to the Ambassador's Hotel, where he was staying, and sent up my name. As luck would have it, he was in. He was in a small bedroom on the un-fashionable side of the hotel.

I wasted no time. 'Cecil, I've just been lunching with Bessie Marbury, and she says you paint your face.'

'*What?*'

'You heard me the first time.'

The next few sentences should be written by Ouida, for Cecil's features really did 'darken'; his mouth really did 'set in a grim line'; and he really did clench his fists 'till his knuckles showed white'.

He sprung to his feet, and flung open the door to the bath-room. 'Perhaps you'd kindly look at *this*!'

I walked across and peered inside. There, on a glass shelf, was a cut-throat razor, a stick of shaving soap, a toothbrush, and a tin of Calvert's Carbolic tooth-powder. There was not even a tin of after-shave talcum powder. Those were the sum total of Cecil's aids to beauty. Personally, I should have re-garded them as grossly inadequate.

'You can tell that old bitch . . .' began Cecil. Then, suddenly, he started to laugh. So did I. We sat down on the edge of the bath, and laughed our heads off. Within a few weeks Bessie had seen the error of her ways, and was one of Cecil's staunchest supporters.

And now we can return to our two ladies.

We were motoring down to the country with Syrie Maugham and Elsie de Woolf. And though Elsie has—we hope—come to life, we cannot really understand her without introducing her greatest friend, Bessie Marbury—the woman who spread the malicious rumour about Cecil.

Bessie was one of the dominating figures of New York. She lived in a charming backwater called Sutton Place, a cluster of small Georgian houses looking out on to the East River. Although she was always more than civil to me, she frightened me. There was a sort of brooding menace about her. And though she had a questing, active brain, the whole of her life was dominated by her adoration of Elsie.

Let us use the technique of the screen to introduce her. The camera shows a close-up of a woman's hand clutching a snapshot. We cannot for the moment see the snapshot, but we note that the hand is trembling. The camera pans back, revealing a monstrously fat woman of about seventy, who is staring at the snapshot with a strange mixture of fascination and disgust.

This is Miss Bessie Marbury. Whenever I think of her I recall Hugh Walpole's story *The Old Ladies*; she might have been the inspiration for the one who coveted the piece of amber. Sitting there, by the fireplace, a hulk in black bombazine, she would gaze up to the ceiling, to the room where Elsie was dressing, and her eyes would slowly travel across the ceiling, and then through the wall, in the direction of the staircase, and slowly downwards; and at last the door would open and Elsie would come in, and I am quite certain that Bessie had summoned her by some strange magnetic influence.

In spite of Bessie's size and her lack of mobility—it took her ten minutes to get down the stairs at her Sunday luncheon parties—she was still, in the twenties, a force both in American politics and in the American theatre. Her life had been a curious blend of the two; as a young woman she had acted as agent for Oscar Wilde; in middle age she was often consulted by the heads of the democratic party on matters of policy. She was a frightening woman. When I met her she was nearly seventy, and as broad as she was long, but she once fixed me with a gleaming eye and said: 'You know, Beverley, I could

still have a baby.' She said the same thing to John van Druten
late one night, and we have never been able to decide which of
us fainted first. There was an awful suspicion that she might
be telling the truth.

Bessie had never had her baby; her inclinations were otherwise directed. Her whole existence had been dominated—until
the bitter last years—by her adoration for Elsie de Woolf.

We can now come back to the snapshot, which we must
remove from Bessie's clutch, because her hand is trembling
with such violent indignation. What is there so terrible about it.
The setting is a plage on the South of France. We see a young
man in bathing slips, tanned and muscular, of the variety who
grinds his stomach muscles every week, with such evident
discomfort, on the covers of *Health and Strength*. He is holding
aloft a young lady in a bikini . . . but stay ! What have we here ?
A *young* lady, was it ? As the camera comes closer we see that
the lady is very far from young. True, she is balancing upside
down in mid-air, perilously upheld by the stomach-grinder's
hairy arm. True, her lips are stretched in a professional smile.
But the sun in the South of France (when it comes out) is
pitiless, and it reveals the fact that this is no young lady; it is,
on the contrary, her ladyship. It is none other than Elsie de
Woolf, now Lady Mendl, aged—let us be gallant—sixty-five.

'Isn't it disgusting ? Isn't it sickening ? At *her* age ? '

The voice comes from Bessie—deep and growling and
strangely masculine.

'How can she allow herself to be seen in such a position ? '
She peers at the picture more closely. 'And how much does she
have to pay that dreadful young man ? And what does *Sir*
Charles think of it ? Not that *Sir* Charles cares tuppence about
what she does as long as she pays the bills ! When I think what
a mess she has made of her life . . . '

She let the snapshot fall from her fingers, and stared into
the fire. She looked like some huge primitive image, squat and
foreboding. She was consumed by a black jealousy—jealousy
of the little girl who had escaped from her enveloping love, at

an age when a woman of lesser character would have given up any attempt to do so.

'What a mess Elsie has made of her life!' Most women would hardly endorse Bessie's verdict. To make a great fortune by one's own efforts, to spend one's life among exquisite objects, to become a world celebrity, to inhabit one of the most elegant houses in Europe, to marry in one's sixties a highly civilized man twenty years one's junior . . . and through it all to enjoy perfect health, finally expiring, with the utmost grace, at the age of ninety-four, if this is failure one would like to know how Bessie would define success.

This record is all the more remarkable because Elsie began with few natural or social advantages. She was always rather common. She had a vocabulary that made one flinch, full of glossy little words like 'smart' and 'chic', which she pronounced 'chick'. Her gestures were barmaid; at any moment one might receive a sharp blow on the knee or a resounding slap on the back.

She was also very plain. She had a poor skin, an indeterminate nose, and button eyes. Her hands were so ugly that she wisely kept them concealed; she never appeared in public without gloves.

To complete the catalogue she had the nastiest of voices, pinched and grating and sour.

How was it that she managed, in the end, to create an illusion of beauty? By what sorcery did she persuade quite a large number of people—not only café society people—to accept her as elegant? And why, when she died, did so many people feel that the world had lost a symbol of gaiety and courage?

The shortest answer is the best; she *became* beautiful, and she *was* elegant, she *was* gay and courageous. As the years went by the monkey face—admittedly with the help of surgery—was transformed into an ethereal mask, which had nothing to do with nature but satisfied the demands of decoration. At the same time the jerky little body, with the help of Mr

Gaylord Hauser's dietary system, was disciplined into grace. When I last saw Elsie, at her house in Hollywood, she was ninety-two. But she was a beautiful woman. And when she slapped me on the back, it was no longer a barmaid gesture; it was the fluttering of one of the last leaves from an age that has gone.

One could not go about very much in London or Paris or New York, in the twenties, without meeting Elsie de Woolf, or at least picking up her trail. In the world of interior decoration she occupied rather the same position as Lord Duveen in the world of art. There were always millionaires in the background, to whom she was selling tapestries or carpets or *boiseries* or porcelain. These sales—apart from her business in New York—were conducted in an atmosphere of the greatest *luxe*, at luncheon parties in the house at Versailles, or the apartment in the Avenue de Jena, or the villa which she rented in the South of France. How she ever found time for people like me is a mystery; I could not have afforded to buy a teacup and I had no grand relations. All the same, she did.

Here is a vignette of an evening with Elsie, which may have a certain nostalgic appeal for a few people. One night there was a long distance call from Paris. Elsie speaking . . . 'Beverley darling, I am flying over tomorrow from Paris for Willie's[1] first night. Can you come? Beverley darling, that will be wonderful. Now Beverley, I shall be staying at Claridge's and I am incognito . . . repeat *incognito*.' (The word crackled over the wire like a spluttering firework.) 'So please don't tell anybody that I am coming, most of all Syrie.[2] Why not? Well, Beverley darling, that's a long story, but there's a Bessarabian carpet . . . no, darling, *Bessarabian* . . .' (more firework noises) . . . 'that Syrie's got her claws into, and I want it for the Aga Khan, and it would be just too embarrassing

[1] Somerset Maugham.
[2] Mrs Somerset Maugham.

to have to go into all that at Willie's first night, so good-bye, darling, and it will be Claridge's at seven o'clock, *heavily veiled.*'

(That phrase, 'heavily veiled', is an authentic echo of the twenties. We all used it in our little *contes scandaleuses.* 'Who d'you think I saw having supper at the Ritz last night? Robin and Baba! But of course they were both *heavily veiled* at the time.')

And so to Claridge's on the following evening, and into a softly lit room smelling of all the scents of the twenties, which have faded from my memory.

And there, advancing towards me with arms outstretched, was Elsie, in a dress shimmering with *paillettes* . . . and bright green hair.

The hair really was a brilliant, acid green; it seemed to catch the glitter of the *paillettes.* Here was a social dilemma. Should I comment on it? Should I say, 'Elsie darling, I think the hair is beautiful'—which in a way it was—'and I know it will be a sensation'? But how would that fit into the 'heavily veiled' rôle?

Elsie solved the problem. A terrific slap on the back. '*What* fun, darling! Help yourself to a sidecar.' (The sidecar was very much a drink of the twenties . . . equal quantities of brandy, cointreau and lemon juice.) 'I sent Willie a telegram from Paris, just to put him off the scent. He won't be there anyway; he'll be prowling round the *boites* in Piccadilly in an agony of nerves, poor darling. So we'll just be all on our own and nobody will know we're there!' (A sharp dig in the ribs.) 'Oh Beverley, I never knew what fun it was to be incognito.' A step towards the long looking-glass. 'I feel like a *conspirator*!'

So we went to the first night, and we had seats in the middle of the third row, and Elsie, in her dragonfly coiffure, made her entrance just before the lights were dimmed, and expressed suitable astonishment that she was recognized, because she had only turned round about six times to wave to friends behind her.

To me, one of the most interesting things about Elsie is that her memory does not 'date'. One might write a whole volume in an endeavour to analyse the causes of 'dating', but one could probably sum up those causes in a single phrase . . . whether we are discussing personalities or works of art, the second-rate dates, the first-rate doesn't. Gladstone is a museum piece, Disraeli, in spite of the ringlets and the rhetoric, is a contemporary figure. Thus, at our first night, Elsie and I sat next to Michael Arlen, who was having a sensational success on both sides of the Atlantic with his novel *The Green Hat*. Michael was the very last word in 'modernity', and he probably thought that Elsie, even in those days, was a raddled old stick of a woman. And yet Elsie is still a contemporary figure, whereas Michael . . . !

Listen to this, from *The Green Hat*, of which an inscribed copy was lying beside Elsie's cocktail tray at Claridge's. Iris Storm, the palely promiscuous heroine, is speaking:

'I am a house of men,' she begins, 'of their desires and defeat and death.' Which, one would have thought, was enough to go on with. But no. She continues: 'You laid your foot down on the soil of kindness, but where your foot fell there leapt up a dandelion . . . and in the heart of the dandelion a tiny little rose, but what, my friend, is just one little rose surrounded to suffocation by a huge dandelion?'

My own answer to this question would be just one little lemon; one just has to rub one's little eyes after reading such stuff. Was this indeed the prose that captivated the twenties? Was this the author on whom the most respectable critics fawned, writing of him in the same sort of terms which they nowadays reserve for Mr Graham Greene? The answer is yes, and a very encouraging answer it is for those of us who have never been the critics' pets.

Now that we are on the subject of critics, let us pause to consider another member of the audience who is sitting only a few feet away from us—a stubby little man with a florid complexion, a balding head, and an expression of professional pugnacity. Mr James Agate, the celebrated dramatic critic of the *Sunday Times*.

For many years, in this great newspaper, Agate expressed his opinions with vigour and—so I imagined until experience taught me otherwise—with integrity. He did not confine his attentions to the drama. He wrote a weekly book page for the *Daily Express*, in which he surveyed the whole field of literature with a lordly eye. As if this were not enough, he contributed a feature on gramophone records to another journal, innumerable articles to magazines, and a seemingly interminable series of autobiographies entitled *Ego*, in which he played the part of his own Boswell. (He was, indeed, a sort of pinchbeck Johnson.) How any man, who was also a *bon viveur* with an abnormal capacity for alcohol, could be expected to give a measured judgement on a play, a book, or on anything whatsoever, is something of a mystery. The fact remains that he did, and many of us were thereby considerably the worse off, in prestige and in pocket.

Agate, I imagined, had nothing against me, personally. Then, towards the end of the decade I wrote a play called *Avalanche*. I usually mistrust an author who states that a work is 'written with his heart's blood'; even if the claim is true it is not necessarily a certificate of merit; passionate sincerity can be, and often has been, productive of a great deal of sorry rubbish. But as it happened *Avalanche*—which was a dramatic presentation of the argument for absolute pacifism—was written with this type of ink, and Agate knew it. Till late at night, in various raffish little pubs and bars, we had argued for and against the doctrine of total non-resistance, and whatever his opinions of my work as a dramatist he had no cause to doubt my integrity.

After the usual vicissitudes *Avalanche* was eventually put on for a trial run in Edinburgh. Normally London critics do not make the long journey to Scotland in order to see plays in their preliminary stages, but Agate decided to come, and by doing so, killed the play. The local notices were brilliant; his notice in the *Sunday Times*—the only paper that mattered, as far as the London managers were concerned—was damning. Not only did he damn the play, as a play, but he accused me of making a joke out of the horrors of war, an accusation which he knew was totally false. A week later, the play 'folded'.

This is not quite such a little personal storm in a teacup as the reader may suspect. On my return to London I happened to walk into the Garrick Club, where I picked up a copy of that admirable magazine *Country Life*. As I turned over the pages I suddenly found a long notice of *Avalanche* by a dramatic critic whose name was unfamiliar—George Warrington. It seemed that Mr Warrington had also attended the first night, and that he had found much in the play to please him. Mr Warrington then proceeded to take Mr Agate to task, and to show him, in no uncertain terms, where he had been at fault.

So what?

Just this. 'George Warrington'—as I discovered a few days later—did not exist. There was 'no sich person'. Mr Warrington was James Agate himself.

I do not tell this story in order to repay an ancient grudge against a dead man who cannot answer back. I tell it in order to offer some belated consolation to those many young actors and writers who were wounded by his pen, and are destined to be wounded by the pens of the Agates of today and tomorrow. Here was a man who wielded a very considerable influence in the theatre, not only during the twenties, but throughout the thirties and the forties. And he led a double literary life. He praised with his right hand and damned with his left, and that is enough to make me suggest that there was no health in him, nor in his modern counterparts.

In common with a great many other young dramatists whom Agate had attacked, I was to enjoy a minor revenge when he rashly ventured to assume the mantle of a dramatist. The occasion was a comedy in which he had collaborated with another writer whose name I forget. We will call him X. The audience which assembled for the first night was tense; here was the great man who for so many years had been telling us all how to do it, laying down the law, strutting the boards with a squirt of vitriol; now, at last, he must prove his qualifications. How would he fare? Mr Agate himself seemed to have no qualms. He sat in the front of the stage box, smoking a large cigar, waving to friends, beaming about him, flushed with anticipated triumph.

Then the curtain went up, and within five minutes it was painfully evident that we had been summoned to witness a watery little farce of almost incredible ineptitude. The plot was ludicrous, the characters were caricatures, the dialogue was flat and coarse. So bad was it that the audience sat stunned. At the end of the first act, there was near silence. I glanced towards the stage box, expecting to see that Agate had beat a tactful retreat. But no. He was still there, waving and beaming. Was it conceivable that he had not sensed the audience's reaction? It was. When the final curtain fell he marched on to the stage, puffed with elation, to be greeted by a fusillade of boos, not only from the gallery but from all parts of the house.

A few days later I met Agate and could not resist the temptation to say that I thought he had been ill-advised to make a speech at the end of his play.

'My play? Why do you call it *my* play?'

'It was described as such.'

'Pooh! I had practically nothing to do with it. That was why I took a curtain. I was going to tell the audience that all the credit should go to X.'

Certainly, a man of resource.

Further and further away drifts the melody of *And Her Mother Came Too*, but Somerset Maugham's letter is fluttering before us. The damnable thing about it is that I haven't a transcript of the letter, only my memory of it. But that is vivid enough. Willie had made Syrie's entry into business an occasion for the most delicate irony, and his letter indicated that it was a last desperate effort to keep the wolf from the door. Nowadays, of course, such an idea would be far-fetched; everybody has a niece who works at Woolworth's or a first cousin who appears, in the middle of luncheon, to tune the piano. But in the twenties, when a 'woman of society' went into business, the fact was news.

So Willie told Ned that poor Syrie had been obliged to go to work, selling old pieces of furniture. He trusted that this enforced labour would not overtax her strength. Himself, he must stay in his garret, churning out prose which some editor, he hoped, might be persuaded to accept. One had the impression that Syrie Maugham, at that moment, was auctioneering a worm-eaten commode in the Caledonian Market, and that Willie was bombarding the editor of *Tit Bits* with snappy paragraphs. In fact, he was the most successful dramatist writing in the English language, and his fee for a story in *The Cosmopolitan* was £1,200. As for Syrie . . .

But this digression has gone on far too long. We will close it with Ivor sitting down at the long black piano—after the room had received another impregnation of Omy—and singing the last verse of *And Her Mother Came Too*.

Ivor was very beautiful. The adjective is more apt than 'handsome'. I never cared for his face myself, though I was devoted to the man behind it. But the face was too good to be true, with the impeccable nose, the raven locks, the huge eyes, the chiselled lips, and all that neck. In spite of this catalogue of perfections Ivor was not a conceited man. His only weakness was that he was apt, by a sort of instinct, to turn into profile; presumably he had turned so often, before so many cameras, that the habit had become a second nature. When he did this I used to say to him 'Stop doing a profile, Ivor'. Whereupon he would turn back with a charming smile, and apologize.

All through the twenties—and indeed until the day he died —people used to ask themselves about 'the woman in his life'.

Who was she? Was it his latest leading lady? Was it that little
girl who suddenly stepped out of the chorus and did a solo
number? Or was it somebody who had nothing to do with the
theatre at all? Surely there must be *somebody*; it was incon-
ceivable that any young man so personable, so rich, so talented
and so romantic should not have a 'woman in his life'. Who
was she? They might have spared themselves the trouble of
asking that question. There were no women in Ivor's life—
not in 'that' way. There were dozens of women who were
devoted friends and good companions—most of them were
old enough to be his mother—but his love-making stopped
when he stepped off the stage. This was a source of frustration
to countless young females who could not understand why he
behaved so strangely to them in taxis and on divans, or rather,
why he did *not* behave so strangely to them in taxis and on
divans. They could not grasp the fact that here was a man
whose life was made up of music and limelight, a man who
really dwelled in Ruritania. That is the essential reason why
Ivor's spectacular romances—which, let's face it, were rather
silly, when analysed in cold blood—were so convincing on the
stage. He believed in them implicitly himself; he had Ruritania
written on his passport.

Yet he was not a Johnny-Head-in-the-Air; he had a shrewd
grasp of the contemporary scene—always provided that it was
in some way connected with the theatre. His play *Party*, for
instance, is as taut and nervously effective as Noel Coward's
The Vortex, and some of the plot is not dissimilar; it tells of an
ageing actress of genius who discovers that a young actress—
also of genius—is taking drugs. The originals of the older
character, in real life, was Mrs Patrick Campbell and since
any excuse is good enough for telling a story about the
immortal Mrs Pat, here it is.

While Ivor was writing *Party* he used to see a good deal of
Mrs Pat; he wanted to saturate himself in her personality—
which was not difficult; she oozed personality to such an extent
that sometimes one felt as though one would be drowned by it.

P

One night they were having supper when they were suddenly joined, much against their will, by a boring American entomologist, who began to talk about ants. This was such an unexpected intrusion that for the moment Mrs Pat was startled into silence.

'Ants, my dear Mrs Pat,' boomed the American, 'are the most astonishing creatures. They have their own social services, their own nurses, their own hospitals, their own sanitary system. Ants have their own architects, their own engineers, their own police force, they have their own army . . .'

Mrs Pat could bear it no longer. 'No *navy*, I presume?' she boomed. And that was that.

Here are two stories about Ivor, shortly before his death. I was motoring near Redroofs one hot Sunday afternoon, and I thought that I would drop in to see him. Ivor was in bed resting, so I joined some other guests who were having tea on the lawn. A few minutes later there was a call from the house; it was Ivor standing by his bedroom window, beckoning to me to come up and see him.

So I went up and sat down on the edge of his gigantic bed, and we talked. He was in cracking form, and he looked the picture of health. Suddenly, for no reason at all, I glanced towards the window, through which one could see the branches of a glorious old apple tree. I found myself saying:

'This would be a wonderful place to die.'

'It's *going* to be a wonderful place to die,' said Ivor cheerfully. 'It's all settled. I'm going to expire in this bed, in about forty years time, with the utmost grace, looking at that apple tree. The only trouble is that I can't decide what season of the year it should be. What do you think?'

I said that I would choose the spring, with somebody outside the window singing *We'll Gather Lilacs*.

That was the last time that I ever saw him. A few weeks later he died. There was no apple tree for him to look at, only the walls of a London flat. All the same, it was a wonderful way to die, with the cheers of a great audience still ringing in his ears, and an unfinished glass of champagne by the side of an open piano.

The other story about Ivor was told to me by Lady Juliet Duff. The enchanting name 'Lady Juliet' has always seemed to me a musical echo of her own personality; it has the grace and gaiety of a chime of bells. Juliet has always adored the theatre and the men and women who work in it, and through her friendship many of the young artists of the twenties were made acquainted with a way of life more spacious than they would otherwise have known.

Lady Juliet was a guest at Redroofs on the last week-end that Ivor ever spent there. The weather was golden; the company enchanting; and on the Monday morning, before she went back to London, she decided to commemorate the occasion by taking a snapshot. They lined up on the sunlit lawn—Ivor and Bobby Andrews and two others whose names I forget. She bent over the lens to focus. Then she frowned. Ivor had disappeared.

'Ivor,' she said, 'do get into the picture.'

Ivor's voice came back. 'But I *am* in the picture, darling.'

She looked up. There he was, smiling at the end of the line.

'I'm so sorry,' she murmured.

She looked down in bewilderment. But Ivor had gone again. There was no reflection of him in the lens. Quickly she took the picture, telling herself that it must be a trick of the light.

That night he died.

Some weeks later I saw this photograph. If this were a ghost story instead of a piece of reporting, there would have been, of course, no Ivor in the picture when it was developed. As it was, he came out very clearly. That was the dreadful part about it; for his face was the face of one who was already far away, for whom the last lilacs had been gathered.

CHAPTER SEVENTEEN

ENVOI

LADY HORE-BELISHA once leant across a dinner-table and informed me in crisp, ringing tones that she always regarded me and her husband as two people who had 'missed the boat'. This led to a brief coolness between us; women, however charming, should not say things like that about one, particularly if they happen to be true. I have been missing boats all my life; Leslie Hore-Belisha really only lost one. How and why he lost it will always be something of a mystery.

When Leslie came down from Oxford in the early twenties he was widely tipped as the future Prime Minister. He did nothing to discourage this legend, and he gave it clearly to be understood that the particular Prime Minister he proposed to emulate was Disraeli. Even at Oxford there was a bust of Disraeli in his rooms, and in those days he could recite long passages from *Sybil* and *Coningsby*. In London he used often to hold court in the Café Royal, where he always sat at a table in the corner, which was reputedly the favourite table of Oscar Wilde.

As it happened, this was not the favourite table of Oscar Wilde . . . a fact which leads us to yet another digression.

One spring evening in 1925 there was a loud knock on the front door of my little house in Ovington Street. Gaskin was out so I went down to answer the summons. There on the doorstep stood a tall youth of about twenty, with bright golden hair.

'Good evening,' he said graciously, 'you are Beverley Nichols?'

I could not deny it.

He nodded and stepped past me, uninvited, into the tiny hall. Over his shoulder, in a casual aside, he said: 'I am the reincarnation of Dorian Gray.'

When young gentlemen announce themselves in this manner, it is wise to telephone for the police. However, he was already half-way up the stairs.

He explained his mission in the most charming manner, reclining on a sofa, smoking a gold-tipped cigarette. He had just been sent down from Oxford, owing to a disagreement with his tutor. This gentleman, it appeared, was unsympathetic to the theory of reincarnation, particularly as it involved his pupil in an exclusive study of the poems of Lord Alfred Douglas when he ought to have been reading law. No . . . not quite exclusive; for in addition to the works of Lord Alfred he had been studying the works of Nichols, or rather one work, a novel of undergraduate life called *Patchwork*. This book, which is now mercifully lost in oblivion, had greatly impressed him. 'It should have been printed on rose-petals,' he observed graciously. He said this twice.

The upshot of this singular conversation was that I was invited to luncheon to meet Lord Alfred Douglas at the Café Royal. 'We shall lunch at the same table which was always reserved for Oscar and Bosie,' he said. I longed to ask if we could have ortolans, washed down by hock and seltzer, and accompanied by . . . what was it? . . . 'one of those scarlet melodies by Dvorak'? It is years since I read *Intentions*, but Lord Henry Wootton said something silly of that sort.

A few days later we lunched. The table responsible for this digression was not downstairs in the corner, it was upstairs by the window. We did not have ortolans, nor hock and seltzer; we had rump steaks and stout. And Lord Alfred, whom one had thought of—when one thought of him at all—as a slim golden youth in a straw hat, was a podgy, crusty old man in a bowler.

So this, I thought, is the fact that all the fuss was about! This podgy, alcoholic blob, with the mean eyes and the double chin and the sinister signature of arterio-sclerosis in the veins at the sides of the forehead!

The deterioration in the brain was as marked as the deterioration of the body. Of wit there was none, charity was lacking, malice ruled the board. He talked in jerks, gruffly, like a Ronnie Squire impersonation of a Freddy Lonsdale duke. He cursed the younger generation, the modern girl, and the Labour party. He sneered at the unemployed. He came out with all the old bitter cliches such as . . . 'These fellahs don't *want* to work; they'd rather live in luxury on the dole.'

He was a very, very nasty little man. He was particularly venomous about Wilde. He gave it to be understood that he, Douglas, had been responsible for the best epigrams in *Lady Windermere* and for the finest passages in *Salomé*. He raked up old debts which Oscar had never paid him, and he ended by saying that if only Oscar had listened to *him*, when the trouble came, the trial would have had a very different ending. He left one with the impression that Oscar Wilde was altogether a common-place sort of person who owed his success to the tireless efforts of Lord Alfred Douglas.

As I listened I felt myself closing up like a clam, and growing colder and colder inside. I had long ago emerged from the temporary phase of aestheticism through which most inquiring youths must pass; I had grown out of Beardsley and I no longer thought it amusing to hang the walls of the bathroom with etchings by Felicien Rops. At the same time I had not reacted so far as to forget that Wilde was—*pace* St John Ervine —a considerable genius. Admittedly, he should have been shaken till his teeth rattled, and told to be not such a damned fool, and plunged into ice-cold baths to discipline himself, and even sent to Enton to get some of the fat off. He should have been forcibly led in front of looking glasses and made to stare at his flabby paunch, and kicked in the buttocks and told to get

on with his work and stop talking all that rubbish about his
soul being 'a stringed lute on which all winds could play'. If
he had ever had a decent friend, apart from Robbie Ross, who
was hardly the muscular type, he might have been saved from
himself by these somewhat public school methods, and we
might have had another *Importance* . . . and been spared the
succulent death agonies of *De Profundis*. As it was, he got Lord
Alfred Douglas.

Yes, he was a very, very nasty little man. And now we can
get back to Leslie Hore-Belisha.

As I was saying, Leslie's missing of the boat is one of the
unsolved mysteries of British history. Here was a man who, in
the crucial early days of the last war, seemed destined for the
highest honours. He held the vital post of Minister of War. He
was young, as politicians go. He was a brilliant orator, in an
assembly which was mostly composed of mumblers and stut-
terers; he had a vivid and dynamic imagination, at a period
when most of our leaders—with the eternal exception of
Winston Churchill—were stuck in a rut; moreover, he had
the ear of the masses. The man-in-the-ranks felt that he was
'one-of-us'. For the generals, the admirals and the whole
collection of brass hats, the man-in-the-ranks had little use. But
Leslie was different. He was 'one-of-us'.

In this conviction the man-in-the-ranks was singularly mistaken. True, Leslie had a genius for publicity; he had been
through the hard school of Fleet Street, and he was an excellent
window-dresser. But he always saw himself, privately, as an
aristocrat, which of course he was not. Moreover, his concep-
tion of aristocracy was strangely out of date, and more than a
little 'ham'; one felt that he hankered after fobs and flowered
waistcoats and long black sticks.

Thus, if we take him back to the beginning and sit him down
at his table in the Café Royal, we shall find him discussing, of
all things, a coach-and-four.

'For the proper dissemination of my policy, my dear Beverley,' he is saying, 'I need a coach-and-four.'

'Of course, Leslie. What else?'

An airy wave of the hand. 'The rest will follow. Once one has a coach-and-four, the rest will follow.'

This was not the amiable fooling of a *poseur* after a glass or two of wine; it was an *idée fixe*. So much so that when in later years he was contesting Devonport, he got his coach-and-four, at much trouble and expense, and rolled round the streets in it, with a loud flourish of trumpets. Disraeli, one supposes, might have done the same sort of thing. In any case, the coach-and-four seemed to appeal to the voters, for he won his election.

When a man of Hore-Belisha's genius and ambition misses the boat in so spectacular a manner, some moral weakness is usually to be suspected. In Leslie's case this weakness was a profound laziness, that grew more marked as the years went by, until in the end it was a deep-seated neurosis. I had personal experience of this laziness even at Oxford. Among my various activities was the creation of a magazine called *The Oxford Outlook*, to which I persuaded Leslie, who was then President of the Union, to contribute a series of articles. They were not long articles; they involved no research; a competent journalist —and he was a very competent journalist—could have completed them in a couple of hours. But they were never ready. The days would go by, he would prevaricate and invent excuses, and always, in the end, I would be obliged to go to his luxurious rooms in St John's College, and get him out of bed, and stand over him while he wrote the article, with many sighs and protestations.

This laziness nearly involved him in a considerable scandal. Towards the end of the decade he was hard pressed for money, and since he was not prepared to work for it, he lent his name to various enterprises in the City which were, to say the least of it, disastrous for the shareholders. One of these, for example,

which was launched in October 1928 with glittering pro-
mises, was wound up a year later, the shareholders receiving
2½d per share. Another, of which he was the chairman, and
for which he prophecied the rosiest future, was in liquidation
within eighteen months. Company after company with which
he had been associated showed the same record of bankruptcy
and total failure. Years later, in January 1940, just after he had
resigned from his office as Secretary of State for War, these
facts were published in *Truth*, and a deplorable effect they had
upon public opinion. Incredible as it may sound, when Leslie
heard about the first article he could not be bothered to get
a copy of the newspaper himself—he was in his country house
and it was snowing. He telephoned to a woman friend in
London, requesting her to motor down with the article. When
she arrived he pleaded fatigue . . . perhaps she would be so
kind as to read it to him? With some embarrassment she did so.
When she had finished she said to him: 'What are you going
to do about it?'

'Nothing.'

'But surely you must do something?'

'Nothing.'

And that was that.

I narrate this story not to blacken Leslie's memory but to
defend it. The effect of the *Truth* articles, whether intentional
or not, was to persuade a large section of the public that he had
been engaged in a number of extremely shady transactions.
But one vital fact was not mentioned, or rather was not stressed
as it should have been . . . the fact that the failure of most of his
companies occurred within a few weeks of the financial debacle
of 1929, which engulfed the whole world. I am entirely convinced that Leslie was an honest man. The explanation of this
unhappy business lies in his fantastic inertia. He was simply too
lazy to read a prospectus.

Towards the end of Leslie's life his laziness was pathological.
Six years before he died I lunched with him at his extraordinary
house in Wimbledon—extraordinary because it was a country

farm-house, surrounded by woods and fields, only twenty minutes from Piccadilly Circus. After luncheon he took me upstairs to read me the first chapter of his autobiography. I was enthralled. Here was work of exceptional quality. The style was elaborate and ornate, with a faint echo of de Quincey, but the setting of the background, the drawing of the characters, the sense of historical perspective . . . all these were masterly.

'This is great stuff, Leslie,' I exclaimed.

'You really think so?'

'But of course. When will it be finished?'

As soon as I had asked the question I realized that I had made a mistake. He pushed the manuscript aside with an impatient gesture, and muttered something about his 'commitments'. And that was that.

But Leslie had no 'commitments'. That was the tragic part of it. From time to time, over the next year or so, I used to telephone to him and ask how the book was going. I did this for the simple reason that I wanted to know; the single chapter that he had read to me had whetted my appetite. But always the answers were elusive, and usually they were in French. '*Ça va*,' Leslie would say. Or . . . '*on verra*'. I came to the sad conclusion that *ça* did not *va*, and that *on ne verrait plus*. The conclusion was correct. When Leslie died, there was a blank space under the heading Chapter Two.

And yet he clung to the illusion that some day, somehow, he might make a come-back. To the end, even at the most common-place luncheon party, he would command silence with a gesture and indulge himself in sonorous rhetoric, as though he were addressing a phantom audience. Even when his public engagements of any importance were almost nil, he still kept two secretaries. They can hardly have been over-worked. Or were they? A very lazy man can take a lot of looking after, and as I suggested above, Leslie's laziness was pathological. The last story I heard about him is laid in the South of France. Leslie announced that he wished to spend the morning writing letters. He retired to his room and emerged two hours later with a couple of envelopes which needed stamping. His host provided him with the stamps. Leslie took them and stood there helplessly, looking from the stamps to the envelopes. 'But who'—he was asking the question in all seriousness—'but who is going to stick them on?'

One might write a whole chapter about men who missed the boat—men who, in the twenties, seemed marked for the highest destinies, only to fall into oblivion and contempt.

I can best illustrate this by the story of two weddings at the beginning of the decade. On April 21st, 1920, at St Margaret's, Westminster, a young ex-Grenadier guardsman, who was then acting as ADC to the Governor-General of Canada, married a tall, pretty girl called Lady Dorothy Cavendish. Although the groom was a commoner, and although his post as ADC was not very exalted, the bride was the daughter of a duke, and society arrived in force. There was even Queen Alexandra, who was then an old lady of ghostly and tenuous beauty, with the roses flaming all too brightly on her parchment skin. (Most middle-aged people, when they recall the name of Queen Alexandra, instinctively attach to it a curious adjective—'enamelled'. We were all told, as children, that she 'enamelled' her face, and we accepted this as a fact of nature. 'But how does she smile?' I once asked my mother, 'She does not smile,' replied my mother gravely. 'If she did she would crack.')

Enamelled or not, Queen Alexandra went to the young ADC's wedding, and his name was Harold Macmillan, and we all know what happened to *him*.

A few weeks later there was a much grander wedding, for though the bride was only the daughter of a marquess, the groom was one of the most gifted of all the younger members of parliament. The ceremony was conducted in a blaze of glory at the Chapel Royal, St James'. King George was there, beaming approval, and Queen Mary, in the toque to end all toques, and the King and Queen of the Belgians and heaven knows whom else.

There was only one discordant note, which was discussed by one of the gossip writers under the heading . . .

BRIDE DEFIES SUPERSTITION

'In choosing pale green for her bridesmaids' dresses,' wrote this observant person, 'and also in having the leaves of the Arum lilies embroidered on her wedding gown in their natural shade, the bride flouted superstition. She also gave proof of her disbelief in popular notions by fixing on the month of May—generally regarded by brides with disfavour, for her wedding.'

Perhaps there was indeed some malevolent influence in the leaves of those Arum lilies. Thirteen years later the bride was dead, and seven years after that the groom was in gaol. For his name was Oswald Mosley. And we all know what happened to *him*.

Or do we? Seldom in history has so complete a pall of oblivion fallen over a figure of such glittering promise. Mosley was the most eloquent speaker I ever heard, and I have heard the lot; moreover, the quality of his mind was by no means the coarse home-spun of the average dictator; if he had been a crude bully he would not have rallied round him, even for a brief period, humane and civilized men such as Harold Nicolson.

Moreover, he had good reason to suppose that his movement was in tune with the mood of a very sizeable section of the British people. The first years of Italian Fascism were regarded by the democracies with a comparatively friendly eye; Mussolini had not yet revealed himself in his true colours . . . and in actual fact those colours, in his early years of leadership, were not so black. When an attempt was made on his life, in November 1925, the *Sunday Dispatch* was probably echoing the opinion of the average Conservative in the following leader:

In no country will Signor Mussolini's escape from the assassin's hand be welcomed more cordially than in Great Britain, for nowhere else, outside his native land, has the Italian leader more numerous or more ardent admirers.

Enthusiastic young men in our islands have banded themselves into Fascist corps. Whatever may be thought of the wisdom or policy of this movement, it is at least a testimony to the impress Mussolini has made. If he had fallen by a shot from that levelled rifle, he would have been mourned scarcely less deeply in Britain than in Italy itself.

For it is to Europe, not to Italy alone, that Signor Mussolini belongs. He stands for the forces of strong government and ordered progress against those of anarchy and lawlessness.

When Mosley read that sort of thing in one of the most popular Sunday newspapers, he might well be excused for believing that he was destined to lead a movement that might sweep the country.

And yet the gods destroyed him, with the whole-hearted co-operation of himself.

And now? A few days ago I took a taxi from Whitehall to Victoria. As we passed Downing Street I noticed that there was a bigger crowd than usual outside Number Ten; the Prime Minister's popularity seemed to be growing. At Victoria I got out and walked down the squalid Vauxhall Bridge Road; I was looking for a certain junk shop. And suddenly I found a shop, though it was not the one for which I had been searching. It was called the Union Book Shop, and I realized that I was standing before the last outpost of British Fascism. The paint on the door was chipped, and the little array of propaganda volumes looked in need of a dusting. I pressed closer to the railings to see what was being published. The titles had a hollow ring, as though they echoed from a distant world. *The Answer of a German*—an open letter to the Archbishop of Canterbury by Hans Grim. *Wagner and Shaw*—a synthesis by Sir Oswald Mosley. *Stuka Pilot* by Hans Ulrich Rudel. A copy of *The European*, described as The Journal of Opposition.

And *Government Tomorrow—The Problem of Power*, by Sir
Oswald Mosley. What a sad and curiously pathetic little list!
And what a mournful footnote to a career that had been so
bright with promise! To say that Oswald Mosley missed the
boat is something of an understatement.

However, he has not lost quite everything. He is still in
Who's Who, and he is still a member of Whites' Club.

'But is it not true,' I asked myself, as I wandered away,
'that all of us who were young in the twenties have lost the
boat? Has a single cause for which we fought been won? Is
the world a whit the better for all the sacrifice? Are we in any
way richer, in any way safer, in any way wiser?'

The honest answer must be, of course, that we are in every
way poorer, in every way in greater peril, and that we have
learned nothing whatsoever. When a man is young the full
horror of history is not apparent to him, unless he is a person
of exceptional sensitivity; because it is printed and bound
between the covers of a book it is one step removed from
actuality. Only when one is growing old does history appear
as the horrible thing it is . . . a dirty tale scrawled on a wall by
men whose tools grow ever sharper with the years. And by
then, most of us are too tired to care.

I am afraid that I have not, as yet, quite reached that stage
of indifference. The contemplation of the last three decades still
arouses in me undignified agonies of apprehension. 'If such
follies are possible,' I ask myself, 'is there any hope at all?'
Consider only one aspect of this history through which we of
the twenties have lived . . . the bewildering changes in alliances
and counter-alliances which have been necessary in our
struggle for existence. When we were at school the Japanese
were our 'gallant companions' in the struggle against the
'unspeakable Hun'; we lived to see them branded as 'the
arch-traitors of mankind', and we applauded their extermina-
tion, in large quantities, by the immaculate Americans. They

are now, of course, a 'vital bulwark' in the struggle against communism. As boys we learned to sing the Russian national anthem, a beautiful song that turned into the hideous jingle of the Red Flag . . . but in the last war we were taught to march to that tune too . . . for a time! When we were young the Turks were 'oriental fiends', but the *maquillage* of power politics has converted them into gallant Western gentlemen, just as it has turned the 'unspeakable Hun' into one of the 'fortresses of Western democracy'. France has been friend, foe, and friend again, and so has Italy; we were the saviours of Greece, we are now their 'oppressors' . . . but why go on? This frenzied shuffling and reshuffling is dignified by the phrase . . . the Balance of Power. It is in fact a gigantic dance of death, in which the partners seem to have no volition of their own, but spin round to the bidding of an insane fiddler, hidden in the wings.

Therefore, if I were a young man today, and if—because I had lived through them—I truly appreciated the horror of the past thirty years, I should be prepared for greater horrors. And greater ironies too. I should be prepared to see a grand and shining alliance between Britain, the republic of China and the black republic of Africa against those two arch-confederates, the USA and Soviet Russia. It would afford me no surprise to see the Red Flag entwined with the Star-Spangled Banner, nor to hear an ageing King Charles urging the Canadians to bomb New York. Why should it? Stranger, very much stranger, things have happened in my life time.

So what is the young man to think about it all? As I asked that question, I remembered what I had thought about it thirty years ago. I set down those thoughts in a book called *Twenty-five*, and on the last page I wrote:

> I have enjoyed the writing of this book too much to indulge in any sudden moralizations. But I know my generation, this post-war generation which has so baffled the middle-aged on-lookers who, from the gallery, have watched the dance whirling

beneath. And I know that the one thing of which we are always accused—that we live for the moment only—is the one thing of which we are innocent. We are none of us living for the moment.

No, we were building for the future. Our white Temple of Peace still gleamed by the shores of Lake Geneva. Our horizon was limitless, and lit by the rays of a rising sun. If we were Tories we could still sing *Land of Hope and Glory* with conviction ('Wider still and wider, may thy bounds be set'! In the age of lunar satellites such a slogan falls rather flat.) If we were Socialists we could still dream of a society liberated by equality and made beautiful by fraternity, without any of the disillusioning experiences of socialism in practice. And if we were merely care-free, irresponsible young people, we could sail the seas and roam the distant spaces, without having to obtain permission, to explain ourselves, to touch our hats to some Treasury official as though we were schoolboys seeking an increase in our pocket money.

So if the young men of today are living for the moment, nobody can blame them. Why should they make provision for an old age that may never mature? Why should they deny themselves the pleasures of today in the hope of benefits to come? What is the point of cultivating a garden which may be blasted out of existence before the saplings are waist high? That is really the Sixty-Four Thousand Dollar question—a question that in the twenties we had not the agony of being obliged to answer. Surely, it can only be answered in one way.

And yet, one wonders. There is a streak of divine obstinacy in the human heart which urges men to continue in the race long after it is lost. This would not be the first time, in the history of the world, when the youth of the world seemed to be obviously and irrevocably doomed, and it would not be the first time when youth contrived to ignore the fact. I can even ignore it myself, with all my middle-aged apprehensions and all my loathing of being obliged to live in an age of science fiction. On the day when the first satellite was launched I received from America a packet of rare seeds from an exotic tree that takes, with luck, some sixty years to mature. This, I regret to say, is a period somewhat in excess of my normal expectancy of life. A sensible man would have thrown the seeds into the waste-paper basket. I did no such thing. I planted them with the greatest care. I await their germination, and I look forward to their flowering.

Once more I turn to the last page of *Twenty-Five*. Thirty years ago, this curious bundle of talents and prejudices called Beverley Nichols wrote the following envoi to his little book of memoirs. I quote it in order to make a tardy comment:

> *And thus, abruptly, I end. A line drawn, a cigarette thrown out of an open window, a pile of manuscript pushed into the corner of one's dsek. And thus, I suppose, youth ends. A line drawn under one's eyes, a sudden realization, as one is laughing or drinking, that the 'stuff which will not endure' has worn itself threadbare. To what purpose? God alone knows, not I . . . Accept the joke of life for what it is worth. It is not such a brilliant one, after all. And was there not a man called Browning, who wrote 'Grow old along with me, The best is yet to be'?*

Even in those days I secretly suspected that Browning was talking through his hat. Today, I know.

Q

INDEX